Management in Institutions of Higher Learning

Management in Institutions of Higher Learning

Edited by
Erwin Rausch,
Didactic Systems, Inc.

with

Robert A. Laudicina ... [et al.]
Elliot I. Mininberg
Richard J. Nichols
Bernhard W. Scholz
Nathan Weiss

LexingtonBooks,
D.C. Heath and Company
Lexington, Massachusetts :
Toronto

Library of Congress Cataloging in Publication Data

Main entry under title:
Management in institutions of higher learning.

1. Universities and colleges—Administrations—Addresses, essays, lectures. 2. Management—Addresses, essays, lectures. I. Rausch, Erwin, 1923-
LB2341.M26   378.1   79-1650
ISBN 0-669-02856-8

Published simultaneously in Canada.

Printed in the United States of America.

International Standard Book Number: 0-669-02856-8

Library of Congress Catalog Card Number: 79-1650

Contents

Contents

List of Figures
and Tables

Figures

Tables

Preface and Acknowledgments

This book represents an attempt to demonstrate how the modern management techniques contained in the Linking Elements Concept can be applied successfully to management in institutions of higher learning. The Linking Elements Concept has found wide acceptance in many industrial organizations as well as in health-care institutions and government agencies. It is proving itself to be a valuable guide for managers who wish to achieve higher levels of performance in their organizational units. However, the Linking Elements Concept is not a simple concept. It is a rather complex one, and use of it to significantly enhance the management function in any activity requires extensive and continuing attention to many details.

When we first started to work on this book, we all questioned whether Linking Elements ideas would really apply in the environment of an educational system. However, as we explored in greater detail the skills, techniques, and strategies that are actually used to guide the various departments and divisions of an educational institution, it became increasingly evident that Linking Elements thought processes can indeed become practical guides for people with responsibilities in all functional areas of an educational institution.

One of the purposes of a preface is to pay tribute to the many people whose efforts or contributions to society's store of knowledge have provided the foundation on which our thinking rests. We owe a considerable debt to the contributions of the many management and behavioral scientists who provided the foundations for the Linking Elements Concept and for other thoughts expressed in this book. Indeed, there are very few thoughts in this book that are entirely new. This book's value, it is hoped, will come from the new perspective it provides toward the important work of others.

We also owe a significant debt to the thousands of working managers at all organizational levels in industry, government, and health-care institutions who participated in seminars in which the entire concept or portions of the Linking Elements Concept were presented. Their thoughtful questions, suggestions, and criticisms helped to sharpen the ideas so that we were better able to apply them to the problems and opportunities of managing in institutions of higher learning.

In addition, it is only fair that we acknowledge the contributions made by those who helped to shape the ideas that form the Linking Elements Concept, as described in the book *Balancing Needs of People and Organizations: The Linking Elements Concept*, Bureau of National Affairs, 1978.

The contributors, and especially the editor, are indebted to Emil Sadloch of Didactic Systems, Inc., to whom fell the large and thankless task of conducting the necessary research and organizing the initial chapters so that they presented the Linking Elements Concept in a setting useful for the purposes of this book.

Similarly, we are all grateful to Dr. Bernhard Scholz of Seton Hall University, who graciously volunteered to contribute the historical introduction to chapter 6 when it became apparent that such a segment was needed and none of the contributors could muster the extra effort within the limited time available.

Finally, thanks are due the staff members of our respective offices, who worked diligently typing the many revisions of this book, and to the publishers of other books applying the Linking Elements Concept—the National Fire Protection Association and the Bureau of National Affairs—who made much of the art work available. It is probably not necessary to stress that any errors of commission or omission are solely those of the contributors and especially the editor, but for the sake of completeness, it is stated.

Erwin Rausch
Robert A. Laudicina
Elliot I. Mininberg
Richard J. Nichols
Nathan Weiss

Management
in Institutions
of Higher
Learning

1

The Linking Elements Concept: Introduction and Overview

This is a book for managers about effectiveness on the job. It is intended for those in institutions of higher learning who recognize the fact that in every environment, in personal life as well as in one's work, the establishment and the accomplishment of goals is an important element to success. (The title *manager* is used here and throughout the remainder of this book in its broadest sense and, thus, covers all persons with supervisory or leadership responsibilities. Included in this term are managers of administrative departments and academic leaders, for example, deans, department chairpersons and committee chairpersons, who do not always see themselves as managers.) The book, however, is not for all managers; it is only for those who are willing to devote considerable effort to the pursuit of greater competence. If you are such a manager, you will undoubtedly find many useful ideas as you read. They will require serious study, however, because the model presented in the following pages is complex.

This book offers a thorough and comprehensive framework, not a simplistic picture. It does not suggest easy solutions to problems, but it does provide a roadway through the complex issues that face managers who wish to improve the performance of their organizational units. While it is clear that supervisors and managers in administrative departments have managerial responsibilities, department chairpersons, committee members, and committee chairpersons in academic functions traditionally have not considered themselves to be managers. Because many have been elected to leadership positions by their peers, they often consider their role to be primarily that of a spokesperson or a representative of their constituencies. As such, they sometimes fail to see that their positions or assignments require the discharge of managerial responsibilities. In their roles as "academic leaders," many department chairpersons, for example, believe that their leadership situation is so unique that the general principles of management that are useful in other environments—in business, industry, and government, and even in the administrative departments—do not apply to them. Many assume managerial positions with little managerial training or experience yet make little effort toward developing an understanding of the basic principles essential to successful performance of management functions.

This attitude, to some extent, ignores the reality that all academic leaders do perform managerial functions. When the responsibilities of deans

1

and department chairpersons are examined, it becomes clear that their work requires many of the practical skills that are useful to any manager. For example, department chairpersons exercise managerial skills when they assign courses to their respective colleagues, guide individuals who have difficulty with students to greater understanding of alternative ways to solve those problems, guide department members toward establishing a common position with respect to issues facing the department, and marshal the department's resources to work most effectively toward goals they wish to achieve. Therefore, it is important that academic leaders, once elected or appointed, recognized that they will be significantly more effective if they gain greater acquaintance with management concepts.

As the academic world comes under increasing pressure to make more effective use of available resources, the demands on academic leaders, and on managers in other institutional departments, for better decisions, clearer direction, and a more enlightened leadership will intensify. There is little question that the public will demand ever geater efforts toward high-level performance, not to mention accountability. It is inevitable that all academic leaders will soon realize that the choice is not whether to be a manager, but merely whether they wish to be competent in their function. Inherent intelligence and good intuitive judgment are no longer enough. Management principles encompass more than common sense. A thorough understanding of the concepts discussed here and an enhanced ability to apply them can be a foundation for reaching significantly higher levels of achievement, even excellence.

Leader, Supervisor, or Manager?

In most business and government organizations, the title *supervisor* is used for those who supervise the work itself. Higher-level supervisors are generally referred to as *managers*. In some organizations, the distinction is less clear, and higher-level managers may be referred to as *department supervisors*. In either case, it is important to clearly see that it is possible to *manage* an activity or lead a unit without *supervising* anyone. Supervision refers to directing the work of other people, an activity that is not necessarily a management function. If someone supervises the work of other people, however, that person automatically managers, because supervision of others requires specific planning and goal setting and the organizing, directing, and evaluating that is so essential to the management task.

It would therefore appear to be more appropriate to speak of first-line supervision, middle-level supervision, and top-level supervision and to reserve the title of manager for those who manage some function but supervise no one. Thus, a "manager" could be in charge of planning or legal matters, or small individual research projects.

In the academic world, a third title is used. Deans and department chairpersons are "leaders of colleagues." They are not considered, and usually do not serve as, supervisors in a strict sense. They do, however, preform many management functions, as was previously discussed. In this book, the term *manager* is applied to them whenever appropriate. For the sake of simplicity, and to comply with general use of the broader meaning given to the word *manager*, it is used throughout this book. Most of the discussions in this book are addressed to those individuals in institutions of higher learning who actually supervise the work of others. In most sections, an attempt also has been made to demonstrate how the same concepts can apply to academic leaders.

The Linking Elements Concept Defined

The Linking Elements Concept, which is the core of this book, is an attempt to synthesize theory and practical experience into a workable, although difficult, guide to action. It combines the thinking of behavioral scientists and management theorists with the viewpoint of the practical manager or academic leader. Thus it offers a systematic, practical approach for managerial problem analysis in the search for greater effectiveness.

The Linking Elements Concept starts with a truism—that the level of performance of an organizational unit, to the extent to which it can be influenced by the unit manager or leader, depends on the skills with which the manager or leader can balance the needs and characteristics of the people in the unit with the needs and characteristics of the unit itself. These skills are the linking elements. From this definition, this book proceeds to analyze, linking element by linking element, what managers and leaders in higher education should know, and do, to improve their skills and thus achieve a better balance.

The Linking Elements Concept works. It is a pragmatic, realistic system that helps managers develop their human resources and create a climate in which people can find motivation for achievement. Linking elements ensure that the roles of managers and employees are defined clearly so that credit for contributions to the organization is given fairly, based on competence and effort, not luck or other extraneous matters.

You probably will not immediately agree with everything that is said here. At first, some of the ideas may seem, to conflict with what you have come to believe. However, if you keep reading with an open mind, a comprehensive picture will most likely appear. It will answer some of your objections and explain some of the contradictions between theories, or between theory and what you might consider to be practical guides to action.

When theorists ask that a manager adopt a participative leadership style, the idea is great—as an ideal—but how practical is it for the average manager or leader, who must meet quotas or performance standards, many of which are dictated from above? Similarly, if you have had management or leadership responsibilities for some time, you have read about management by objectives (MBO) or management by results (MBR). (The abbreviation MBO will be used to designate all goal programs. This book concerns itself primarily with fundamental issues; no attempt will be made to distinguish between management by objectives, managing with goals, or management by results. Those who have originated these various concepts use them to describe essentially similar management techniques. Apparently, different names are used to avoid any negative connotations that may have built up in the minds of people who have worked on unsuccessful programs and are therefore disenchanted with the program name.) You may have attended a seminar or two at which MBO was discussed at length, or you may be working for an educational institution that has a goals program of some sort. In any case, you know that a goals program holds great promise for helping your institution achieve greater control over its future and, at the same time, for bringing greater job satisfaction to employees and managers as well as better service for students. However, you also know, or probably have found, that MBO very often can degenerate into a great deal of paper work or just another attempt by high-level administrators to gain tighter control over the actions of people at lower echelons or in other fields.

You also have probably become acquainted with Maslow's "hierarchy of needs," which seems to provide a blueprint for motivating people. Yet, if you have thought about how you can actually apply it, you probably have come to wonder whether you can really "motivate" anybody to become more achievement oriented. You also may have questioned whether real people actually fit into Maslow's framework. You may have tried to determine how money fits into the scheme or what self-realization (or self-actualization) really means for your secretary or for the other people who report directly to you. If you asked some of these questions, you undoubtedly found answers difficult to come by. Your people are probably like most of us; they do not know where they can find self-realization. It is no accident that "finding one's self" is such a frustrating experience and leads many people on a futile odyssey or to a psychiatrist. The theory is tantalizing—but where is the practical end? How can you help others achieve so elusive a goal?

In theory, it is clear that planning is highly desirable and that people should be rewarded for planning their work and working their plans. What happens, though, when you reward those people who achieve the goals in their plans and fail to reward those who fall short? For example, do people strive harder to stay within budget or improve their performance? Or do they, instead, devote considerably greater effort to gamesmanship so that their responsibilities will be more comfortable the next time around?

It is not only with theories that you have undoubtedly often felt uncomfortable. Have you thought from time to time that you should have handled a situation differently? That you should have made a better decision? That you could have established a better environment for some people so that they would have been more willing to accept the responsibilities of their positions?

The Linking Elements Concept will answer some of these questions. It will *not*, however, provide easy or simple approaches to resolving practical problems. Nor, for that matter, does it claim that any of these problems can be resolved in their entirety. In their enthusiasm over their findings, theorists often do not emphasize sufficiently that there are many influences on the behavior of people, from body chemistry to the environment. Obviously, not all these are under the control of the administrative manager or the academic leader. A person who lacks motivation or dislikes the work cannot be turned into a zealous achiever, no matter how knowledgeable or competent the manager or leader may be.

The lack of balance in theories has lead to the assumption, which underlies most management-development programs, that it is within a manager's power to motivate most, if not all, people and that people will get to enjoy tasks they dislike just because the manager treats them "properly." The Linking Elements Concept is not based on such an assumption. The concept, in fact, suggests that it may be best not to be too concerned with the reactions of specific individuals, but rather, to concentrate on the "climate" in the organizational unit, so that it will become one in which most people can find higher levels of satisfaction from working. In such a climate, some people will respond immediately with higher levels of achievement, while others will be reached more slowly; still others may never respond. The effective manager or leader is not overly concerned if one or two people in the unit cannot find true motivation. If others around them have positive attitudes, they too will become better producers than they would be in a less positive climate.

Bridging the Gap between
Comprehension and Application

The Linking Elements Concept is a practical theory with many points that can be applied directly, and immediately, to help improve the performance of a unit in an educational environment. However, it is a complex concept with a deceptively simple facade. It therefore requires a certain amount of effort for complete understanding, and only when it is completely understood can it fulfill its promise. Shallow understanding leads to partial implementation and frequently to disappointments. For example, when you first attend a management seminar, many of the thoughts expressed have only limited meaning and may not seem directly applicable to your work environment. Gradually, however, as you gain greater experience, some of these thoughts begin to encourage deeper insights, and opportunities for practical application appear more frequently.

Good theory is that way. Limited contact usually brings some benefits, and deeper study brings many. Greater confidence in the theory's applicability, when many veils hide the fundamental issues, can come only after a thorough understanding has been achieved. One of the problems you may face in your work as an administrative manager or academic leader is that you never know whether you are achieving the best that can be achieved, somewhat less, or a great deal less. Fortunate environment or circumstances may bring good results when competence is low. Conversely, even the most competent manager can barely avoid serious problems in highly unfavorable situations. The old, spuriously modest adage "We must be doing something right" is a treacherous guide when conditions change.

If deeper comprehension of the more complex concepts has not been thoroughly integrated into a manager's personal style, awkward situations can sometimes occur as the manager tries to use unaccustomed approaches. There is a tongue-in-cheek story about a computer-services office that was brought on-line with a new system. The office hired several new supervisors, some of them straight out of college. While it was customary for the institution to send new supervisors to a management-development course before they were assigned their duties, at this particular time, the need was so great and the course so crowded that it was decided to put some of them to work directly. Among them was a young man named Jim. One day during his first week in the office, he walked down a corridor and saw one of the employees sitting off to the side having a cup of coffee and smoking a cigarette. He walked over to her and asked, "What are you doing?" The employee replied, "Can't you see? I'm having a cup of coffee and I'm smoking a cigarette." The young, new supervisor, recognizing an infraction of rules, responded, "This is no time to take a break. These are working hours. Please go back to your job or else I will have to discipline you." The employee, knowing better than to argue with the supervisor, doused her cigarette, put down her cup of coffee, and went back to her work. This conversation was observed by Jim's manager, and before the day was out, Jim and he were having a discussion about good management. The upshot of it was that Jim was sent to the supervisory course after all.

A week later he returned to the same position. At about the same time, on his first day, he was walking down the same corridor. There was the same employee sitting off to the side, having a cup of coffee, and smoking a cigarette. Jim walked over to her and said, "What are you doing, may I ask?" The employee replied, "Just having a cup of coffee and smoking a cigarette, as you can see." To which Jim replied, "Now? These are working hours. Please return to your work or else I will have to discipline you." No sooner were the words out of his mouth, though, when he remembered some of the things he had learned in the course. He walked over to the woman, who was preparing to return to work, smiled at her broadly, and said, "How was your weekend?"

This is, of course, an exaggerated example, but it may not be as far from what sometimes happens in real shops and offices as it may seem. Employees and colleagues can recognize when a manager or leader is not fully sincere with them, even when he or she is not as blatantly manipulative. One of the errors many managers make after returning from a seminar or course on some aspect of management or leadership style, or some facet of the behavioral sciences, is to quickly put some of their new "insights" to work. Such efforts are often self-defeating, because they are not thoroughly integrated into the manager's style. They are therefore likely to be in contradiction with the image that other people have of the manager. More than intellectual comprehension is needed for effective implementation of a change in style. A way has to be found to make the change compatible with one's total personality and with the expectations of the people being supervised.

How the Book Is Structured. Besides this introductory chapter, there are eight other chapters in this book. Chapter 2 traces the history of management as a discipline, a science, and an art from its informal and formal beginnings to the twentieth century. It starts by discussing the four foundations of modern management theory (management science, behavioral science, the management cycle, and management by objectives or results) and by examining the work of some of the leading theorists in these areas. Chapter 3 provides a very brief overview of the entire Linking Elements Concept, which combines management science, management by objectives (MBO), and the behavioral sciences into one all-encompassing framework. Chapter 4 discusses MBO, or management with goals—a major segment of the Linking Elements Concept. Chapter 5 discusses the remaining linking elements; this chapter completes the foundation and general principles of modern management concepts and theories.

Chapter 6, which discusses governance of institutions of higher education, provides a transition into the remaining chapters, which identify how the Linking Elements Concept can be used by managers and leaders to set goals and lead their respective units to higher achievement. Chapter 7 relates the concept to the roles and responsibilities of leaders and managers in academic affairs. Similarly, chapter 8 discusses applications in the various departments that comprise student affairs. Finally, chapter 9 reviews the administrative function in terms of the Linking Elements Concept.

Assumptions Underlying the Linking Elements Concept

Five assumptions are central to the Linking Elements Concept. These are

1. A manager's actions are shaped by three primary influences: the environment, the people who report to him or her, and the manager's personal characteristics.
2. A person cannot "motivate" other people, but can only create an environment in which the others can find motivation.
3. Decision-making and communications skills are required for all managerial activities; as these skills are improved, it is likely that other skills will improve as well.
4. A major determinant of success for an organizational unit is the extent to which unit needs are aligned with the needs and characteristics of people in that unit.
5. There is some measure of validity to the findings of all serious, prominent researchers and theorists, and a comprehensive concept must take these findings into consideration.

The Primary Influences on Managerial Action

The first assumption underlying the Linking Elements Concept is that three primary influences shape your behavior as an administrative manager or academic leader:

1. The *environment* in which you manage, including the changing situation of the moment. This means that what may be a correct action right now may be far from the best action a half hour later if changes have taken place that significantly affect the situation.
2. The *people who are affected* by your actions. These people influence your decisions. Whether dealing with individuals or groups of people, colleagues, employees, or students, you need to consider their relationship to you, their level of knowledge, their capabilities and emotional maturity, and their access to information.
3. *You*—your capabilities, including your knowledge, skill, and aptitudes. This also includes the way you are perceived by others.

Of these three, you have immediately direct control only over the third one—and you can, if you work, bring about significant change. However, to suddenly make extensive changes is neither easy nor desirable.

Even minor changes sometimes come across as forced or unreal. In your role as manager or leader, as well as in your other roles in life, you are most effective when you are yourself. At the same time, if you seek increasing control over your environment and your destiny, you must gain increasing awareness of yourself, of the various characteristics of your personality, and of your strengths and weaknesses, as well as of your impact on the people around you. This can help you cushion and reduce the effect of any undesirable aspects of your decisions and actions while you strenghen and gain increasingly greater advantages from those which are beneficial.

Motivating People

A second fundamental assumption of the Linking Elements Concept is that people cannot motivate other people. You certainly do not want someone to "motivate" you. Managers and leaders in an academic environment, however, can establish a psychological climate in which people can develop a desire to achieve and which will encourage them to strive to improve their performance. In short, a manager or leader who tries to "motivate" an employee or a colleague is likely to fail—although the employee or colleague may be induced, cajoled, or forced to the desired actions. However, managers *can* help their people find greater motivation in their work.

Decision Making and Communications

The third assumption involves the roles of communications and decision making. Both these skills overlap all other managerial skills and are enormously broad subjects. While some general principles can be isolated that are universally applicable, these principles, by themselves, are not sufficient to help managers improve their performance significantly. (See appendix A for an overview of decision making.)

If you want to become a better communicator or a better decision maker, your best bet is to brush up on and practice communications for specific purposes, such as selection interviewing. After one application has been mastered, you can proceed to the next one. This is not meant to deny that there are fundamental principles, such as those concerned with listening, speaking, questioning, and so on, that must be understood before one can study, practice, and master a specific type of communications. However, communications is no different from other comprehensive subjects. For instance, only very few highly talented people can learn several musical instruments from the study of the fundamentals of music and from practicing on one instrument. Nor have there been many mathematicians who have become skilled in the various fields of mathematics without extensive experience in each one. Yet, when it comes to decision making and communications, there appears to be a lingering belief or a strong hope that managers have the innate capability of transferring knowledge of principles and skill in one area to all the others.

Better communications in interviews come from detailed study of interviewing and practice of interviewing techniques. Good decision making in a specific field, whether it concerns scheduling or some facet of personnel management, requires the application of some general principles. What is more important, though, is that good decision making is usually the result of considerable experience with, or careful study of, the factors that are important to decisions in a particular field of work. Various aspects of decision making and communications are covered in many places in this book, and a brief overview of the major fundamental principles of decision making is provided in appendix A.

The Foundation for Success

The fourth assumption concerns the truism that an organizational unit will be as successful as it can possibly be if its manager can achieve a high degree of alignment between its needs on the one hand and the characteristics and needs of its members on the other hand. (*Success* is defined here as the ability to cope with the environment and to achieve growth and/or excellence to the extent to which either is desired or possible, to survive where survival is the best that can be achieved or to dissolve in ways most beneficial to the mission and the future of the people involved, to gain maximum control over the changing environment, or to seek out and adapt to a new, more favorable environment.) This is not meant to imply that it is the manager's task to mold everyone to fit the organization's needs or that the organization must conform to the characteristics of its members. On the contrary, it refers to the dynamic process of continuous adjustment and mutual accommodation (not compromise) that somehow achieves a total far greater than the sum of its parts.

The Linking Elements Concept
and the Finding of Research

One more assumption completes the foundations for the Linking Elements Concept—and it is an obvious one. It concerns the findings of theorists and researchers in the management and behavioral sciences. The Linking Elements Concept builds on these findings because it assumes that important insights stem from every serious piece of work. It attempts to resolve existing contradictions and important objections that have been raised. As a result, in a few instances, the models originally suggested by the researchers have been significantly modified. In general, however, these changes are primarily along the lines of further explanation.

Common Misconceptions

There are some common misconceptions that have to be discussed briefly in an introductory chapter to a comprehensive management text because they exert considerable influence on attitudes about continuing management development. The following sections consider these misconceptions.

The Starting Point for Good Management

Many administrative managers and academic leaders believe that good management must start with the president of the institution because they feel that at their levels it is virtually impossible to practice leadership styles that are not in keeping with those of their superiors. That this is not always the case, however, is obvious from the fact that some managers and leaders achieve better results than others in the same environment and in the same situation. Clearly, these managers are either better leaders or better managers, or both. Intuitively—or because they have acquired greater knowledge about good management techniques and approaches—they lead their units to higher levels of achievement.

The ideas suggested in this book can be used at any level in an educational institution. Admittedly, they have wider application at higher levels, and when practiced there, it is easier for lower-level managers to use them. However, these ideas are *not* restricted to use by administration. Even the smallest institutional unit can benefit if its manager or leader commits himself or herself to their use.

Influencing Top-Level Administrators

Another common belief held by many administrative managers and academic leaders is that the upper levels of academic administration are not receptive to their ideas and suggestions. Here, too, there is some truth to the belief, and usually, little can be achieved unless these people are in a receptive mood. However, if receptivity were all that is involved, how might it be explained that some people exert greater influence than others on those to whom they report?

The Applicability of General Principles

As mentioned earlier in this chapter, many academic leaders do not recognize that general management principles apply in the educational environment. While general principles do need interpretation and translation to be effective in any specific environment, the basic principles of management apply just the same.

In every environment, management is concerned with the establishment and accomplishment of goals through the efforts of people. Managers, particularly at high levels, have always been aware of the great similarities in managing different organizations. They know that the required technical skill and knowledge exist among the people in the organization and that they can draw on that expertise in order to accomplish what they would like to achieve. At lower levels of management, however, managers usually must possess some of that technical expertise themselves. Direct supervision of work requires that the manager understand the intricacies of the work at least sufficiently to recognize what is right and what is wrong. Those who advance through the management ranks must supevise more and more different types of functions and, naturally, can no longer be personally knowledgeable in each one of them. This is why, for instance, the higher levels of government can and do draw their managers from all walks of life: education, industry, labor, and other governmental agencies and institutions. A competent manager who gains experience in one industry will often do well in a high-level position in another industry or in government, and a manager from a high governmental position may do well in private industry or an institution. This interchange of managers between different professions and occupations is evidence that because fundamental management principles exist, it is usually possible for competent managers to adapt quickly to new environments.

Management and Common Sense

Another widely held belief is that common sense is an adequate guide for most management decisions. People tend to believe that they will do the "right thing" intuitively when the need arises. Intuitive reactions may seem right because they come about naturally, but very often they can be deceptive and thus lead to poor results. Examples of erroneous intuitive reactions are easy to find. We need only to step suddenly on the brake when driving a car and watch the reactions of our passengers. Inevitably, they will brace themselves by stiffening their arms against the dashboard or the seat in front of them and, with both feet, push hard on an imaginary brake as though an accident were about to happen. This is an intuitive natural reaction, yet it is wrong. Nothing is potentially more dangerous than an attempt to prevent the impact of a high-speed collision with arms and legs that are too weak to resist. If an accident were to occur, such stiffening of the limbs would only lead to more severe injuries. Once the arms and legs give way, the body is thrown into the windshield with additional force. The correct position is exactly opposite the position just described—that is, lean forward loosely and brace the head and body against the dashboard or seat in front.

Similar intuitive yet incorrect decisions are made by salespeople who charge ahead when a prospect or customer voices an easily refutable objection. Rather than attempting to find the concern that prompted the objection in the first place, such salespeople address the words that may be only a weak reflection of the prospect's actual feelings. The same is true of a department chairperson who, when faced with pressure from higher levels of administration, immediately passes that pressure along. The department chairperson acts intuitively, and sometimes wrongly, as does the business manager who cuts advertising when business slows down or the teacher who chides students for asking "silly" questions. The examples are legion, yet the conclusion is obvious: Intuitive reactions are often not the best. A few moments of thought between impulse and action can often bring about better actions—and better results.

For good management decisions, managers and leaders need a conceptual framework that provides logical consistency while making it possible to act quickly. That framework is usually based on a theory. To quote the words of the English economist John Maynard Keynes, "Practical men who believe themselves to be exempt from theoretical influences are usually the slaves of some defunct theorist."

Process and Content

Finally, one distinction that managers sometimes fail to see clearly is that between *process* and *content*. Although the distinction is simple, it is sometimes difficult to keep in mind. For example, if a professor is teaching theories of growth and development, then the topic, that is, growth and development, is the content of the activity. At the same time, there is a process going on: the acquisition of information by the learners, that is, the learning process. The inadequate or inexperienced instructor may concentrate solely on explaining the topic (content). Such an instructor is likely to lecture and possibly not be aware that some of the learners have fallen asleep, although their eyes may still be open. The competent instructor, in contrast, while being occupied with discussing content, would watch the process of information transmittal or acquisition of information by the learners. Such an instructor would constantly be asking what else could be done to help students learn more effectively, how students could apply the information so it would be more meaningful to them, and how students could search for the portions of the topic they still did not understand in order to gain a broader comprehension of the subject.

For most management tasks, the content of an activity concerns the specific job that has to be done and the steps that are necessary to achieve it. The process that the competent manager keeps in mind, though, concerns the effectiveness with which a team coordinates its activities, how the team responds to the environment, what major problems occur that need to be dealt with in the future, and so on. (*Effectiveness* is not the same as *efficiency* and should not be confused with it. *Efficiency* refers to the ratio of output to input. The higher is the rate of output to input, the higher is the efficiency. Efficiency can be measured in pieces produced per hour, lower costs, and so forth. *Effectiveness* is a much broader term than efficiency. Effectiveness concerns not only the immediate results, but also the impact of today's actions on the future. For example, an effective manager is one who makes efficient use of personal time, who follows policies and procedures that will bring efficiency in the use of materials and in the use of the time of subordinates, but who does not sacrifice actions or expenditures that build for the future in order to have better results today.) Both administrative managers and academic leaders need self-discipline to keep process in mind while performing routine daily activities, whether these activities concern conducting of an interview, chairing a meeting, or planning a project. A constant awareness of process helps provide the foundation for planning for the future. It is in process that long-term effectiveness is developed—an effectiveness that constantly improves an individual's or a team's ability to cope with the environment.

2

The Four Foundations of Modern Management Thinking: Management Science, The Management Cycle, The Behavioral Sciences, and Management by Objectives

Good practices often exist long before people become aware of the theoretical foundations on which they rest. Bridges were built and ships navigated the seas in the days when there was no science involving strength of materials and when astronomy was more myth than discipline. The pyramids of Egypt, the Great Wall of China, and the magnificent cathedrals of Europe all attest to the competency of the skilled managers of their times. The successful construction of the pyramids—the planning efforts, the methods for moving the huge blocks of stone, the supervision of the thousands of men and women who toiled directly and indirectly in the construction work itself and in the supply of tools, materials, and food—could never have been realized without the efforts of many knowledgeable managers. Unfortunately, there are few records of the techniques these managers used to guide their work forces. There is, however, a passage in the Holy Scriptures that hints at formal organization: "And Moses chose able men out of all Israel, and made them heads over the people, rulers of thousands, rulers of hundreds, rulers of fifties and rulers of tens. And they judged the people at all seasons; the hard cases they brought unto Moses, but every small matter they judged themselves." Exod. 18:25 and 26.

Management before Management Theory

Despite the tremendous size of some of the spectacular projects in the early days of civilization that required managerial skills, most management functions were performed on a small scale. Then, as now, individuals managed their personal activities by themselves. However, few people thought of this as management. For example, farming was not considered to be management of an enterprise because most of the production went for personal use. It was much less complicated than it is now because there were no complex machines to worry about, no special fertilizers, no pest-control chemicals, and no bank loans or multipage tax forms.

Although there were some people who might be thought of as managers, real managers were few. Noblemen often employed the services of tax collectors (similar in function to today's credit and collection managers) to collect goods, rent, or taxes from tenants. This, however, can hardly be thought of as management as we know it today. Moreover, the type of management needed for barter trade with faraway places, while it required planning, organizing, and executing, was hardly complex enough to warrant development of a formal theory. It, too, followed a pattern and was done the way it had always been done.

Nevertheless, supervisors in the large governmental organizations and offices, in the early armies and navies, and on large estates were concerned with obtaining the largest possible output from the workers. They also were involved with other managerial activities. For example, the *span of control* must have been given serious consideration not only by Moses, but also by navies and armies and large governmental organizations. There is no doubt that managers and military officers were aware of the problems in controlling many people; they knew that a wide span of control (many subordinates reporting directly to each manager) meant that they would be closer to the line and maintain better vertical communications. They were equally aware that a more limited number of direct subordinates meant more levels between themselves and the action and that longer lines of communication made them slower and less reliable. Along similar lines, the *extent of delegation* of authority and responsibility always was dependent on the varying capabilities of subordinate managers. Those who were in charge of large organizations always had to give careful thought to how they delegated, when, and to whom.

In addition, *communications systems* had to be carefully designed and required thought and constant monitoring. Without this, supervisors could not possibly maintain cohesion among the many groups that a large organization spanned. Furthermore, *salary administration* had to be equitable in relation to most of the same principles that guide salary administration today. *Financial systems* had to exist to ensure that adequate monies (or substitutes) were available when and where needed to meet payrolls and the demands for payment for supplies and services purchased (or bartered) from outside the organization.

Planning and production had to be organized just as well then as now in order to place huge armies into the field, to erect large structures, or to conduct large-scale trading operations. Moreover, *administrative lines* had to be drawn. Line and staff functions were separated and limits were set to authority, at least to a degree. (However, the tales of intrigue and conspiracies that have been recorded are ample evidence that the checks on authority did not deter the ambitious and unscrupulous.)

The Foundations of Management Theory

The limited number of managers in antiquity and down through the Middle Ages did not make management a topic of popular concern. Not until the industrial revolution did the increasing complexity of management and the growing number of managers lead to the development of management theory.

Management theory as we know it today has evolved gradually from four major foundations: management science, the behavioral sciences, the management cycle, and management by objectives. *Management science*, whose establishment as a separate discipline is credited to Frederick Winslow Taylor, concentrates on the efficiency of the work processes and the way the individual employee performs tasks. The *behavioral sciences*, which developed considerably later than management science, explore the way people behave in their work environment and the influence their behavior has on the amount and quality of work output. The *management cycle* concerns an entirely different aspect of management. It steps away from analyzing the employee and concentrates on the manager's task—on how to make the manager's work more effective so that the people who report to the manager will achieve improved results. The *management by objectives* concept, or management with goals, is an outgrowth of the management cycle. It is a significant refinement of, and in some major ways supersedes, the management cycle, although many managers today view it as an independent concept.

The Linking Elements Concept builds on all four foundations and uses them to create one comprehensive framework that can provide guidance for managers and leaders in higher education who want to improve the performance of their units. Thorough understanding of the Linking Elements Concept requires an appreciation of the history of management theory. The development of the two major foundations, management science and the behavioral sciences, is therefore outlined very briefly here. The management cycle is described in this chapter, and management by objectives is such an integral part of the Linking Elements Concept that it is discussed together with the latter in chapter 4.

Management Science

The Impact of the Industrial Revolution. With the advent of the industrial revolution came many changes that affected the work patterns of the average person. Hand looms faded from existence and were replaced by textile mills. Potters gave up their wheels and went to work in pottery factories.

The small crafts and guilds, the people working at home in their cottages, and the little shops that previously turned out cooking utensils, clothing, needles, and other necessities were replaced by something new to civilization—the mills, plants, and factories that came into being during the industrial revolution.

The transition from cottage to factory changed farm hands and small entrepreneurs into factory workers. Now the large mills, plants, and factories needed managers to ensure effective operation. Not too much was recorded at first about the management practices of the day. This was primarily because few people could read, fewer could write, and the general public had little or no knowledge of scientific subject areas beyond rudimentary arithmetic.

Throughout the nineteenth century, awareness of management as a distinct discipline grew, but it was not until the end of the century that this awareness was formalized in the work of Frederick Winslow Taylor. Management science, or "scientific management," considered to have begun with the work of Taylor, concentrated on the way the work of employees could be organized to obtain greater output. Management science included several topics: *methods study*, which was concerned with the way an operation should have been performed and how the work place should have been organized; *work measurement*, which attempted to determine how long various tasks took; and *work standards*, which specified the "normal" or "standard" time it took to do a task.

Work standards formed the basis of piece rates (payment for production of a unit of work, a piece) and other incentives. These were intended to induce employees to work faster and harder, but also provided an opportunity for higher earnings. It is interesting to note that management science provided the earliest form of performance evaluation, which was based completely on results and linked directly to compensation.

Management science branched out from the basic types of measurement just described into the mathematical techniques widely used today to determine the ways of doing things. Operations analysis, inventory-control principles, linear programming, production-line balancing, and scheduling techniques all sprang from the broadening search for better work arrangements. Management science led to computers, to today's self-correcting machinery, and to many mechanical devices that perform so much of the monotonous, repetitive, or menial work in modern society.

Methods Study, Time Study, and the Modern Manager. What is the significance of the findings of early management scientists for modern managers? The answer to this question, of course, depends in part on one's point of view. There are those researchers and theorists who feel that setting standards for people is likely to be demotivating, dehumanizing, and there-fore self-defeating. People naturally resist the regimentation of standard setting. They are likely to strive for the lowest possible standards because that gives them either the widest freedom of movement or the highest in-come, or both. If they can obtain easy standards, they are often likely to restrict their work output to come close to those standards, even if that can be done in a small part of the workday, to avoid raising questions about the validity of the standards.

Researchers opposed to setting standards will concede, of course, that there is value to methods study that simplifies work so that in most situations formal study by people other than those doing the work is not necessary. They maintain that employees have the inherent intelligence to find the best work method if management will only give them the chance to do so.

Other experts take a somewhat broader view. They see many manufac-turing plants and offices in which one person is dependent on the output of another, and they feel that it is essential that the work load be divided up fairly and evenly. Specialized skills in time study, as well as methods study, are essential in order to achieve these results, and only people formally trained in these skills can set high-quality standards. Those who hold such views do not consider it practical to train all employees so they can be equally proficient in standard setting.

Summary and Perspective. Management theory was born as management science. Emphasis was on efficiency—on methods, on time study, on piece rates, and on scheduling. The search was for better ways to do things so that society would have more goods and services with the same amount of effort. The concept that more production leads to greater wealth, originally from Adam Smith, was the guiding principle. It was assumed without question that higher income was the most important motivator. Better work methods lead to higher revenues and profits. They, in turn, permitted higher wage payments. Various incentive plans were shaped to share the increased in-come and at the same time, so it was hoped, stimulate maximum motivation in employees. This was all that was considered necessary to bring a better world. There were problems with people, of course, but the causes were believed to be with inadequate precision in methods and time studies and in incentive-payment systems.

The search for solutions kept management scientists looking for ways to overcome the problems. The result was a focus on *techniques*, with little at-tention to the *psychological needs* of people. Not until, almost by accident, this search led to unexpected results did the attention of management thinkers shift away from single-minded concentration on financial rewards to the broader needs of people at work.

The Behavioral Sciences

The second major foundation of modern management theory can be found in the behavioral sciences. Although the behavioral sciences became part of management theory almost accidentally, their impact has been very large indeed. As the level of education of employees rose and machines took over more and more of the repetitive and easily measurable tasks, appreciation for the importance of motivation as a prime determinant of output increased by leaps and bounds.

The roots of the behavioral sciences lie in two areas: (1) formal psychology, and (2) the humanistic movements, such as those of the Ricardian socialists and Utopians of the early nineteenth century, who believed that societies could be formed in which the relationship between work and life could be more harmonious than that which they saw around them. Both roots contributed philosophical considerations as well as a pool of knowledge on which the early behavioral scientists could draw.

The development of behavioral science, which was not so called until after it was well established, started during the first third of the twentieth century with attempts to determine how the work environment influenced productivity. The questions to which some of the management scientists wanted answers dealt with the effect of work breaks on productivity and the impacts of lighting and other environmental factors. The most famous investigations were conducted at the Western Electric Company's Hawthorne Plant in Chicago between 1927 and 1932. Western Electric's scientists found that work output did not change, as they had predicted, when they manipulated the physical conditions. They called in Dr. Elton Mayo of Harvard University to conduct further studies. The results of many experiments in the Hawthorne studies were startlingly diffferent from the researcher's original hypothesis. In the most famous experiments, six young women were detached from a department where hundreds of workers assembled a simple telephone-relay component. Working in a separate room under careful observation and friendly attention from the researchers, they were given rest periods of differing durations at various times in the working day. As predicted, their work output began to increase. However, when the rest periods were eliminated, the work output continued to increase dramatically and kept rising almost without interruption with every change in working conditions—whether the changes were favorable or unfavorable.

The Work of Elton Mayo. Dr. Elton Mayo of Harvard interpreted the Hawthorne experiments in a series of papers and books that made him famous. According to Mayo, in experiments like the one involving the telephone component, assembly workers demonstrated the importance of informal social groupings that were often more meaningful to them than the formal organization of the company, changes in physical surroundings, or money incentives. The young women assemblers, he explained, increased production because of the friendship and trust they developed among themselves and because of the special recognition given them as a group—when they were singled out for the experiment, they felt special and acted that way. Mayo also pointed out that some of the other informal groups observed in the experiments operated to limit production and fight controls, even when better efforts would have brought about higher pay. The reasons, Mayo suggested, lay in the suspicion and distrust these groups felt toward management and the need they felt to build barriers and intragroup rules for their own protection.

Mayo's broadest conclusions were highly controversial. He disturbed many readers with his sweeping view of the informal group as the workers' last refuge in a cold, inhumane society. His prescriptions for management, involving tactics with which managers could identify and control informal workers' groups, angered many liberal observers who interpreted these prescriptions as antiunion. Whatever the arguments against Mayo, he had publicized a remarkable series of experiments that included more than 20,000 individual interviews with workers and their supervisors. These interviews underscored the existence of a psychology and a sociology of work previously unexplored and thus laid the major foundation for the complex, interdisciplinary behavioral sciences that gradually emerged.

With the advent of the Hawthorne experiments, management theory had been extended beyond physical movement and efficiency questions to a study of questions concerning how workers behaved and why. The study of management had thus grown in one leap to embrace a large segment of behavioral science inquiry into motivation, communications, the nature of leadership, the social characteristics of organizations, and the best conditions for employee development and career growth.

Scientific management and industrial engineering had by no means been displaced by this human relations school of management. Extensive follow-up on the findings of the Hawthorne experiments was delayed many years by the higher urgencies brought about by the Great Depression and then World War II. During this time, the term *human relations approach* gradually appeared and declined in use and the term *behavioral science approach* grew in popularity.

The Management Cycle

So far this chapter has discussed only management science and behavioral science, two of the legs on which management theory rests. Management science, as was pointed out, focuses on the work of employees. As society needed more and more managers to manage increasingly complex tasks and the larger number of people in industrial and government work forces, more thought had to be given to the work of the managers themselves.

Henri Fayol's Work: The Basis of the Management Cycle: Of all the people who studied how a manager's work should be organized, few showed greater understanding or wrote about it more clearly and intelligently than a French mining director named Henri Fayol. Fayol spent his entire business career (over 50 years) as the industrial manager of a coal mine. He used the same scientific, rationally derived methods of attacking management problems as Taylor, but in an entirely new area. In his book *General and Industrial Management* (written in French in 1916 and translated into English in 1949), he outlined what managers should do, how they should do it, and how they should relate to each other. Fayol saw the role of management as a cycle that keeps repeating itself. Managers perform a specific set of functions that gradually lead every project or task to a satisfactory completion.

Management Skills: Fayol divided a manager's duties into five primary functions: (1) planning, (2) organizing, (3) commanding, (4) coordinating, and (5) controlling. These functions, as Fayol saw them, form a cycle of management because they blend in with one another to form a total concept of management (see figure 2-1).

Other theorists who have studied and written about a manager's duties have used various terms to overcome the misunderstandings and problems that Fayol's original definitions sometimes created. For example, although

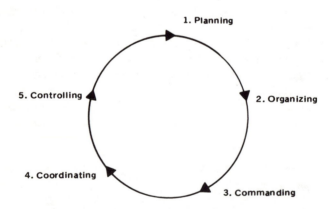

Source: From Henri Fayol, *General and Industrial Management*. Copyright © 1949 by Pitman Publishing Company. Reprinted by permission of Pitman Learning, Belmont, California.

Figure 2-1. Pictorial Representation of Henri Fayol's Management Cycle

planning and organizing are commonly used for the first steps, some theorists follow these with steps such as "executing," "implementing," "staffing," "leading," "follow-up," and "evaluating"—all words that describe one or the other of the remaining functions in the cycle.

Even though the mangement cycle applies to specific projects or activities, as well as to a manager's overall responsibilities, it is not as practical as it may at first seem to be. While it recognizes the importance of the manager's team, it provides little guidance for the manager's relationships with team members and concentrates on the disciplines that managers should impose on themselves to increase their personal effectiveness. Despite this shortcoming, the management cycle has been a major foundation for management education and training for over 50 years. It continues to be taught as a fundamental concept in many management-training programs today.

Management by Objectives

Management by objectives (MBO) is the fourth major foundation of management theory. It will be discussed in great detail in chapter 4. The brief discussion here serves only to complete the historical picture.

Management theorists have always spoken about objectives and goals. So, for that matter, have people from areas other than management. There is, therefore, some question as to where the formal concept of MBO originated. Most people credit Peter Drucker, the famous author and consultant, while others point to Chester Barnard.

Chester Barnard, for many years vice-president of the Jersey Bell Telephone Company, spoke of the need for managers to develop a cooperative system that would be capable of satisfying the personal objectives of employees as well as meeting the objectives of the organization. Barnard thus recognized the existence of two separate sets of objectives and that the success of an organization depended on satisfying both.

Peter Drucker spoke more specifically about an organization's objectives, particularly those of a business, since Drucker's main work was, at that time, at General Motors. He identified eight key areas in which objectives of performance and results have to be set: market standings, innovation, productivity, physical and financial resources, profitability, workers' performance and development, work performance and attitude, and public responsibility. He was aware that some of the goals or objectives in these functions could be quantified quite readily, while others were much more difficult to state precisely and without ambiguity.

While Drucker and Barnard were speaking primarily of the objectives of the entire organization rather than specific work and development objectives for each unit, possibly even for each individual employee, their thinking is fundamental to much of modern management theory. Moreover, as noted earlier, that portion of it dealing with MBO is relevant to the Linking Elements Concept, which is described in the next chapter. The Linking Elements Concept can furnish practical, sound approaches to management problems and management tasks to those managers and leaders who have mastered it. It can do this because it satisfies all the criteria for a comprehensive theory of management:

1. It accommodates all four foundations of management theory: management science, the management cycle, MBO, and the behavioral sciences.
2. It gives appropriate consideration to the organizational unit's need for performance (productivity, quality, response flexibility) *and* to the individual's right to gain maximum satisfaction.
3. It provides for consideration of three influences (situation, manager, and subordinate) on all decisions.
4. It applies with equal validity at all organizational levels, even though at lower levels freedom of action is limited to a greater degree.
5. It provides a guide for accurate diagnosis of performance problems.

3

How the Linking Elements Concept Works

Changing Views of the Management Function

It is interesting to note that in the case of each of the management theories discussed in the last chapter—that is, management science, the management cycle, behavioral science, and management by objectives—it was hoped that a relatively simple system could be devised to help managers manage more effectively. It seemed as though, with intelligent and reasonable people, not too much would be required to help overcome what appeared to be relatively minor obstacles to better management.

The management scientists thought that a lack of understanding of how to set standards prevented people from achieving more. After Fayol, it was inadequate awareness of the manager's role that had to be overcome. The management cycle, it was hoped, would bring better performance. Then, with the advent of the human relations approach to management, it was showing managers how to be more democratic that would unlock the door to higher achievement and greater job satisfaction at the same time. Today, few people seriously believe that significant changes in behavior, particularly in managerial competence, can be achieved with a program of 5 or 10 days, or even 30 days.

It has become abundantly evident, for instance, that there is more to motivation than just good leadership style and that management by objectives is not the simple concept it once seemed to be. There is no longer any hope that easy answers can be found. It is clear that good management requires either thorough understanding or a high level of innate ability to balance a far larger number of considerations than had heretofore been thought necessary.

The old definitions still hold, though—management means getting things done with and through people—but the meaning of this has changed. Not too long ago, this definition was believed to mean that a good manager who delegates properly is doing the best job possible without having to work hard. Gradually it has become clear that this is not really true, because a manager's function is to provide support and help to immediate subordinates. Even with excellent delegation, there is a lot left to do, from searching out opportunities for improvement to helping subordinates overcome those stubborn problems which are beyond their capabilities or resources.

Moreover, good management is not simply a matter of being democratic or autocratic, task-oriented or people-oriented. One form of management or one specific leadership style will not do for all situations. It is now obvious that the three influences referred to earlier—the situation, the characteristics of subordinates, the characteristics and styles of managers—create a highly complex environment and no single idea can serve as an adequate guide. All three of these influences must be considered in decision making, and managers must feel comfortable with a wide range of leadership styles, from the highly participative to the highly autocratic, from the highly supportive to the rigidly demanding. Managers also must either have high competence in one of the technical fields that is important to their organizational units or have exceptionally good diagnostic and analytical skills so that they can determine where their unit's performance is weakest and quickly get to the source of problems as they develop. Even more important is the need to perceive the frontiers of the field so that they can help their teams identify significant opportunities and take advantage of them.

In addition to being good leaders, modern managers also must be good planners, good organizers, and competent decision makers. These are difficult tasks and appear, at times, to be almost impossible. However, they are really no more difficult today than they were in the past—just more complex. For instance, there is no doubt that in the past, different styles of leadership were called for in a maintenance unit with unskilled or semi-skilled people, in a lab with highly educated scientists, or in an admissions office with widely traveling recruiters. But today there are more technical variations, higher employee expectations, and more demanding competitive requirements. The manager who is bent on rapidly improving competence must dig through the wealth of existing theories and gradually shape a philosophy and a framework that can serve as a guide.

However, how many capable managers have the time and the inclination to do so? It would seem that there is a need for a blueprint with which managerial as well as self-development decisions can be made. The Linking Elements Concept presented in this book can furnish such a guide. It stands squarely on research and research findings, and it covers most, if not all, the skills managers need to be effective. It does not sidestep the contradictions that exist between theory and practice, but faces and resolves them as best as can be done within the limits of existing knowledge. This does not mean, though, that the Linking Elements Concept provides an easy road to greater effectiveness. It is mainly the roadmap for very difficult self-development and self-discipline that can bring results to the manager who persists in developing the awareness and habits needed.

The Linking Elements Concept

The Linking Elements Concept is based on the fundamental truth that an organizational unit will achieve the highest level of performance that its environment permits if the manager can bring a high level of alignment between the needs of the unit and the characteristics and needs of the people in it.

The Organization

As illustrated in figure 3-1, the Linking Elements Concept begins by stating the obvious—that an organizational unit, whether it is an entire company, a governmental agency, an educational institution, or a voluntary organization, wants to achieve a high level of performance, whatever meaning the word *performance* has for it. For an educational institution, for instance, performance might be measured in many terms, among them quality of instruction, efficiency in providing services to students and to the community, and quality as an employer, as a customer to suppliers, and as a member of society at large. High-level performance depends greatly on three requirements: control, technical competence, and morale.

Control. The control requirement consists of three main elements. First, the unit must have direction. It must know where it wants to go and how

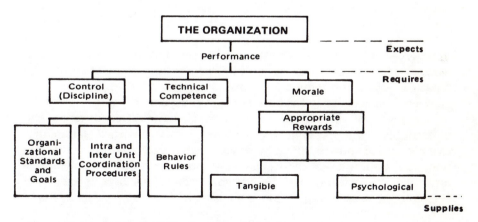

Source: Courtesy of National Fire Protection Association.

Figure 3-1. The Organizational Basis for the Linking Elements Concept

fast it wants to get there. That is, it must have *goals* that it wants to achieve and *standards of performance* so that everyone knows what to contribute toward the achievement of these goals. Control also means *discipline*—not discipline in the sense of punishment, but discipline in the sense of a disciplined team where every individual recognizes the needs of the team and is willing to forgo personal interests for the sake of achieving the goals of the team.

Besides direction, an organizational unit needs *coordination* if it is to have control. Coordination means that everybody knows what to do relative to other people. For instance, everybody in the Registrar's Office can agree that all students should receive prompt confirmation of their class schedules, but if coordination is lacking, a lot of wasted effort will prevent such rapid acknowledgement. In addition, for good control there must be *behavior rules* for the individual that establish what the unit can expect from an employee and tell employees what is expected of them.

Technical Competence. An organizational unit must have high technical competence if it expects to achieve a high level of performance. Each individual on the team must have the necessary capabilities, knowledge, and skills to perform well on the assigned tasks. For example, financial aid officers and their staffs must be fully aware of sources of financial assistance and the respective governmental regulations in order to serve the students effectively. Likewise, if instructors have extensive knowledge and are very skilled in teaching methodologies, then they will be better equipped to motivate their students to learn and to help them reach higher levels of scholastic achievement. (In this book, the term *instructor* will be used to include all teaching personnel, from part-time adjuncts to full professors.)

Morale. An effective unit must have a high level of morale. Morale depends on the satisfaction that people get from their work. There are two kinds of satisfaction: tangible and psychological. An organizational unit must provide adequately for both kinds of satisfaction.

An organization unit can achieve control, technical competence, and morale only if the people in the unit have the characteristics and abilities that are needed and are willing to devote them to the goals of the organization. The relationship of the individual to the organization is a critical factor in the achievement of performance goals, and the manager or leader, the person in the middle, can do much to shape it.

The Individual

Figure 3-2 illustrates the characteristics and needs of the individual that the manager or leader must balance with the characteristics and needs of the

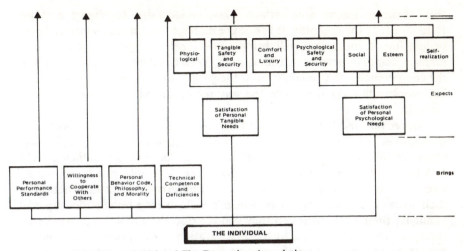

Source: Courtesy of National Fire Protection Association.

Figure 3-2. The Employee Basis for the Linking Elements Concept

organization. Individuals come to an organization with *personal perfor-mance standards* and a willingness to work—which may or may not meet the requirements necessary to achieve organizational goals. If willingness to work on required tasks and assignments is sufficient to meet unit needs, then the manager has very little to do. If, however, it is not, as frequently is the case, then there is a whole series of skills that a manager or leader must apply to gradually bring an employee or colleague to more willingly accept organizational goals.

The coordination an organization needs so that all subunits can move toward goals in an organized fashion requires *cooperation*. People must work smoothly with each other and with other teams. Good coordination depends on willing cooperation. There are many obstacles to cooperation between individuals and between teams. A manager must be able to recognize serious problems and must have the skills to remove all obstacles to cooperation and coordination.

An individual brings *attitudes and a philosophy of life*, or a morality, that may be compatible with organization rules. Often, though, individuals feel that some rules are wrong or that they should not be applied in a certain situation. When this is the case, managers have difficult decisions to make. Sometimes they will have to grant privileges by waiving the rules temporarily. At other times, they must demand adherence to the rules. Not only must managers be sure that all members of their teams understand the rules, but they also must make sure the rules are right for their people. In many cases, managers have to work towards obtaining changes in the rules if they consider them no longer appropriate. This, incidentally, highlights a major foundation of the diagram. It is not the manager's or leader's task to force people into a mold that will bring some ideal arrangement, but rather, managers and/or academic leaders must work to adapt the organization to the competencies and capabilities of the people while at the same time helping people adapt themselves to the way the organization can be most successful.

Moreover, individuals come to an organization with both *skills and deficiencies*. As a matter of fact, throughout their lives most people have some deficiencies relative to the tasks on which they work, and they usually lack the knowledge and skills needed for higher-level jobs which they would like to obtain and which they hope will bring greater work satisfaction to their lives. It is a manager's or leader's task to help people identify and eliminate these deficiencies so they can develop their abilities in ways that increase their effectiveness in the organization. The manager also should help them as they prepare themselves for jobs or assignments from which they will gain greater work satisfaction as they progress in their careers.

Finally, every individual expects from the organization the satisfaction of a complex set of both *tangible and psychological needs*. On the tangible side, there is the need for adequate income to satisfy the physiological needs of food, clothing, and shelter as well as some of the safety and security needs and a certain level of comfort and luxury. On the psychological side, there is the need to feel secure, the need to belong and to be respected, and the need to find a measure of satisfaction in one's work. There is a great deal that managers and leaders can do to raise the satisfaction their employers and colleagues obtain from their work.

The Linking Elements

Linking elements are the skills and strategies a manager or leader must apply so that the organization's needs and the rewards it can supply achieve the greatest possible balance with the characteristics and expectations of employees and/or colleagues. Each set of arrows shown in figure 3-3 demands competence in at least one specific managerial skill—the linking element. In the next two chapters, each of the linking elements will be explored in detail to describe what skills and strategies it includes and what managers and leaders can do to sharpen the skills that will continue to help the organizational unit improve its performance.

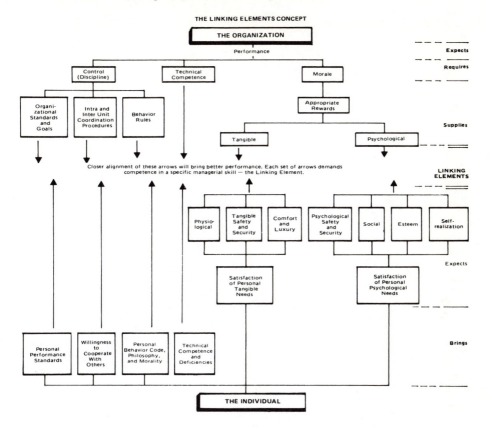

Source: Courtesy of National Fire Protection Association.

Figure 3-3. The Linking Elements Concept. Note the relationship between the individual and the organizational unit.

Working toward Goals

The Goals of an Organizational Unit

Most managers will agree that a day started without a plan, without some goals to achieve, will result in less accomplishment than a day for which objectives have been set. The concept of goals and objectives is such a simple one. It seems so logical that setting appropriate goals with and for employees and subordinate managers, and to some extent with colleagues, should at the very least clarify what demands concentration and what is to be handled in a more routine manner. Goal setting can and should provide the discipline to help managers and others think through the things that need to be done and thus help to establish a regular habit of planning. Appropriate participation in setting a goal by those who will work to achieve it can ensure that their knowledge, not just the manager's or leader's, is brought to bear on the problems and opportunities that face the team.

The advantages that a regular goals program can bring—in communications, in putting first things first, in establishing a clear view of respective responsibilities, in developing employees—are so significant that it would seem that the concept of managing with objectives, or toward results, should have swept like wildfire through the industrialized nations and have become a standard process everywhere. This, however, has not happened.

In an article in *M.B.A.* magazine, Stephen Singular explained that organizational goals programs often appear under different names. According to Singular, these programs are most frequently called "Management by Objectives" ("MbO" or "MBO") or "Managing by Objectives/Results," or they are hidden behind labels such as "Performance Appraisal" or "Performance Objective" programs. The different names are used because the words *goal* and *objective* have different meanings in different organizations. For purposes of this text, however, the words *goal* and *objective* are used synonymously; distinctions are covered later in this chapter in the section entitled Hierarchies of Goals.

Whatever the label, Singular cites a research study by professors Fred Schuster of Florida Atlantic University and Alva Kindall of the Harvard Business School that estimates that fewer than half the largest 500 industrial companies listed in *Fortune Magazine* manage their businesses with systems that can be termed MBO based. According to Singular, this is so in spite of the fact that MBO "is a technique based on real planning and thought and is, most agree, the best theoretical management program ever conceived." Moreover, on the basis of research results, "less than 10 percent of those 500 corporations—somewhere between 36 and 50 companies—have MBO-based programs that are considered a success. And only 10 companies, or 2 percent, have programs that are considered highly successful."[1]

This chapter will explore the concept of managing with goals as it applies to institutions of higher education, whether it is called management by objectives, management by results, or some other name, as a central strategy in achieving the desired balance between the needs of those institutions and their people. It will review several reasons why managing with goals has failed to approach its potential for creating more effective organizations and will briefly discuss possible solutions to the problems that MBO has in the past brought about.

The Management Cycle and MBO

Although it is frequently not recognized, MBO is a fairly practical approach to applying the management cycle to a manager's everyday work. When you, as manager or leader of your organizational unit, go through the process of selecting goals for the coming period, you are really doing little else but good planning. The action plans that lead to the achievement of the goals make up the balance of the planning process.

In the language of planners, you conduct a situation analysis to determine the strengths and weaknesses of the current situation, as well as the opportunities inherent in it, so that you can select appropriate goals. Then you prepare strategic and tactical plans to achieve these goals. Whether you approach this operation in an informal or formal manner, it still is planning. A thorough set of goals and an appropriate (though not necessarily detailed) set of action steps constitute a complete plan—and probably a better plan than one not specifically expressed in terms of goals. Arriving at agreement on goals, deciding who will assume responsibility for the achievement of each goal, and providing the necessary resources are the steps that are generally included under the term *organizing* in the management cycle. Implementing action plans falls under *implementing* or *executing* in the cycle, and progress reviews of a goals program fall under the *follow-up* or *controlling* phase of the cycle. In this last phase, the steps needed to improve low achievement are determined, and plans and goals are revised.

Goals for Individuals

Everybody has goals, even people who do not realize they set them. Some take their goals seriously; others do not. But almost everybody, even most people who lead very simple lives, have some vague, general idea about where they would like to be sometime in the future.

For people who think seriously about the future, though, and who expect to accomplish something in life, goals are not merely guesses about the future; they are real and meaningful targets to strive for. Some of these goals are complex and distant. Others are simple and short-term. For instance, if you have decided to go on a vacation in three months, you have set a goal. It is a very clear and direct goal, and you probably see clearly what steps you must take to accomplish it. Obviously, you have to decide on destination or itinerary. You must arrange for tickets and money, possibly for traveler's checks, and for the clothing and sports gear you may need. If no emergency arises, you will then be able to leave on your vacation as intended.

Not all goals are as easily accomplished. Many goals are not as specific. They may not have a date when they should be accomplished, and even the goal itself may be somewhat vague. For instance, consider the example of a college graduate with a degree in education whose career goal is to become a high-level leader in higher education. This goal, of course, is clear, but nowhere near as specific as the one in the preceding example. It does not state the exact position, the size of the institution, or a date by which it will be accomplished.

There are some fundamental differences between the two types of goals just described, differences that significantly affect planning. Taking a vacation is a short-term goal, and it can be achieved easily unless an emergency or really unusual circumstances interfere. Becoming a high-level leader is a long-range objective. It usually would not be very productive to tie it down with specifics such as the school, the level, or the date by which it is to be achieved. It is clearly important to distinguish between long- and short-term goals and to work with them differently.

Hierarchies of Goals

Most organizations working with goals have tried to identify different kinds of goals. Some talk about objectives as being general, long-range targets, while they view goals as specific, relatively short-range targets. Other organizations reverse these definitions of goals and objectives. For the purpose of this book, as has already been pointed out, the words *objective* and *goal* will be used interchangeably. The distinction between long- and short-term goals is fundamental, but beyond this there is a need to further identify the various types of goals. Thus goals may be arranged in two hierarchies, one in time and one in scope, as shown in figure 4-1.

Each hierarchy rests on *action steps*, the specific tasks that have to be accomplished so that the goals will be reached. Action steps are not goals.

*Action steps are not goals. Their significance is explained in this and later chapters.

Source: Courtesy of Bureau of National Affairs.

Figure 4-1. Hierarchies of Goals

While distinctions between the various levels of goals are not of great significance, the distinction between goals and action steps has broad implications. From the point of view of making a goals program successful, the distinction between action steps and goals is of crucial importance. Whereas goals are ends to be reached, action steps are the means to these ends.

Philosophical Goals/Mission Statements

In the hierarchy of goals, philosophical goals (mission statements) for organizations represent the highest-level goals. *Philosophical goals* are not meant to be achieved. They include such qualifying words as *best*, *fastest*, and *most*. They aim toward the future. For instance, one philosophical goal for an educational institution could be to provide the best instruction for its students or to provide the best possible intellectual climate for students and faculty. A school can have philosophical goals in many areas. Some could refer to students, others to the interests of employees, faculty, the community, and so on.

Philosophical goals exist for organizational units as well as for the entire institution. For example, the Student Activities Department could have as its philosophical goal the objective of providing the highest-quality programs and activities possible. Philosophical goals describe in the broadest possible terms the overall aims of an organization or a subunit. Thus the term *mission statement* is often considered an accurate definition of philosophical goals. The individual members of an organization seldom are directly concerned with achieving the organization's philosophical goals because these merely define the environment within which more specific goals should be set. People work primarily on operational levels, and as the goals at these levels are being achieved, the entire organization also achieves strategic goals and thus moves in the direction of its mission statements.

Although philosophical goals are rarely guides for action, they do offer a sense of direction and purpose. Frequently they are not in writing and exist only as a consensus within the organization. Individuals, of course, often have mission statements for which they strive. "To be an excellent career-placement counselor" is such a statement. Individuals also work toward achieving their own personal philosophical goals, in their careers and in their lives, by setting their own strategic and operational goals. For instance, in order to achieve the philosophical goal of becoming an excellent career-placement counselor, an individual would have to set such strategic goals as obtaining appropriate degrees, serving an internship in an appropriate discipline, being successful in a series of positions with increasing responsibilities, and so forth. Operational goals within these strategic goals would concern taking specific courses, obtaining good grades, establishing good performance records in respective positions, and so forth.

How the hierarchy of goals relates to an institution of higher education is shown with the help of the Registrar's Office of a fictitious school called Warren and Lewis University. Use of the Registrar's Office for this example has the advantage that it requires both quantitative and qualitative goals and thus can serve equally as a foundation for the discussion on administration (chapter 9) as for the one covering academic departments (chapter 7).

The following background information on the Registrar's Office will be useful in this example. The office, which operates with a relatively formal goals program, is set up in three separate units: Unit A is Scheduling, Unit B is Records, and Unit C is Class Assignments. For this example, the work of the Records unit will be traced. This unit has set goals in the following areas so that higher levels of performance can be achieved:

Recording: Currently, student records are updated within 10 days of receipt from instructors.

Error rate: Errors occur at a 4 percent rate.

Issuance of reports: Reports that the unit provides faculty are frequently late.

In accordance with the institution's mission, the office has defined its own mission as (1) to provide all necessary services pertaining to registration (that is, scheduling, recording and storing data, issuing reports, and academic analysis) accurately and promptly, and (2) to provide these services at the lowest possible cost.

Strategic Goals

Strategic goals are the big goals, usually fairly long-range, which help to move an institution, an office, or a department in the direction of its mission. In support of the mission, the Registrar's Office established the strategic goals shown in figure 4-2 for the coming year.

As figure 4-3 shows, the strategic goals of the Registrar's Office are specific enough that each respective unit can set strategic goals that are relevant to its specific function. Note that in this example, all strategic goals merely specify requirements for operational goals. Such goals are very common because they, in effect, define the areas in which operational goals could, and often should, be set regularly. Strategic goals also can be of a different nature, though, pertaining to results that are to be achieved only once. Here are some examples:

Develop a remedial program for new students who are deficient in English and mathematics.

Prepare programs that adapt existing records for entry into a new computer system.

Achieve faculty agreement on a new policy.

Solve a major scientific problem.

Mount an expedition to explore something (whatever is called for by a specific situation).

A unit's strategic goals can then be allocated to the various subunits, individuals, or managers in such a way (see figure 4-4) that they will be accomplished if every subunit achieves its own goals. How this allocation of goals takes place and how the decisions are made concerning who gets what will be discussed later in this chapter. If all subunits achieve their strategic goals, then larger organizational units will achieve theirs all the way up the entire organizational structure.

It is important to keep in mind, as this picture becomes more complicated, that the organization referred to in a diagram might be the entire institution, a department, or even a single office. Wherever a goals program originates, mission statements, expressed or implied, exist, and strategic goals should be prepared in a more or less formal way if people are to communicate effectively with higher and lower levels, as well as the same level, of an organization hierarchy. Each strategic goal, then, should be supported by strategic goals of the various lower organizational units or managers; these managers must accept their share of the particular goal. Please note that this discussion is intended only to ensure a common viewpoint on the structure of the goals hierarchy. In no way does it suggest how many goals should be set or how formally they should be expressed. These

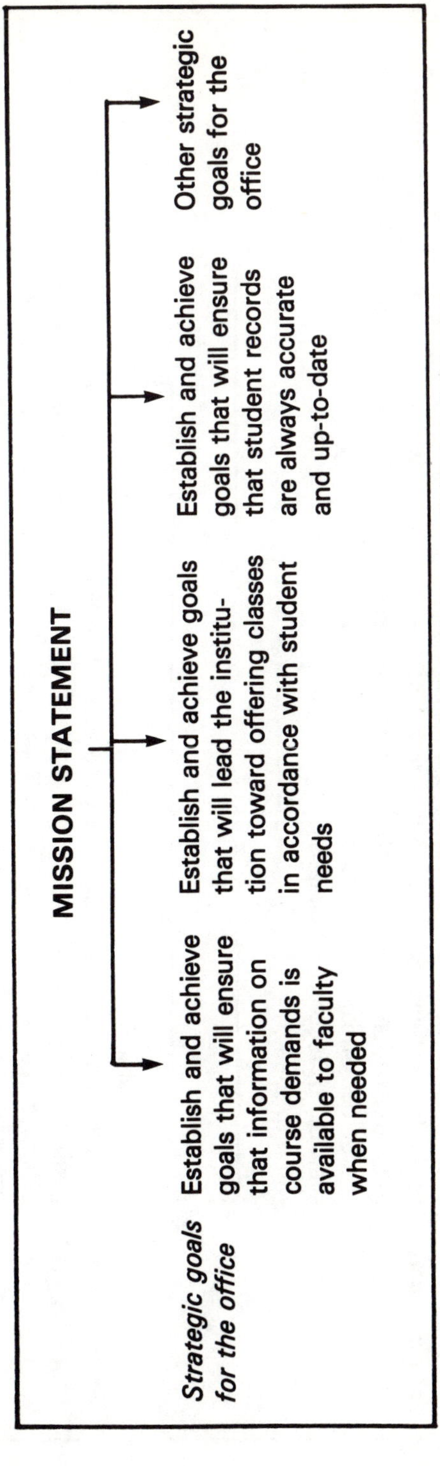

Figure 4-2. Registrar's Strategic Goals in Support of Mission Statement

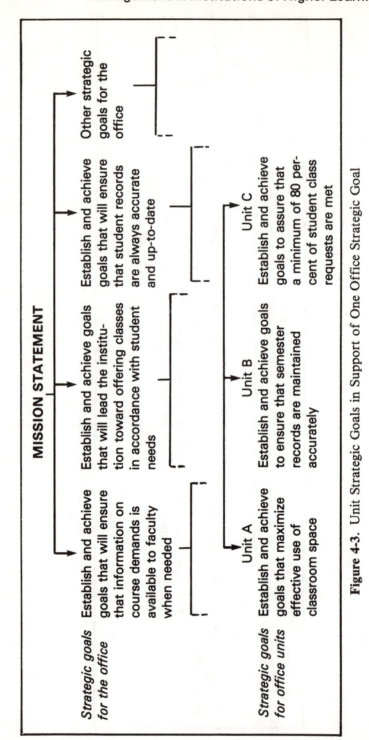

Figure 4-3. Unit Strategic Goals in Support of One Office Strategic Goal

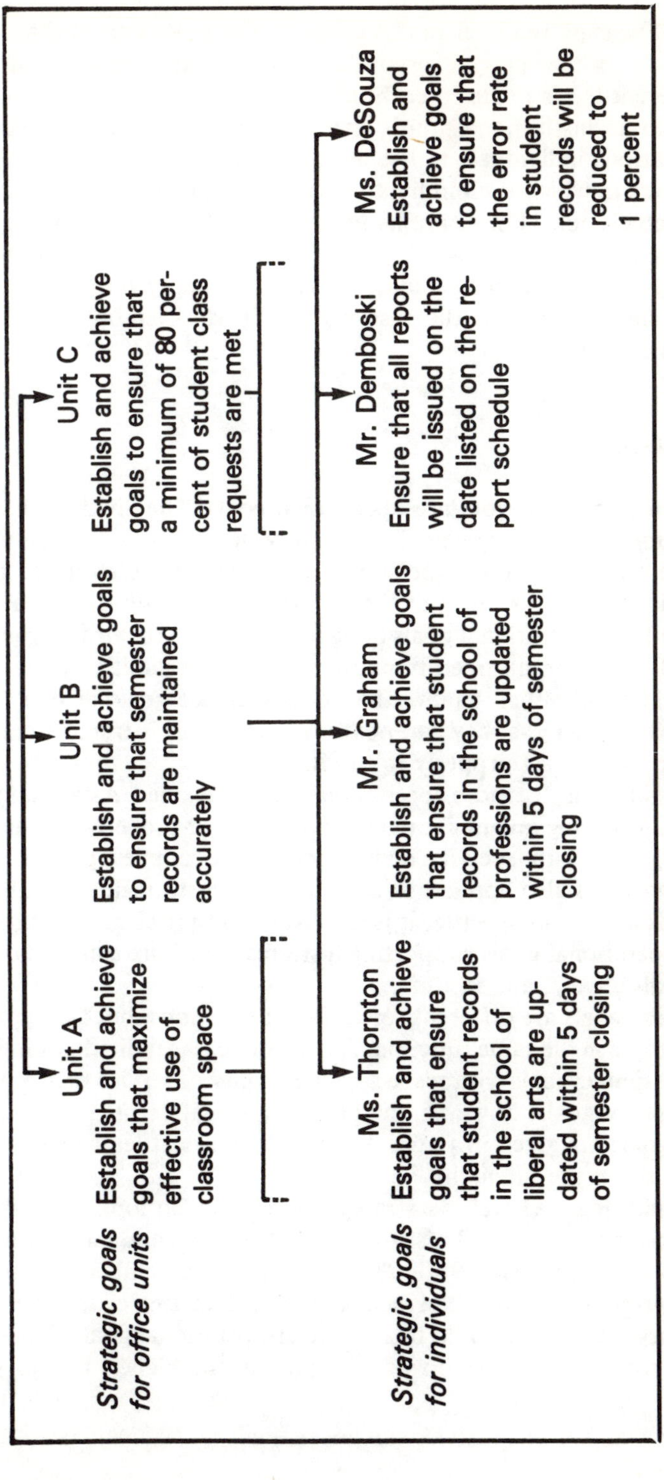

Figure 4-4. Strategic Goals for Individuals in Support of One Unit Strategic Goal

Strategic goals for office units

Unit A
Establish and achieve goals that maximize effective use of classroom space

Unit B
Establish and achieve goals to ensure that semester records are maintained accurately

Unit C
Establish and achieve goals to ensure that a minimum of 80 percent of student class requests are met

Strategic goals for individuals

Ms. Thornton
Establish and achieve goals that ensure that student records in the school of liberal arts are updated within 5 days of semester closing

Mr. Graham
Establish and achieve goals that ensure that student records in the school of professions are updated within 5 days of semester closing

Mr. Demboski
Ensure that all reports will be issued on the date listed on the report schedule

Ms. DeSouza
Establish and achieve goals to ensure that the error rate in student records will be reduced to 1 percent

questions will be explored later in this chapter. The point here is that for a goals system to work properly, everyone should understand how the various goals in different levels relate to each other.

Very often an institutional unit's strategic goal is simply parceled out among the various individuals in the unit. This is especially true of those functional units in which each individual assumes a proportionate share of the unit's strategic goal. For example, in figure 4-4, Ms. Thornton and Mr. Graham share Unit B's responsibility for updating semester records. Some strategic goals are not parceled out, though, but apply only to one individual or one unit. This is the case with both Mr. Demboski and Ms. DeSouza in figure 4-4.

Operational Goals

Supporting each strategic goal are operational goals. The dividing line between operational and strategic goals is not very sharp, nor is it necessary to have a sharp one. While everyone should be aware of the strategic goals relevant to his or her work, most of the time the activities of individuals are concerned with the operational goals designed to achieve the strategic goals. If all the individuals in an operational unit achieve the unit's operational goals, then they will either achieve the unit's strategic goals or else be as close to achieving them as they can possibly come. This is true, of course, only if the goals were set properly in the first place.

Operational goals are more specific than strategic ones. As a matter of fact, much that is being taught about the importance of properly stating and quantifying goals, with specific completion dates, applies primarily to operational goals. It also applies, to some extent, to strategic goals, but if strategic goals are not as specific, it is not likely that problems will arise as long as the operational goals supporting a strategic goal are clarified quantitatively, qualitatively, and in time.

Operational goals are different for different functions, but can be quite similar for people in the same function. For example, the individuals in Unit B might have similar goals with respect to the quality of service they render. Their quantitative goals, however, might be totally different. Examples of operational goals are given in figure 4-5, which shows at least one goal at each level of the entire hierarchy.

Operational goals as well as strategic goals can be long- and short-range. For instance, in the Admissions Office, the operational goal of increasing by 6 percent for the 1981-1982 school year the number of entering students who rank in the top 10 percent of their graduating classes can be a short-range goal, but there could be the longer operational goal of increasing by 15 percent the proportion of freshmen in the highest category by

1984. There is, of course, nothing wrong with considering the latter goal as a strategic goal or with calling all goals supported by operational goals, strategic goals.

Usually it is not necessary to have a clear picture of the line that separates strategic from operational goals. Sometimes that line is quite fuzzy, and at other times it is unimportant. What is important, though, is that all operational goals be clearly measurable.

One other point deserves mention here. Many managers consider all short targets as goals, and, of course, they are—even the daily, almost routine tasks of completing a specific project. In the Registrar's Office, for instance, processing a "normal" number of forms or reports is a goal, although an extremely short-term one. However, as far as the managerial work of the unit is concerned, this is a routine task and should not be included in a goals program. Major problems or opportunities concerning them, on the other hand, may properly be treated as goals. For instance, increasing the level of "normal" activity, reducing the number of "normal" errors, or introducing new methods are meaningful goals. They may deserve the priority that inclusion in the goals program will give them. This is discussed in greater detail in the section on quality of goals later in this chapter.

Action Steps: The Working Ends
of a Goals Program

Although the distinction between goals and action steps might seem to be of no greater consequence than the distinction between strategic and operational goals, this really is not the case. There are major differences in the way managers and leaders should look at action steps, and these differences have implications of great significance to the success or failure of a goals program.

As previously explained, goals are statements that describe ends to be achieved. At the operational level, goals should always be measurable, significant, and attainable—but also challenging. *Action steps*, the specific steps necessary and desirable in order to come closer to accomplishing a goal, are not ends to be reached; rather, they are the steps necessary to achieve the end results.

Action steps also must be measurable, of course, but it does not matter whether they are challenging. Action steps, by definition, are achievable. Examples of action steps for the goal of ensuring that a qualified person will be found by the end of June to replace keypuncher Hudgins include notifying the Personnel Department and other specific recruiting and selecting activities. Note that many such steps could possibly be taken without finding

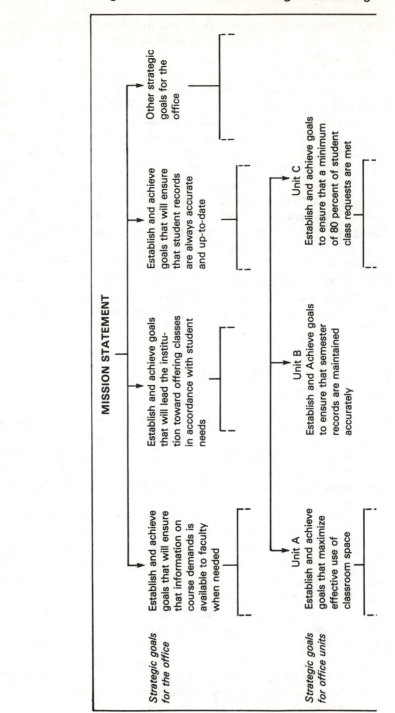

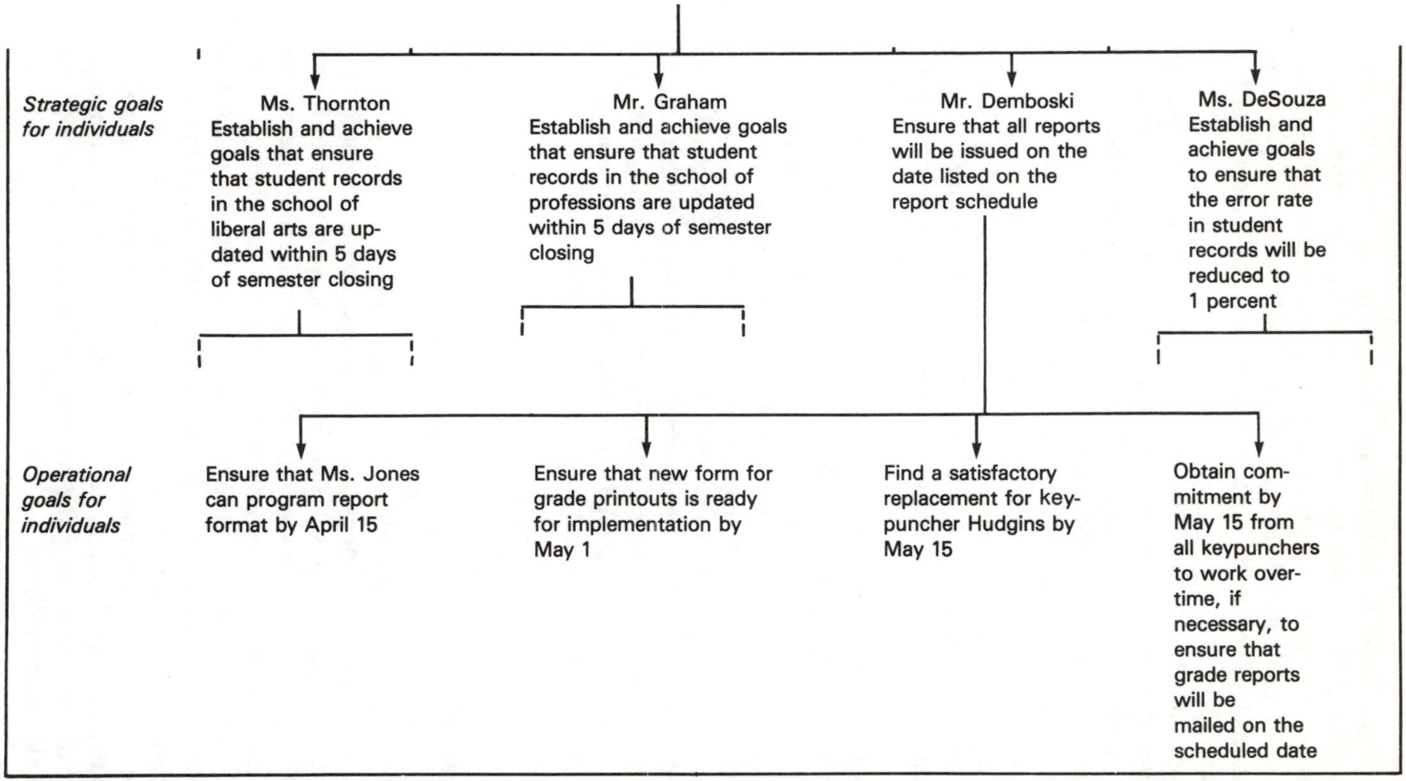

Figure 4-5. Relationships between Strategic Goals at Different Organizational Levels and Operational Goals at the Lowest Level. At each level only a few goals are shown in support of only one of the goals at the next higher level. Many others, of course, could exist at each level.

a qualified replacement for keypuncher Hudgins by June 30 at the salary that can be offered. This is why the distinction between a goal and an action step is so important. Action steps for the goal of ensuring that adjustments and changes are made include entering changes, scheduling the weekly adjustment sheets into keypunch, sending "Notification of Change" cards to students, and so forth.

The most important characteristic of action steps is that they are generally *under the control* of the person or group that has been assigned and/or has accepted the responsibility for carrying them out. Thus the individual or group can properly be held responsible for the completion of action steps. Goals, because they are also subject to external and uncontrollable events and circumstances, may never be achieved, even if all appropriate action steps have been taken. The goal of ensuring that all transcript requests are filled in a timely manner, for example, can be achieved only if enough qualified people are available to accomplish the goal.

Action steps can be large or small, short- or long-term. The length of time or the size of task is not the key factor. The only thing that is of importance is that an action step is essentially under full control of the person or people responsible for it. Sometimes what appears to be an action step prior to its completion may turn out, in retrospect, to be a goal. The action step of driving to a certain place and arriving there at a certain time can turn out to be a goal if exceptionally inclement weather or a major, sudden obstruction prevents the trip from being completed on time. As a rule, it is fairly easy to tell whether someone can be held accountable for completing an action step, because only unusual and unexpected events will prevent its achievement.

Defining Goals Clearly

Some goals, however, cannot be defined clearly. This is particularly true in research or technical fields. For example, if a goal concerns development of a new computer program that will significantly improve the output format of a specific report, it may be very difficult to establish clearly measurable and specific criteria to determine whether the goal has been achieved. It also may be difficult to set a reasonable time limit for achieving the goal. A great deal of research work may be needed, and trials may have to be run.

In such a case, in which goals cannot be defined with a reasonable forecast because there are too many unknowns, it is very often possible to tentatively define the goals in terms of the first few action steps that must be taken. For the goal concerning the computer program just described, the first few action steps might be

1. To compile a list of items that must be included in the report.
2. To discuss with programmers the various formats that might be appropriate.
3. To take specific design steps.
4. To develop sample forms to be evaluated by users.

Upon completion of these action steps, the next step would be to set a specific goal for completion of the program.

Making Goals Programs Successful

Owing to the relative simplicity of the concept of managing with goals, it might seem that the problems involved in the setting and carrying out of goals could be easily resolved, and that all goals programs should be successful. Obviously, however, the real world of goals programs is far more complicated. There are no easy answers and no quick solutions. Goals programs within institutions of higher education are no exception. The problems attendant on goal-setting programs are the same in any organization—whether that organization is a private company, government agency, educational institution, or hospital.

The remainder of this chapter explores the eight problem areas that usually arise in goals programs and discusses how these particular areas might apply to the managers in an academic environment.

The Eight Potential Problem Areas in Goals Programs

Analysis reveals eight areas in which goals programs can fail to achieve their potential and thus lose the opportunity to become a way of life. In any organization, all eight areas are rarely involved at the same time, although they can be. The eight problem areas can be summarized by the acronym *EQIFAPPO*, as shown in the following list:

1. *E*xtent of goal setting
2. *Q*uality of goals and goals statements
3. *I*nvolvement by managers in the way employees and lower-level managers work toward achievement of their goals
4. *F*requency of goals reviews
5. *A*ccountability of subordinates—the bases on which performance will be evaluated
6. *P*articipation by subordinates—the voice that subordinates have in setting goals that affect them

7. *P*erformance appraisal/evaluation—the relationship between the goals program and the performance-evaluation process
8. *O*perational/developmental goals considerations—where developmental goals for individuals fit into the goals program

Improving the ability to cope with all eight of these problem areas can help a manager or a leader achieve higher morale and better performance, the results of a successful goals program.

All eight problem areas are briefly summarized in subsequent paragraphs. In all areas, emphasis will be on the way the Linking Elements Concept can provide practical suggestions to a manager on how to make better decisions in all these areas. As you read on, please keep in mind that the way the potential problems are approached depends on the three considerations emphasized throughout this book as crucial to all decisions: (1) the manager's own capabilities, (2) the capabilities and competencies of subordinates, and (3) the particular situation. These considerations are especially important with respect to all the aspects of goal setting.

The Department Chairperson's Role in Goal Setting: Each of the eight problem areas will be discussed in terms of the "manager/subordinate" relationship. There is, as was pointed out in chapter 1, another type of relationship in higher education: the leader/colleague situation that exists primarily in the academic departments. Deans, department chairpersons, and committee chairpersons make managerial decisions and, in certain instances, have limited authority over their colleagues. The managerial skills to be applied in each of the eight problem areas, however, also may be applied in varying degrees by academic leaders in their relationships with colleagues.

With respect to goal setting in the academic departments, a chairperson's work concerns primarily those administrative and instructional matters which pertain to the unit as a whole. His or her responsibility clearly is to ensure that the department functions at a high level and moves toward achieving the goals of both the department and the institution, while at the same time creating a climate in which the members of the department can come as close as possible to achieving their goals. The chairperson has a very limited responsibility for monitoring what goes on in the individual classrooms. The goal-setting process really applies to major shifts in the department's course offerings, the development of new courses by certain times, participation in institutionwide activities where there would be goals for the department's representatives, and, of course, goals for new instructors in the department, who may need guidance and help in adapting to the needs and requirements of the department.

A department chairperson is usually in a position where he or she has to set goals only occasionally rather than on a continuing basis with most members of the department, particularly with those who are established, tenured members and who function way over on the left-hand side of the Hersey-Blanchard diagram (figure 4-6). With these department members, goals must be set only when there is some significnat change in the course offering of the department or when their help is needed in achieving some departmental goal. However, with respect to individual new members, the chairperson's involvement would be significant both in the goal-setting process and in the way they work toward the achievement of these goals. For example, in a basic course that is taught by several instructors, the students of one particular junior professor may have achieved markedly lower grades on the department exam than students of his or her colleagues. In this type of situation, the chairperson could work with the professor to set goals so that the required degree of uniformity of topic coverage might be achieved.

This example shows that while the chairperson may not have responsibility for the quality of instruction, in certain situations his or her involvement may be warranted. However, involvement is a difficult line for the department chairperson to tread. He or she has a responsibility to uphold and protect the academic freedom of his or her colleagues to conduct their own classes. This is also important because there should exist a climate in which the needs of the individual members of the department are satisfied; there is nothing more important to an experienced professional in a discipline than the freedom to express his or her views and to lead classes

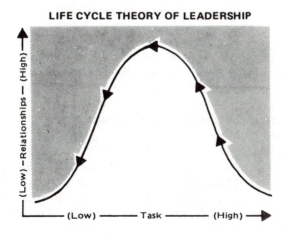

LIFE CYCLE THEORY OF LEADERSHIP

Source: Reproduced by special permission from the February 1974 *Training and Development Journal*. Copyright © 1974 by the American Society for Training and Development. Artwork courtesy of the National Fire Protection Association.

Figure 4-6. Representation of the Life-Cycle Theory of Leadership

in the ways he or she sees fit. Any external interference, unless it is warranted by serious complaints or other serious considerations, is a significant encroachment on that freedom.

While these responsibilities are not easy for a department chairperson to balance, department chairpersons who apply the Linking Elements Concept in their work can apply appropriate strategies to ensure high departmental accomplishments as well as protect academic freedom.

Extent of Goals to Be Set

In order to determine the number of goals to be set at the various levels, it is necessary for managers to have a thorough understanding of the meaning and value of goals and a knowledge of how to establish them at the respective levels. Two of the problems involved in determining how many goals to set are (1) the setting of too many goals, thus enmeshing the entire process in a maze of paperwork that can prevent the goals program from generating the enthusiasm it needs to become a way of life; and (2) the setting of too few goals, thus losing the full benefit the goals program can bring. The more successful goals programs carefully identify, from the goals that could be set during a time period, those which deserve priority. They ensure that these priorities are clearly understood by the people involved.

In deciding how many goals to set, it is therefore important to look at the *capabilities* of the subordinate or colleague. Then, to decide what functions or projects should be emphasized with goals, it is necessary to look at the functions being performed and select those which deserve the highest *priority*.

How Many Goals to Set: The Capabilities of Subordinates: A manager can agree on several goals with some subordinates because they are competent enough to work on several goals at the same time. There are others for whom only a single goal can be set. Determining how many goals to set requires an assessment of the subordinate's capabilities in terms of technical competence and maturity.

As far as this book is concerned, *maturity* does not refer to age, nor does it refer to personal psychological maturity, although it does relate to this to some extent. Maturity refers instead to the way in which the person deals with the management process discussed here. A mature person makes decisions on a rational basis, understands and accepts the need to forecast, sets goals, plans the work, and works the plan. Such a person does not resent planning and goal setting as an imposition. He or she is keenly aware of the benefits of thorough analysis and will ensure that emotional reactions are kept out of the goal-setting and decision-making processes. Lack of emotionalism in goal setting does not, however, mean denial of self-interest. On the contrary, a mature person gives high and proper weight to the personal benefits an alternative will bring. If the system is such that low, easy-to-achieve goals are in his or her best interest, then the mature person will strive to set such goals. Conversely, if the psychological and/or tangible reward system favors challenging goals, such an individual will set goals that way. A mature individual usually will not be concerned about exposing lack of knowledge or inadequate training on any topic, or about sincerely asking the manager for help and advice when he or she believes this to be useful for greater achievement.

Technical competence is usually quite easy to assess. Maturity, however, is not simple to recognize, but the findings of researchers can help to provide some guidelines. The theory described in the next subsection looks at the life cycle, traces the maturity of a person from birth to full adulthood, and draws a parallel to the job situation.

Life-Cycle Theory of Leadership: In helping to decide how many goals can be set, an interesting diagram provides some guidelines. It was developed by two professors at Ohio State University, Dr. Paul Hersey and Dr. Kenneth Blanchard. They entitle it "The Life-Cycle Theory of Leadership." The diagram shows the development of an individual from infancy to self-sufficiency, or the development of a new employee from the first day on the job to full job competence.

In considering figure 4-6, it is first necessary to understand the two coordinates, the vertical and horizontal axes. The horizontal axis depicts the extent to which a parent, or a manager, assigns tasks. If near the left end of the line, the manager or parent assigns very few tasks and the subordinate or offspring makes all or most of the decisions about what task to work on. Toward the right end of the line, the manager or parent assigns most, if not all, tasks. In other words, the farther to the right one moves, the more the manager or parent decides what has to be done.

On the vertical axis, the parent's or manager's concern for establishing a good *work* relationship is depicted. At the bottom of the diagram, the parent or manager has little concern about how well the subordinate likes the decisions that are made. At the top of the diagram, the parent or manager shows maximum concern about the way the decisions or work arrangements are accepted by the offspring or subordinate.

It is important to notice that love or warm feelings do not enter this diagram. A parent can have, and show, great love for an offspring and still show little concern about whether a child likes to be told what to do and what not to do. To understand the meaning of the diagram, follow the line, from right to left, first for an offspring:

1. On the lower right-hand side of the diagram, the parent must assign a great many tasks to the infant, and there is little need for the parent to be concerned about whether or not the child likes the decisions that are made.

2. As the child begins to mature and becomes aware of the world, the parent must explain the reasons for decisions. This is shown by the way the curve rises to the left toward greater concern for relationship. In the early years, parents still must assign tasks, but they should allow the offspring increasing freedom to decide what he or she may do. However, as the child grows, parents must show increasing concern for feelings by explaining the reasons why certain rules must be followed.

3. As the child moves into adolescence and becomes more independent and more knowledgeable about the world, the parents must relinquish some of their right to make the decisions for the offspring; but at the same time, if they wish to avoid serious problems in their relationship, they also must be more convincing in explaining the reasons for assignments or rules they still impose.

4. As the offspring moves on to college, parents can no longer be deeply involved in making decisions for offspring because they are no longer in close or continuous contact. The offspring must accept more of the responsibility for decisions. At the same time, the responsibility for initiative in the relationship begins to pass to the offspring, and the parents have less opportunity to shape the relationship the way they would like to see it.

5. Finally, when the offspring is married and is established in his or her own career, the parents can no longer assign tasks at all; the initiative for the relationship has moved almost exclusively to the offspring.

What is true for the child as he or she matures is true for an employee who enters and becomes established in a new job. For example, a new academic counselor must be introduced to the rules and procedures of the Placement Office. The new counselor must accept these rules and requirements without a chance to affect them. However, as time and experience help the counselor become acquainted with the job, the director of the Placement Office will find it increasingly necessary to explain the reasons for decisions and procedures and allow the counselor freedom to suggest and implement changes where desirable. Depending on previous experience and personal capabilities, the new placement counselor will move more or less rapidly to the left of the curve. The effective manager sees it as his or her responsibility to help and encourage the other person to move as rapidly as he or she is capable, along the curve to the left.

How fast and far along the curve a person can move, from right to left on the curve, depends on ability and potential. The majority of employees in a technologically advanced society such as the United States, however, once established in their jobs, work either near the peak of the curve or somewhat to the left of it. Their superiors must still assign much of the work, but assignments must be made with a high degree of concern about how employees like them and with appropriate explanations of the reasons for them.

Most managers and highly educated professionals in higher education work on the left side of the curve. They are capable of accepting assignments in more general terms. They make many of the decisions about what they should do, when it should be done, and how it should be done. At the same time, their superiors cannot have as much concern about the relationships that exist between them, and the subordinates themselves have to accept a considerable amount of responsibility for these relationships. This places a fairly heavy responsibility on them to establish their own goals in consultation with their superiors, to work independently toward the achievement of the goals, and to keep their superiors informed of progress. As was pointed out earlier, the curve does not depict warmth in the relationship, nor does it show such matters as trust and mutual confidence. These are outside the scope of the diagram in many ways. The diagram really applies only if there is a good interpersonal relationship, characterized by friendliness, mutual respect, and in case of family, the love and warmth that family life should provide.

Conclusions from the Life-Cycle Theory: With respect to the extent of goal setting, the conclusions from the curve in figure 4-6 are fairly clear:

1. With a new employee or one who is limited in potential for personal development, only very few goals can be set.
2. With more experienced, competent, and mature individuals, several goals can be set at one time. It is clear that toward the left bottom of the curve goals can exist for most of the important activities and responsibilities.
3. A major goal for every manager is to help every person in the unit continue to move along the curve to the left, that is, the path to maturity.

Figure 4-6, of course, does not supply clear-cut guidelines, but a manager who understands the diagram fully can find in it a guide to the number of goals that can be set with a subordinate.

The life-cycle theory, therefore, primarily concerns the influence the competence of subordinates has on the extent of goal setting. It determines how many goals should be set. The manager's capabilities and the situation also are involved in deciding the functions or projects for which goals should be established—and this involves *setting priorities*.

Setting Priorities: Deciding on priorities is necessary to ensure that the limited number of goals set are for the most important functions or projects and not for those with lower significance. Priorities are useful not only for a goals program, but also for good management of time. There is no question that managers who want to make best use of the time available to them must allocate their time to activities in proportion to their respective priorities. Competent managers attempt to spend as much of their time as possible on the high-priority matters and delegate accordingly.

Adequate attention to priorities can ensure that when more work has to be done than the available time permits, those goals which deserve maximum attention indeed receive it, and that if anything has to remain undone, it will be the project with the lowest priority. This means that the manager has to decide, sometimes alone and sometimes in conjunction with others, what operational goals deserve highest priority for the upcoming period. Sometimes these priorities are easy to set, but sometimes many complications exist that make setting them difficult.

Several factors must be considered when setting priorities. The most significant are (1) the urgency of the goal and (2) the importance of the goal. Sometimes goals are both urgent and important. Sometimes they are urgent but not important—for example, filling low-level vacancies quickly whenever they arise. The latter type of goal obviously cannot qualify as a goal on which effort should be concentrated during the upcoming period. However, sometimes goals are important but not urgent. An important project, for instance, might have a completion date in the distant future.

Other less significant considerations for determining priorities are

1. How quickly the particular goal can be achieved. There often is a desire to work for those goals which can be achieved quickly because this simplifies scheduling and allows full concentration on goals that are more time consuming.
2. The extent to which completion of the goal might help with other goals. For instance, if, during the next period, one goal calls for obtaining agreement on new procedures, then such a goal would deserve a higher priority than goals that will be easier to achieve once the new procedures are in effect.

Most of the time considerations related to priority are not easy to sort out, and consequently, goals that appear to be urgent often receive higher priority than they deserve. Goals on important matters that are not urgent are thus postponed longer than they should be, resulting in crises at a later time. Figure 4-7 can help, to some extent, to dramatize the necessity of keeping important matters in mind. First priority must go to those matters which are both important and urgent; they appear in area B of the figure.

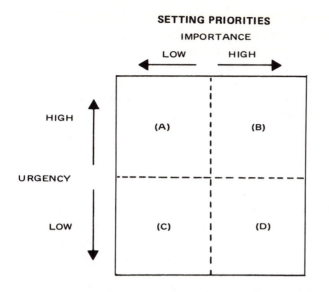

Figure 4-7. An Importance/Urgency Diagram to Help Determine Priorities
for Particular Goals

In setting goals that belong to this category, it is necessary to exercise
restraint; otherwise these specific production or quality goals for the upcoming months are the only goals that will be set. As one articulate rancher
once phrased the problem in referring to people who seem to set all their
goals in area B, "These guys are forever chasing the cows, and no one ever
builds the fences so they can stop the chasing." Area B matters rarely allow
enough time for significant reviews and do not lead toward improved production in the future; therefore, they do not deserve inclusion on the list of
priority goals.

The next priority seems difficult to decide. How does one choose between low importance and high urgency (area A) and high importance and
low urgency (area D)? Things that are urgent certainly deserve attention,
even if they are not very important. These matters, however, should be
completed quickly, and from the point of view of an effective goals program, if they are not important, they belong with the regular routines of the
job.

This leaves the matters in area D, which require planning so they will be
completed on time. More so than any other projects, these deserve careful
thought in deciding on goals, action steps, and completion dates. Only
careful planning will prevent matters in area D from becoming emergencies
at some time in the future.

Finally, those matters which are neither important nor urgent are rarely involved in goal setting. They are shown in area C. When the work load is heavy, there should be some question as to whether any work at all should be done on matters in this area.

With respect to goal setting, therefore, there is a somewhat surprising conclusion. It is not the matters in area B—those most important *and* most urgent—that require the highest priority for goal setting. These will receive maximum attention anyway. It is the matters in area D that need to be covered with goals so that they assume greater urgency and receive the attention they deserve.

Conclusions on Extent of Goal Setting: It may sometimes appear difficult to limit the number of operational goals that are set with a person and to decide on those which deserve the highest priority. One practical way for you to do this might be to come to an agreement with each individual reporting to you at the beginning of the year on strategic goals for each area of responsibility. As soon as these goals have been set, you and your subordinate could together select one or several operational goals that deserve primary emphasis during the first 1- to 3-month period. All other goals could be lumped under a single goal: "To maintain performance in all other areas of responsibility." The subordinate would have to have a clear view of the action steps and their completion dates only for the goals singled out. Any extra or special effort would be devoted to these goals rather than others. Usual responsibilities would be discharged as well as they had been in the past.

Since you can conduct reviews fairly frequently, a new goal can easily be added whenever the need for one becomes apparent. At the end of the review period, progress on the priority goals for the period is reviewed. New priorities for the coming period are then discussed. This is when other goals may be considered.

In deciding on the number of goals that should be selected with a specific subordinate, you can look at his or her capabilities as well as the requirements of the situation. There is great temptation to set more goals, of course, in order to obtain improvement or above-normal effort in many areas. It should be obvious, though, that this is quickly self-defeating. If more goals are set with a person than that person is capable of working on simultaneously, the results will undoubtedly be disappointing. If more effort is required than the maximum that he or she is prepared to give, then the goals will not be taken seriously and resentment will arise. In the end, less will be accomplished than if the number of formal goals were limited to what is appropriate for the situation and the capabilities of the subordinate.

The strategies identified in this section also can be applied in the academic departments. A department chairperson may have very little need to set goals with a tenured faculty member or may need to set such goals only rarely. Goals with senior professors would be set only when there are specific results which that faculty member is charged to achieve. This could be the case if the faculty member serves as a representative of the department on an institutional committee. Goals also may be useful with senior faculty members who work with student assistants and who have difficulty communicating or working effectively with them. There are also goals for the achievement of departmental objectives that may be accepted by a senior faculty member. They might concern revamping the curriculum of a basic course affecting several other faculty members, or they could concern the establishment of standards or the selection of texts.

However, with new instructors, the department chairperson may be in a relationship similar to that of a supervisor with an employee in one of the administrative departments, and therefore, there may be a need for setting many goals. These might pertain to the quality of instruction, to the development and use of tests, or to coordination with others teaching the same course. In the relationship with these faculty members, it will usually be the case that the senior, tenured faculty member requires a leadership style such as should be applied to individuals who live far on the left side of the Hersey-Blanchard life-cycle curve (figure 4-6). The leadership style required by new, inexperienced instructors, however, might very well be close to the top of the curve or possibly even slightly to the right.

Summary of Extent of Goal Setting: The following guidelines can be used for the extent of goal setting.

1. The number of goals that can be set with any one subordinate depend on that person's capabilities.
2. The more mature and competent a subordinate or colleague is, the more goals that can be set with him or her.
3. Goal selection requires great personal restraint on the manager's part. Setting too many priority goals with any one person can cause serious damage to a goals program's viability.
4. While strategic goals can be set in all areas of responsibility, operational goals should be set only on those matters which deserve highest priority for the upcoming period, until the next review.
5. Goals will bring the best results if they are set on those matters which are important, but not urgent.

Quality of Goals and Goal Statements

So that people will understand goals clearly and goals can become the foundation for serious effort, goals and goal statements must be of high quality. There are several aspects of goals and goal statements that determine their quality, among them

1. The mechanical aspects of goal statements must be in order. This refers to the clarity and precision of goal statements. Goal statements must communicate the same meaning to all parties. To do this, several requirements must be met. First, the goal statement must either state or clearly imply who is to accomplish the goal. Second, the goal statement must have a specific date by which the goal is to be accomplished. Third, the goal statement must specify or clearly imply the quantity that is to be achieved. And last, the goal statement must specify or clearly imply, based on the organization's environment, what level of quality is sought.

For example, a goal statement from the Budget Office may say, "We will prepare a monthly financial report." This clearly is not definite enough, even though it appears to be specific. Such a goal statement is inadequate because it does not name the date by which the report will be provided, nor does it specify either quantity (the information that is to be contained in the report) or quality level of the information in the report. It may very well be that quantity and quality are known because the statement refers to reports previously prepared, thereby specifying standards by implication. However, lacking previous standards and a completion date, the goal statement is inadequate. A more appropriate goals statement might say: "We will submit, by the fifth of every month, a report on the institution's financial activities similar to those previously filed," or "covering at least the following topics," or "of (00) pages, covering at least the following topics. . . ."

2. All goals must be in line with the mission. This was discussed in the subsection Extent of Goal Setting, especially with respect to the selection of priorities. If a manager insists on priorities that are not perceived by subordinates as very relevant to the mission of the organizatonal unit, then subordinates will obviously not take the goals program very seriously.

3. Goals must be challenging. This means that they must be set high, but not so high that they are beyond achievement. Goals that are not challenging usually need not be set. Chances are they will be achieved whether anyone makes a special effort to achieve them or not. However, goals that are so high that they are not likely to be achieved are usually "demotivating." People will rarely strive for something that they feel they cannot reach.

Goals are most beneficial to the organization *and* to the individual when they are set just below the point where they would be unrealistic but where most of them are still achievable. At this level, the joy of achievement will be high and failure is likely to be minimal. Goals may be missed by a small margin or by a short period of time, but that is all.

Helping others set realistic goals is a big challenge for a manager. This is why competent managers are careful and resourceful in coaching individuals in goal setting. Managers must work not only with those who set their goals too low, but also with those who set them unrealistically high. Determining how challenging a goal actually is may be most difficult. It is relatively easy to write each goal statement so that it communicates properly or to choose only goals that are thoroughly relevant to the mission of the organizational unit. It is an entirely different matter, though, to determine in advance what goal will turn out to be challenging. When managers and their subordinates try to determine what quantity or quality levels are to be accomplished and a completion date, they are relying on forecasts or estimates. Depending on the environment, the availability of data, and the goal setters' abilities to forecast, the goals will be more or less accurate. They are targets that appear to be achievable, but are they challenging?

One way managers can tell whether goals are really set at a level that is realistic but challenging is to look at effort as well as the percentage of instances when goals are exceeded. If effort is high, about 50 percent of the goals will be exceeded and 50 percent will not be fully achieved when they are really set at a challenging and realistic level. For the manager, it is partly a matter of judging the situation correctly, but even more a matter of being aware of the attitudes of the individual subordinate. What complicates matters is that certain people inevitably set goals much higher because they wish to please the manager, while others are just unrealistic and feel they can achieve much more than can realistically be expected. Others set goals that lack challenge, either because the environment punishes the setting of challenging goals or because they like to play it safe. The climate of the organizational unit exerts great influence over goal setting. If people are aware that they will not suffer when they do not fully achieve goals that challenge, then there is a much greater likelihood that they will set challenging goals.

One-hundred percent batting averages are impossible in the goal-setting game. The trick is to strive for steady improvement in setting goals that stretch abilities. Managers must be alert to subordinates' needs for coaching and assistance, and they must keep alert for problems. The reluctance of most individuals to set challenging goals is a clear indication that something is not completely right in the motivational climate. The extent to which subordinates are willing to set challenging goals is an important diagnostic indicator of confidence in the manager and the system and in the competence of the manager to cope with the system.

In both nonacademic and academic departments, goals and goal statements must be of high quality. If goals are to be set, they might just as well be set such that they communicate appropriately, which means that goal statements must be of high quality. Moreover, if the goals are worth setting, they should be challenging and realistic. The following are two sample goals:

1. The number of student complaints about misleading questions on tests will be reduced to one-half those in the previous semester during the coming semester.
2. Starting with the coming semester, students will receive summaries of all topics to be covered that are not thoroughly explained in the text. The summaries will be provided at least 3 weeks before that topic will be covered in class.

Summary of Quality of Goals: The following guidelines can be used for the quality of goals and goal statements:

1. Goal statements must be clear, concise, and measurable in quantity and quality as well as in time. Goal statements also should specify or clearly imply who is responsible, particularly if the goal requires more than one person's work to achieve it.
2. Goals must be perceived to be important so that employees do not feel that they are asked to spend extra effort on that which they believe to be trivial.
3. Goals must be challenging, but at the same time they must be realistic so that about 50 percent of them can be achieved or exceeded with intelligently directed effort consistently applied.

Involvement by Managers in the Way Subordinates
Work toward the Achievement of Their Goals

Another area in which a goals program can lose its chance to become a way of life concerns the amount of involvement by the manager or leader in the action steps that lower-level managers, employees, or colleagues set and in the way they implement them. Involvement concerns how much discussion there should be about action steps necessary to achieve a goal and the frequency and detail with which a manager checks on how well the individual implements action steps. What should the manager's or leader's role be?

In deciding how deeply to become involved in helping individuals or in checking how they approach their assignments, managers and academic leaders should keep in mind the Hersey-Blanchard life-cycle theory. Those individuals who have either limited experience or limited capabilities and are less mature, in a business sense, than they might be (who, in theoretical terms, have not grown past the peak of the life-cycle curve) require fairly careful checking to see that they are approaching their assignments in a competent way. More competent or mature people require considerably less of this over-the-shoulder watching, and in fact, to do it would lead to considerable dissatisfaction on their part.

Management involvement in supervision not only concerns the frequency of progress checks but also the detail with which managers expect action steps to be set and the level of formality of the action plan. With some subordinates, as part of their development and training process, it may indeed be necessary to lay out a very detailed action program in writing for each of the limited number of goals that have been selected as priorities. With more experienced and mature people, less formality is required. Detailed discussion of action programs may be needed only on a very few goals. Highly competent and mature subordinates or colleagues can best decide themselves how detailed or formal the action plans should be for almost all goals. The manager might rarely, if ever, check them, except when the subordinate or colleague asks for a review of the action plan to take advantage of any ideas the manager might contribute. However, when a project is critical, it may call for fairly detailed involvement on the part of the manager, even if the subordinates are quite competent, if for no other reason than to show that the manager accepts full responsibility for the results.

With respect to involvement, here as elsewhere, three factors should influence the manager's behavior: the situation, the subordinate's capability, and the manager's own personality and needs. For instance, as one of several goals, a secretary may take a writing course at the college to improve work-related skills. With a highly motivated and mature person, the manager may do little more than occasionally ask how the course is going and whether help is needed. With one who is less motivated or less capable of learning, much more would be appropriate. The manager should probably inquire regularly how the course is going and what help the subordinate may need to gain full advantage from the course. The manager also might attempt to provide work assignments that would put to immediate use any new knowledge the learner had acquired. With the least competent employees, it might be necessary, after every class, to briefly review the lesson and help them clarify the more difficult concepts. Detailed follow-up of this type could be deeply resented by competent people as interference. However, for many who feel insecure or lacking in knowledge but who would still like to do well, such "interference" might be considered very helpful and could be sincerely appreciated.

There is one question that managers frequently ask when it is suggested that they allow their subordinates more freedom in working toward goals:

"How do I know that action plans have really been considered and that they are being followed?" This question is, of course, not always easy to answer, because managers really know very little about the plans of subordinates in whom they have confidence. However, managers have access to some information about progress from day-to-day contacts or from the reports they receive. Furthermore, managers routinely receive considerable information about action plans and how they have been revised during each goals review and whenever subordinates encounter difficulties. A subordinate who does not provide such information voluntarily is not yet sufficiently mature, and more detailed monitoring or checking is required, as well as training or coaching to provide the subordinate with greater awareness of the manager's need for up-to-date information. The highly competent subordinate recognizes his or her responsibility to keep the manager informed so that the manager has a general idea on progress in all areas for which he or she is responsible. One of the major responsibilities of the manager, therefore, is to help subordinates develop a thorough understanding of their responsibility for communicating any obstacles or occurrences that may prevent the achievement of a goal.

Two very common characteristics of less mature subordinates are the desire to be left alone to complete projects as they see fit long before they have achieved the experience and competence to consistently reach good results and an aversion to filing regular verbal or written reports. Competent subordinates, however, keep their managers informed about developments by providing brief synopses of events and progress on a regular basis. They recognize that managers also must report to someone who expects them to be knowledgeable about the status of major projects and aware of significant problems.

Much of what has been said about involvement by managers is conceptually applicable to the relationship between the chairperson and the faculty member. Obviously, with a senior, tenured faculty member, once a goal is set, there should be little need for the chairperson to be involved with the way the faculty member works toward the achievement of the goal. At the same time, of course, the chairperson should be available to provide assistance and guidance or suggestions if the faculty member requests such help.

With a new instructor who is unfamiliar with the environment of the institution, much more guidance in the way action steps are to be set and followed would be needed. Most mature, new instructors would welcome assistance to ensure achievement of goals. When new faculty members are asked to work on goals that involve other department members as well, it is clearly to everyone's advantage to provide some measure of guidance so that the goals of the group are achieved.

Summary of the Involvement of Managers: The following guidelines can be used for involvement of managers:

1. The extent of desirable involvement on a manager's part depends on the capabilities and maturity of people in the unit.
2. The more competent an individual is, the less welcome is managerial involvement, except when requested. The less competent an individual is, the more necessary is managerial involvement.
3. Involvement is viewed as desirable by people in the unit only if it is clearly intended to provide help rather than to evaluate performance.
4. A manager's expressed goal should be to help individuals develop so that progressively less involvement will be needed.

Frequency of Goals Reviews

A goals review is simply this: At least once a year the manager and each subordinate set strategic and operational goals on all the major responsibilities in the subordinate's job. At the same time, they select those few operational goals (see the subsection Extent of Goal Setting) appropriate for the subordinate and the situation for priority attention during the period until the next review, which may come between 1 and 3 months later. This ensures that while goals have been set in all areas of responsibility, at the next review emphasis will be on high-priority goals. During this review, priorities may be shifted or new high-priority goals may be added. As an alternative to this approach, the manager and the subordinate could select only priority goals and lump all other duties and responsibilities under one priority goal stating that all other functions would receive their normal attention.

Some specific purposes of goals reviews are (1) to pinpoint those areas in which the manager should provide additional help or support and to discuss the specific support the manager should provide; (2) to keep the manager informed of progress about goals on which work is proceeding essentially as expected; (3) to review what new goals, if any, should be added for the upcoming period; (4) to review which goals have become unrealistic as a result of changing events and should therefore be modified; (5) to drop any goals that are no longer important enough to keep on the list of goals; (6) to review the adequacy of coordination and communication with the people who are affected by the goal; and (7) to assign priorities to the goals for the upcoming period. Of these, the first purpose is the most important. The manager has to determine how he or she can help a subordinate achieve realistic goals, decide whether additional help should be provided, or allow the goals to slip.

Although regular reviews are necessary for a goals program to be successful, there are few hard and fast rules to guide the number of times per year that goals reviews should be held. Many organizations who have reasonably effective goals programs require their managers to hold goals reviews with each subordinate at least once every 3 months. Within this requirement, however, it is possible to hold reviews even more frequently, such as monthly, biweekly, or occasionally even weekly. With highly competent subordinates who can work on several goals at the same time, a monthly review is beneficial, for there is relatively little need for detailed discussions about how the goals are being approached.

If there is relatively little involvement by the manager in the way the subordinate works toward achieving the goal, then there may be a need for frequent goals-review sessions. In these sessions, progress toward goals is explored, and the subordinate has an opportunity to call on the skills and capabilities of the manager to assist with the difficult problems. At the same time, the manager receives an update on the status of the various projects that are in progress.

There are several significant benefits that fairly formal, regular reviews can bring. First, they are likely to prevent the common complaint that the manager does not really know what employees are doing or what they are contributing to the achievement of the unit's goals. Second, they provide evidence that the manager is serious about the goals program, that he or she supports it, and that it receives the necessary emphasis and is not just a flash in the pan or eyewash for higher-level administrators. Third, regular reviews also provide opportunities for managers to become more knowledgeable about the capabilities and potential of each of their people, so they can help them individually develop greater competence and higher levels of success. And last, they provide more factual data about the way people work toward goals and thus help to make performance appraisals less subjective.

Goals reviews can be less frequent with subordinates when the manager has to be deeply involved in the way the subordinates work toward achievement of goals. These subordinates are constantly in need of help or guidance with the steps that have to be taken. With such subordinates, a manager can hold formal goals reviews once every 3 months because of the constant supervision and knowledge of the project. Similarly, quarterly reviews would be adequate for a manager who works continuously with a small team of subordinates.

A good goals review follows a pattern that ensures that all subjects are covered thoroughly. One useful procedure might be as follows:

1. With respect to all completed goals, a manager might ask these questions:

    How well was the goal achieved?

How difficult/easy was it to achieve the goal?

What was the quality and quantity of effort needed to achieve the goal?

Was there adequate communication on progress toward goal achievement?

How adequate was the support provided the subordinate?

2. With respect to all open goals, a manager might ask:

Will the goal be achieved? If not, what is the problem and what should be done about it?

What support should be provided to help the subordinate achieve the goal?

How adequate are communications, so far, between all parties?

How appropriate is the involvement of those people who are affected by this goal?

Is the goal still appropriate in light of changes in environment?

3. The manager could determine what new goals should be set.

4. The manager also might review priorities and realign them in the light of the current situation.

In deciding on the frequency of reviews, it is important to keep in mind that more frequent goals reviews often provide more factual data about the way subordinates work toward goals and thus help to make performance appraisals less subjective. It is also important to remember that monthy production goals are not valid candidates for the list of priority goals for any one period, although the quarterly production goal may be a priority. Examples of more important goals that must be included are programs that lead to accomplishment of production goals—improvements in work methods and procedures, skills development, work-force plans, communications improvements, and so forth.

An example may help to clarify this picture. The school's Registrar, Ms. Jones, may have set jointly with a subordinate manager, Mrs. Lee, the following strategic goals for Mrs. Lee and her unit for the coming calendar year:

1. Develop and achieve goals that will reduce total hours on routine functions by 5 percent.
2. Develop the capability, by midyear, to absorb schedule changes that are announced on the day before they are to go into effect without causing more than 5 hours of nonproductive time charges.
3. Reduce the amount of time spent on correction of scheduling errors by 10 percent from the preceding year.

4. Decrease cost of supplies used by 3 percent.
5. Ensure better coordination with the Department of Student Advisement and develop ways to measure such coordination jointly with the director of that department.
6. Develop a standards manual by midyear.
7. Establish and achieve self-development goals that will reduce the number of times when it is recognized too late that a specific goal has not been achieved.
8. Establish and achieve self-development goals in the (*relevant*) technology.

If Mrs. Lee were a fairly competent person, she would use these strategic goals to develop some very specific operational goals for the first quarter, which she would review with Ms. Jones. Her operational goals might be

1. Reduce total hours spent in her unit on routine functions by 2 percent by March 30.
2. By February 27, prepare specific plans, including a training-program outline, to improve the unit's ability to cope with schedule changes.
3. Enroll in an evening course and achieve a good grade.
4. Obtain an analysis of causes of scheduling errors by February 10.

Just because Mrs. Lee would pay primary attention to theses four goals during the first month, or possibly even longer, does not mean that she would neglect her normal supervisory duties. She certainly would keep closer tabs on the use of supplies, talk to the Director of Student Advisement about coordination, collect data for the standards manual, and think about how she can recognize when a goal is in trouble earlier. However, while working on these things, she would make certain that none of them interfered with her efforts to achieve the four primary goals for the period.

If Ms. Jones usually meets with her managers on a monthly basis, the end of the January review with Mrs. Lee might show that Mrs. Lee has enrolled in an appropriate course, that she is well on her way to completing the analysis of causes of scheduling errors, that the cost-reduction goal appears to be roughly on target, and that Mrs. Lee has some ideas on how to deal with schedule changes, but she is not at all certain that these will come close to meeting the goals. She has prepared a preliminary outline of the training program that she wants to discuss with Ms. Jones, together with the entire approach to this goal.

During the discussion, in addition to pleasantries and some discussion of matters of mutual personal interest, Ms. Jones might commend Mrs. Lee on enrolling in an excellent course and, if she is knowledgeable, offer any help that she can provide; and ask Mrs. Lee whether she would like to review what could be done to make faster progress on the March productivity target, but not pursue it further if Mrs. Lee feels she can handle it. Further, Ms. Jones might discuss the schedule-change goal in detail and review the training program, make suggestions, contribute any ideas she can think of, and agree to review its status with Mrs. Lee in 2 weeks to see how else she could help. She might decide with Mrs. Lee that the goals on scheduling error analysis can be dropped and that the self-development goal of attaining a high grade also can be dropped since Mrs. Lee will undoubtedly complete the course satisfactorily. Together they might decide that a specific goal should be set with respect to the standards manual, and that a new matter pertaining to a new service has become sufficiently clear and important that a goal can be set for it. Finally, they might discuss the general situation in Mrs. Lee's unit to see whether all priorities are still appropriate and whether any problems or opportunities exist that should receive more attention.

As a result of this review meeting, Mrs. Lee might submit new goals and priorities within a few days, and at the end of February, a new review could follow a similar pattern. During the month, there would be little need for Ms. Jones to follow up with Mrs. Lee on these matters, except for the one on schedule changes on which she had promised further help.

To show how a department chairperson might think about the question of frequency of goals reviews, an example might be useful. For instance, because the chairperson of the mathematics department has received a number of complaints about a relatively new instructor, with respect to the relevance of testing in the course, the chairperson might have sat down to discuss the problem with that colleague. They might have decided jointy that the instructor would try to design future tests to eliminate these complaints, and they might have set a goal of reducing complaints about tests to a maximum of four per year, since that is a reasonable figure in comparison with the experience of other instructors.

The question that would then face the department chairperson would concern how often reviews with the instructor should take place to look at the progress made toward achievement of that goal. EQIFAPPO suggests that the department chairperson, taking into account the factors discussed in this section, should indeed sit down shortly with that instructor to review what the instructor has done to achieve the goal. Another informal review in 3 months also might be appropriate to provide assurance to the instructor that the chairperson is really supportive and willing to help overcome difficult problems.

While department chairpersons often will not be in a situation where they set goals with colleagues of senior status, the really competent chairperson is likely to do so. When he or she has identified the problem, an informal goal-setting session with the colleague may take place, and depending on the "maturity" of that professor and the extent to which he or she is willing to work toward agreed upon goals, more or less frequent reviews would be necessary.

With a less mature colleague, more frequent reviews would be required in order to ensure that the professor really understands that he or she should be thinking about specific action steps and should be able to articulate those and work toward their completion in an effective way.

Summary of Frequency of Goals Reviews: The following guidelines can be used to help determine the frequency of goals reviews:

1. Goals reviews are important to an open communications climate.
2. There are many purposes that goals reviews satisfy. They provide, for instance, perspective on the total situation and foster an exchange of views that helps to satisfy everyone's needs—the manager's, the subordinate's, the unit's.
3. Goals reviews should be scheduled regularly; there should be at least one review each quarter.
4. The frequency of goals reviews depends on the situation (the closeness of contact between manager and subordinate and the importance or complexity of the goals), on the capabilities of the subordinate, and on the need to obtain adequate factual data for performance evaluations.

Holding Subordinates Accountable

The questions involved here ask what it is that a manager or leader can reasonably expect from employees or colleagues:

> To what extent can anyone be held accountable for accomplishment of goals if outside interferences prevent their achievement despite intelligently directed and extensive effort?

> When goals are not achieved, whose fault is it?

> What will be the consequences of establishing accountability?

If managers want their subordinates to have confidence in them, it is important that they hold them accountable only for those matters which are under the control of the subordinate and that they are factual and fair in this. They should not forget that goals are primarily forecasts, and even the best forecasts are only estimates of what will occur. This means that even carefully planned and well-implemented steps still may not bring full achievement of a goal.

Can someone be held accountable, for instance, if unexpected emergencies pop up? For instance, if a supervisor in the Computer Center is striving to improve quality and, just as he or she is making progress, the two most competent programmers, the ones with the best quality record, are in a car accident together that keeps them out of work for several months, how should this supervisor be rated if quality deteriorates temporarily and then again resumes its upward trend—without making the goal? How good is performance? Is the performance poor because the goal was not reached, or is it excellent because an improving trend existed before as well as soon after the accident?

The question of accountability concerns the extent to which an individual can be expected to achieve a goal and how performance can be judged if the goal is not reached. Many goals programs fail, as do larger attempts at organizational planning, at least in part because they are not able to deal with accountability.

It does not seem particularly useful for managers to place *full* responsibility for the achievement of goals on the people who have accepted them. Higher-level managers and administrators, it would seem, must accept their share of the responsibility. It is often meaningless to observe that 80 or 90 percent of a goal has been achieved or to note that the goal has been achieved exactly on the day planned or a few days earlier or later. The original goal may have been totally unrealistic and impossible to achieve, or it may have been very easy. In either case, to measure percentage of achievement for each goal or for the number of goals achieved does not represent a useful way to judge a subordinate's performance. However, there are many activities or categories of action steps related to goal achievement that a subordinate can and should be held specifically accountable for. Use of these can make it easier for managers to place less reliance on actual achievement of goals when deciding what to expect from subordinates. There are eight major activities related to goal achievement that are fully under the control of the person working on a goal and for which he or she can accept complete responsibility:

1. Setting challenging but realistic goals
2. Setting thorough action steps
3. Maintaining continuity and consistency in planning
4. Ensuring the quality of action steps
5. Keeping to schedule
6. Solving problems
7. Communicating problems in a timely manner
8. Maintaining good relationships with others

Setting Challenging but Realistic Goals: Participation by subordinates is desirable when setting goals; however, goal setting is meaningful only if subordinates are sincere in helping to establish goals that are both realistic and challenging. If a subordinate is forced to play a game to obtain the lowest possible goal so that the least amount of effort is required to achieve it, then mutual goal setting is not effective. Managers therefore need the cooperation of the subordinates in helping to set challenging and realistic goals.

If a goals program exists and the manager wants it to become a way of life rather than a paper program, then obviously the manager cannot expect people to set challenging goals if they are punished when they do not achieve them. Most managers make allowance for effort and do look at events or conditions that are beyond the subordinate's control when reviewing the reasons why a goal was not achieved or why, for that matter, much more was accomplished than had been expected. Rarely, however, do subordinates know what the manager will consider valid or how the manager actually looks at performance. Unless they know the manager's standards, it is not likely that they can develop the full confidence that is needed to go out on a limb with tough goals.

A manager who requires that subordinates set challenging goals must be prepared to look at goals as predictions of achievement and to expect serious efforts to be made to attain them. Some goals, however, may not be achieved even with the best action program and the most untiring effort. If a manager accepts this fact, then subordinates can be held accountable for setting realistic goals that are also challenging.

Setting Thorough Action Steps: Another aspect for which a manager can hold subordinates accountable is the thoroughness with which action steps support all goals. A person working on goals should always be aware of what action steps are necessary to come as close to the achievement of that goal as possible, and he or she should have those action steps fairly clearly in mind. Even though a manager would not frequently ask competent subordinates what progress is being made toward the accomplishment of a goal or what actual steps are being taken, the subordinates would know what these steps are. This does not mean that these action steps must be in writing, nor does it mean that there must be very many of these action steps. However, they should be of the quality that helps to achieve the mission, and the subordinate should be fully aware of what they are. The manager can therefore hold subordinates responsible for having appropriate and adequate action steps for their goals.

Maintaining Continuity and Consistency in Planning: A manager also can hold subordinates responsible for good planning and for the thoroughness with which their planning occurs. A competent person, working against goals, will think of goals at all times. A less competent person will forget about goals during certain periods. The least competent people will remember goals only when they know their managers will ask about them.

Continuity of effort is desirable when carrying out action steps and may be used as a measure of performance. Individuals who are striving to achieve their goals will think of them every day, which will be clear from the way they approach their tasks. Evidence of continuity will be found in the contacts that occur between manager and subordinate in the period between goals reviews. Individuals who regularly and voluntarily update their managers on progress provide ample evidence of their continuing attention to planning.

Ensuring the Quality of Action Steps: When looking at the action steps that a subordinate takes, a manager obviously must evaluate them to see whether they are the best that can be taken. An individual who regularly takes action steps that show improvement certainly deserves to be commended; one who takes inadequate action steps should be held accountable. If inadequate steps are being taken, then it is necessary to provide training. While training proceeds, the evaluation of the individual's work can reflect the fact that full competence has not yet been reached.

This criterion requires somewhat more personal judgment by the manager, because there are no absolute criteria upon which to base the measurement of quality. The manager has to judge whether the action steps are the best that could be taken and whether they are being executed competently. In making such judgments, the manager must rely in part on his or her experience and in part on the results of the action steps.

Keeping to Schedule: Completing action steps on time is also entirely under the control of individuals, and they therefore can be held accountable. If an individual agrees to complete some project by a certain time and then accomplishes it by that time, then he or she clearly has performed satisfactorily. Conversely, if an action step is not completed on time, something is wrong. The quality of the action step or the amount of effort that had to be devoted to its completion may have been misjudged, for example. Once someone has made a commitment to a plan of action, that plan should be implemented as decided; and since, by definition, matters beyond his or her control are not involved, the manager can reasonably expect that steps will be completed as agreed.

Keeping to the schedule—timeliness—is probably the easiest accountability criterion to measure and evaluate. Clear statements of action steps require the specification of completion time as well as quantity and quality. It will be clear at goals reviews whether deadlines have been met. The reviews create a permanent record that may be used for evaluating later performance.

Solving Problems: It sometimes becomes apparent that action steps will not, in fact, lead to the achievement of the desired goal. When this happens, the person working toward the goal should be expected to reconsider the action steps and take any additional steps that may be necessary to reach the goal.

There are many benefits to making it a clear policy that everyone is expected to be creative in solving the problem whenever achievement of a goal is threatened. Such a policy is evidence of confidence in the competence of employees, and it sets the stage for the feeling of accomplishment that comes whenever new approaches prove to be better than previous ones. It is necessary, of course, to make it clear that help is available when difficulties cannot be overcome. The quality of the revised action plan may be used to judge performance fairly and factually. This criterion is also fairly difficult to evaluate and must be based on the evaluator's judgment, even though, as in other instances, goals reviews can provide a basis for judgment.

Communicating Problems in a Timely Manner: Once an organization understands how to work with a goals system, everyone knows that it is essential to notify the manager as soon as it becomes clear that a goal will not be achieved. This gives the manager an opportunity to decide whether to (1) provide additional resources or help in order to ensure that the goal can be achieved and (2) change the goal if it appears that all has been done to achieve it and it still cannot be achieved, or that it does not warrant the additional resources needed for on-time achievement.

For instance, suppose someone must find out what videotape equipment would be best for the institution's needs. The person may have committed himself or herself to completion of the investigation and trials by a certain date, but he or she may find, as time progresses, that more urgent matters have come up and evaluations of the various units will not be finished in time. At this point, the person has several choices. He or she can let the goal slide or inform his or her manager that the goal will not be achieved unless more time is allocated to investigation and trial or unless additional personnel are brought in to help. If this notification is given early enough that the goal can still be achieved, the manager has the opportunity to rescue the goal or to move its completion date back.

If everyone in an organization accepts the responsibility of providing timely notification when a goal is in trouble, then there is greater likelihood that the most important organization goals will be achieved on time. Factually evaluating how promptly employees notify managers of trouble is fairly easy. Notification must be early enough that the manager can still rescue the goal if that is possible or desirable. Since about 50 percent of all goals will not be fully achieved, as discussed earlier, much data regarding a subordinate's actions when missing a goal are available, and a fair evaluation will rarely be difficult.

Maintaining Good Relationships with Others: There is one more aspect of goals programs for which subordinates can be held accountable, and this concerns their relationships with others. Subordinates can be judged on the extent to which they coordinate with others who are affected by their goals, how thoroughly they communicate with these people, and probably even how well they obtain cooperation from others in order to achieve their own goals. Of course, individuals should be judged on the basis of the cooperation they elicit from others and especially the cooperation they give to others.

A number of questions relating to goals reviews appeared earlier. Those which concern communications can aid in evaluating how well individuals maintain their working relationships. Accountability is a complex responsibility that cannot be satisfied by simply checking how well people have achieved their goals. Holding people accountable for the way in which they work to achieve their goals will increase the chances that they will accept goal setting as a useful process.

Goal Setting When Responsibilities Extend beyond the Realm of Authority: In an educational institution it is often necessary for individuals to assume a management task that consists of marshalling resources to achieve a departmental goal. This goal may be rather specific, such as "Prepare by May 1, an outline for a new course on pharmacokinetics," or it may be a rather ill-defined one, such as "Find new direction," or "Determine in what areas adequate funding for new research is available." In any of these cases, the person who has primary responsibility for achievement of the goal is someone who may not have sufficient authority to ensure full cooperation from others involved. Similar situations are often encountered by all managers, but especially by chairpersons of departments and of all institutional committees. In each of these situations, the chairperson's function is to lead the group to an end result, whether it is fairly clearly defined or very loosely specified.

In such situations there may be significant conflicts of interest between the results expected from the chairperson's role and those of single members of the committee. For instance, the chairperson may seek a committee decision on an organizational change that would avoid the damaging long-run consequences of inaction, while individual committee members may wish to protect the benefits the status quo provides the constituents whom they represent. The best interests of the institution and most of its members might be served with a course of action that will result in temporary hardship for a fairly large number of people. In such an environment, the chairperson has the responsibility to lead the group to mature, responsible conclusions that provide progress toward institutional change while minimizing the costs to individuals. The representative of one of the departments charged with representing the interest of his or her particular department, however, may oppose such a solution, preferring a course that places much greater weight on the needs of the affected individuals. Even if the attitudes of committee members preclude significant progress toward the goal to which the chairperson may have committed himself or herself, he or she can still accept responsibility for working toward this difficult-to-achieve or impossible goal. It is important, however, that those to whom the chairperson is accountable understand what it is that they can reasonably expect.

The criteria for performance appraisal suggested by the Linking Elements Concept clarify what can be expected and thus can serve as a guideline for shared goals as well as for those on which action steps concern primarily one person only. When responsibility is defined by these criteria, then it is obvious that the chairperson, as well as the committee member, can indeed be held accountable. There is no reason why someone should not set goals, develop action steps toward the achievement of the goals, keep those action steps in mind, continuously plan for their achievement, revise them when necessary, keep others informed who may be affected, and report back to those who are concerned with the achievement of the goal when it appears as though the action steps will not bring full achievement. Higher-level managers, or the constituents, then have an opportunity to either provide additional resources, make suggestions, or do whatver else is indicated if the goal is important to them and they want to do everything possible to see that it is achieved.

What is true of the committee person or the chairperson is also true of all the responsibilities that all managers have toward goal achievement, whether they are in academic or administrative departments. When assigned leadership in a task that requires cooperation from other people, a manager, leader, or representative can really be held accountable only for serious effort and intelligent, competent application of reasonable action steps. These, of course, include the one to report back at an early stage when a goal is in jeopardy to gain further resources, suggestions, direction, or other support.

The concept of accountability also applies in the academic departments. While a department chairperson may not have the same authority over colleagues as an administrative manager has over subordinates, a chairperson who wants to be seen as a competent leader does have to hold people accountable for taking the appropriate steps toward achievement of goals. For example, a chairperson may have worked with an instructor to set goals with respect to the amount of special tutoring the instructor will provide students outside of class. If, during an informal goals review, the chairperson learns that the instructor is not working toward the agreed upon goals, he or she has several available options to ensure that the instructor complies with the plan.

Since every chairperson has a personal relationship with each instructor in the department, the chairperson might first appeal to the instructor's intellectual integrity and his or her desire to be respected as a competent professional. It is likely, in situations such as this, that moral suasion will be effective; however, if it is not, the department chairperson may have to use other means to ensure the instructor's compliance.

The chairperson may use class assignments, authorizations to attend special meetings, recommendations for service on prestigious committees, or other perquisites and privileges within his or her range of authority to provide rewards in order to achieve greater willingness to accept responsibility for working toward mutually agreed upon goals. In some situations, peer pressure might be brought upon an instructor, while in those institutions where the chairperson has a role in compensation decisions for department members, the chairperson's authority is much closer to that of a manager in an administrative department and he or she can influence directly the individual's salary.

Summary of Holding Subordinates Accountable: A manager can gain higher levels of confidence and greater assurance that subordinates will be willing to set challenging goals if the manager says something like this: "So that we do not misunderstand each other on what I expect from you, it might be well if I explained my standards. I expect you to achieve all the goals on which we have agreed and you have accepted. However, when we review progress, and especially when we find it likely that a goal will not be achieved, I will look at the following. First, I will check whether that goal was set carefully in the first place, that is, whether you had taken the responsibility for setting realistic but challenging goals requiring more than routine thought and effort to achieve. Second, I will look at the thoroughness with which you have laid out the action steps leading to the achievement of the goal. Then, I will look at the extent to which you have kept these action steps in mind. I will also look at how good these action steps were and compare them with those I might have chosen. Obviously, I do not expect you to take the same steps because many roads can be taken to reach the same result, but I will try to determine the extent to which the steps that you have taken were of high quality and reasonable. I will also take a look at whether your action steps were completed as you had planned, or whether many were delayed for various reasons even though they were fully under your control. Since we will be looking especially closely at those goals which have not yet been achieved or are not likely to be achieved, I will be checking whether you have given some thought to changing the action steps that you originally contemplated to see if better ones can be substituted for them. If the new action steps still do not appear as though they will reach the goal, I will look at whether you have given me timely notification that a problem exists with respect to that goal so that I have the chance to do something about it. Finally, I will look at the way you have worked with others and the extent to which you have helped them and kept them informed so that they are able to help you as much as possible. If you have done all these things and the goal is still not attainable, then it is clear that I have to provide additional help or relieve you from the responsibility of achieving the goal on time.''

Participation

The most important step in bringing satisfaction to individuals concerns the amount of participation they have in the goal-setting process. People want opportunities to influence the decisions that will affect their lives in the present as well as in the future. This includes the things that have impact on their working conditions and on the work itself. Managers can and should allow a high degree of participation with some decisions or goals with some of the people who report to them in some situations, but they cannot offer a high level of participation in all situations with all, or even most, goals or with all their people. Goals or decisions made at higher levels, for instance, must be passed on. Rarely can a manager allow participation with these except in the ancillary decisions or goals pertaining to implementation.

A thorough understanding of how a manager can be highly participative without relinquishing the need to maintain control on important matters is a major issue in this book, because it is so crucial to the climate that makes achievement and the satisfaction of people at work two major criteria of success. The key element is the general guideline: a manager should allow the maximum amount of participation a particular situation and the capability of the subordinates permit *to those people who believe that a specific decision affects them and who want to be involved*. It is important to note that this guideline does *not* exclude fully autocratic decisions in some situations and/or with some subordinates.

Every manager has a wide range of participation options. In some decisions, all those who will be affected can and probably should take part at the earliest moment. In other decisions, only those who have the expertise in the particular topic should be consulted. In some, the manager alone should quickly make the choice, while in others, the manager's role should probably be minimal.

In deciding the level of participation that a manager should allow in the goal-setting process, there is much in the literature that can provide guidance. The literature very often calls it decision making rather than goal setting, however. It should be clarified here, therefore, that goal setting and decision making (which will be discussed more fully in appendix A) have a great many things in common. The setting of any goal requires at least one, and possibly many, decisions. Therefore, almost anything that applies to decision making automatically applies to goal setting.

Styles of Leadership: Because of the importance of participation in goals and in other decisions affecting work, behavioral scientists have devoted considerable effort to investigating the way participation should be used. The more important of these theories will be discussed here and related to the goal-setting process so that they can become practical guides to action for the manager who wishes to create the best possible climate.

This discussion of participation in goal setting starts with a famous, widely used diagram. It was published in 1958 by Professors Robert Tannenbaum and Warren H. Schmidt of the University of California in Los Angeles and is called the *continuum of leadership behavior* (see figure 4-8). The problem Tannenbaum and Schmidt addressed was the difficulty managers find in trying to be "democratic" while simultaneously maintaining authority and control. The solution they proposed involved the ability to operate effectively along the whole continuum from boss-centered to subordinate-centered leadership. This, of course, represents a difficult challenge, but one that can be met if the leader pays attention to key ques-

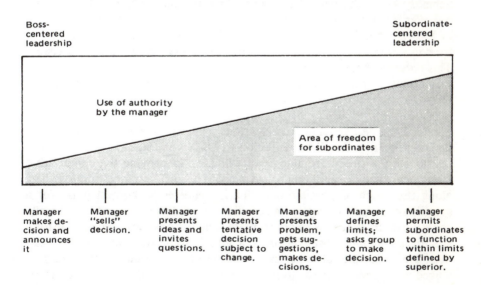

Source: From Robert Tannenbaum and Warren H. Schmidt, "How to Choose a Leadership Pattern?" *Harvard Business Review* (May-June 1973). Copyright © 1973 by the President and Fellows of Harvard College; all rights reserved. Artwork courtesy National Fire Protection Association.

Figure 4-8. Continuum of Leadership Behavior

tions about self, subordinates, and the situation. Some of the questions proposed by Tannenbaum and Schmidt are summarized as follows:

Leader: What are my own values and convictions? Do I have confidence in my subordinates and a desire to see them grow and advance? Do I feel secure in certain situations?

Subordinates: What sort of behavior do they expect from the leader? Do they need independence and want responsibility? Do they feel the problem is important, and do they have the technical knowledge needed to discuss the problem? Do they trust the leader in various styles?

The Situation: What are the demands of organizational policy? What are the time pressures? Is there a need to keep some information confidential?

Such questions may help to clarify the leader's decisions about how to lead at any given time and may, in fact, confine leadership style to a particular segment of the continuum of leadership behavior diagram (as may happen, for example, when both leaders and subordinates do not wish decision making to be shared).

At least two points are considered essential by Tannenbaum and Schmidt: (1) the leader should never shirk responsibility for the decision, however it is made; and (2) the leader should always make clear what style of leadership is being used. There should be no attempt, for example, to trick subordinates into thinking that the leader's decision was their decision. This requires that the manager make it clear, at the outset of every discussion about a decision, what level of participation he or she considers appropriate.

Selecting the Best Level of Participation: The manager who can make good decisions on how much participation to allow will establish a much better relationship with subordinates and will help to provide the climate that motivates them to greater achievement. The difficult question is where along the range of possible participation choices is the best point for a specific situation. Managers who ask themselves this question automatically come closer to choosing an appropriate style for a specific decision or for a specific goal than those who do not give it some thought. Nevertheless, there are no simple rules that can be used to help a manager; the issues involved are far too complex to permit the use of a simplistic formula. There are considerations, however, that allow a more accurate selection of the participation level and timing. These considerations involve issues related to the characteristics of the individual and to the situation.

Issues Related to Characteristics of the Individual: First, there is a question of attitudes and maturity. This concerns the extent to which an individual is willing—and able—to accept responsibility and devote extra effort when required, the level of judgment that person can apply, the willingness to accept the direction in which the goal takes the group, and so forth. If a person generally makes decisions based on emotional rather than factual considerations and does not analyze the facts carefully but instead jumps quickly to conclusions, then that person cannot participate at the same level and in the same number of decisions or goals as someone who has a more objective, rational approach.

Second, in addition to emotional maturity, the level of participation should take into account the extent to which the individual wants to be involved. There are many reasons why a person may not wish to participate in a particular instance. They include the attitudes he or she may have toward the decision or goal. If an individual thinks that the manager merely wants participation in order to have others share responsibility, then there might be a negative attitude toward participation. Similarly, if people believe that a manager asks for participation only on a token basis and does not really want opinions or help with a decision or a goal—is likely to make the decision the way he or she wishes anyway—then they often do not really want to spend time discussing the decision.

Third, besides maturity and a willingness to participate, a thorough knowledge of the subject matter is required. If the individual has little technical knowledge of a subject, then certainly it would not be wise to give that person a large voice with a decision related to that subject. An instructor in a scientific discipline, for example, who uses microscopes infrequently might not be able to contribute significantly to the selection of new equipment. Furthermore, it is likely that this instructor might not want to be involved in a decision about microscopes. Such individuals may feel awkward in participating in a decision in which they can contribute very little and might be concerned about exposing a lack of knowledge.

Often lack of knowledge is not based on education or experience, but rather on the amount of information about the decision that is available and can be made available to them. Without such background data and adequate perspective on the situation surrounding a decision or goal, an individual's contribution often cannot be a large one.

In a way, these three guidelines on the extent to which a subordinate should be involved in goal setting or decision making are related to the life-cycle concept discussed earlier. The further to the left the person has reached on the life-cycle curve, the more extensively and the earlier that person can be involved in the goal-setting and decision-making process.

To summarize what has been covered so far, the extent and timing of participation by subordinates in the goal-setting process should be an important consideration that managers should not take lightly. Managers must give some thought to it with respect to every decision affecting subordinates.

The first question a manager can ask to find the best level of participation and timing is "What is likely to lead to greatest success?" Success here should be thought of in terms of long- and short-term impact on task-related results as well as on people. The timing and the level of participation that will lead to the greatest success depends, in turn, on the capabilities of the individuals who are being asked to participate.

Issues Related to the Situation: In addition to issues related to the characteristics of individuals, considerations related to the requirements of the decision or the goal itself must be included. In order to make a decision or set a goal in the best possible way, two things have to be considered: (1) the technical quality requirement—the knowledge that is required to make the decision successful or to set a high-quality goal—and (2) the acceptance quality requirement—the extent to which successful implementation of the decision or achievement of the goal requires acceptance on the part of the people who are affected. These two considerations were illustrated by Norman R. Maier of the University of Michigan in a grid (see figure 4-9) that, while simple in appearance, is rich in complex questions.

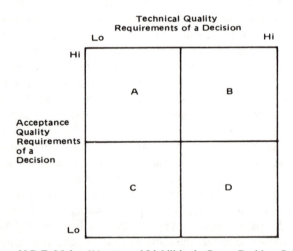

Source: From N.R.F. Maier, "Assets and Liabilities in Group Problem Solving: The Need for an Integrative Function," *Psychological Review* 74, 4 (April 1967):240-241. Copyright © 1967 by the American Psychological Association. Reprinted by permission; artwork courtesy National Fire Protection Association.

Figure 4-9. Simplified Leadership and Decision-Making Grid

Dr. Maier defines the quality requirements as follows:

Technical Quality Requirements are the kinds of specialized knowledge and the amount of such knowledge needed to reach an effective decision.

Acceptance Quality Requirements are the considerations of the amount of acceptance for the decision to be effectively implemented by those who are affected.[2]

According to Maier's grid, a decision with high acceptance quality requirements and low technical quality requirements (quadrant A in figure 4-9) might involve reassignment and rescheduling of working shifts. Little technical knowledge is necessary to make the decision, but a good decision must be acceptable to all the people involved. A decision with high technical quality requirements and low acceptance quality requirements (quadrant D) might involve a choice between two brands of a similar chemical on the basis of elaborate scientific specifications. Only one specialist may have the knowledge to make the choice, and no one in the department would be affected or wish to be involved. Most difficult, perhaps, is a decision with high technical quality requirements and high acceptance quality requirements (quadrant B).

Maier concludes that participative decisions are usually more effective, especially in quadrants A and B, but frequently also in quadrants C and D, because ". . . there is more information in a group than in any of its members. Thus, problems that require the utilization of knowledge should give groups an advantage over individuals. Even if one member of the group (e.g., the leader) knows much more than anyone else, the limited unique knowledge of lesser-informed individuals could serve to fill in some gaps in knowledge. For example, a skilled machinist might supply information on how a new machine might be received by workers."[3] Maier points out, however, that a strong leader may be needed to function as the group's "central nervous system" even when participation levels are highest. The leadership skill in this case involves the ability to keep discussion open, balanced, and fair.

In a way, what Maier may be saying is that a "strong" leader knows what participation level to use in the many situations that arise with the various individuals and groups with whom he or she interacts. What participation level to use is easiest to decide in quadrant D, especially toward the lower right-hand corner, where technical quality requirements are highest and acceptance need is lowest. A knowledgeable manager can set such a goal or make such a decision. A technically competent person to whom the decision has been delegated can do it for the manager, and then the manager merely needs to explain or announce it. The development of a new data-processing program or the preparation of an article for a technical magazine could fall in this category.

For goals and decisions in quadrant C, neither high technical knowledge nor widespread acceptance is required. This quadrant generally involves matters about which nobody really cares what will be done. Everybody wishes that somebody else would make the decision and go on with the business at hand. There are, however, not too many decisions of this type in the work environment. Since goals should be set only on those activities that deserve high priority during a given period, it is unlikely that any goals would fall into this category.

Matters belonging to quadrant A are of a different nature. These require high acceptance for success. A goal in this quadrant could be to reduce absenteeism or increase the attention to certain specific quality details. Most matters involving a significant amount of effort would be in this area, except for those decisions or goals for which, in addition to acceptance, high technical knowledge is required. For instance, the goal of reducing absenteeism by 20 percent does not require technical knowledge. Everybody knows what is involved. That does not mean that everybody can decide that 20 percent is the right amount of reduction to set as a goal, but everybody knows what the implications of the decision are and to what extent it will affect the people who have to implement it. Trivial decisions, such as whether to allocate parking spaces or change the coffee break time, also lie in this box.

It is obvious that any goal or decision in which people believe that they can make a useful contribution and which affects them seriously will turn out better if high levels of participation can be used. If there are differences of opinion among group members, the manager must lead the group to a joint decision that will bring the minimum resentment from individuals so that all will exert the greatest effort toward making the decision successful.

Finally, those goals and decisions which involve many technical problems and which need high acceptance at the same time require the greatest skill on the part of the manager. For example, a word-processing unit might be able to offer a highly desirable service if it could perfect a computer program and obtain the necessary data regularly within a tight deadline. Goals related to these situations must be decided by the people who have the technical knowledge to determine what is feasible. Success of the decisions and achievement of related goals, however, require implementation by several people. If the decisions and goals have high acceptance among these people, then the probability that challenging goals will be achieved is much higher than if such acceptance is lukewarm or lacking.

Decisions and goals of this type are most difficult, and therefore they require the greatest skill on the part of the manager. While it is not immediately obvious what the leader should do in this kind of situation, many managers believe that the leader should obtain a consensus. However, a consensus frequently results in a pooling of ignorance and may bring disastrous results. In such a situation, the leader should help the group identify the people who have the technical knowledge required to do the best possible job and then take advantage of the available knowledge to reach the decision jointly with the experts. Finally, if the manager wishes a decision to be successful or a goal to be a motivating one, the other people involved must be convinced that the decision is indeed the best.

This approach would undoubtedly be the best for goals such as those to improve the institution's fund-raising methods or to offer a new technical service. These goals require consultation with experts first, possibly joint decisions with them, and then good communications to convince others who are affected—or, when possible, the development of action plans and subsidiary goals by those who have to contribute their efforts. Often such additional decisions concern the best ways to achieve implementation and identify as well as overcome those obstacles which can be predicted.

The principles discussed in this segment apply in both the administrative units and the academic departments. With respect to the latter, a chairperson has available many participation options. For example, if a decision concerns whether to use a new textbook in the introductory-level course, the issue regarding participation first is tied to the objective that the chairperson wishes to achieve, to considerations of competence of the members of the group, and to their respective maturity to accept change that they may not favor.

If all the chairperson wants to achieve is to adopt a more modern book and he or she has no clear or strong personal preference for which book should be adopted, then all members of the department could very well be brought into the decision. Conceivably, small subcommittees could be formed to review and recommend specific books so that, from a wide selection, two or three books could be chosen that everyone would have to review in fair detail in order to contribute to the decision. However, this is the relatively simple situation in which everybody is the expert and the outcome should be done in which everybody has essentially an equal voice. The more realistic situation is one in which the chairperson clearly prefers, perhaps, one to three books. In such a situation, the chairperson has to decide whether to offer the group a choice only from those texts or to call together a subcommittee of the more senior members and decide jointly with them what books should be brought to a larger group.

In effect, the chairperson has a whole range of options of whom to consult and in what way, how to use the prestige and authority of the members of the group, how to set the limits within which he or she suggests the group operate (whether to select one or three books or one out of the total range of the available books), among many others. This particular decision, of course, is quite unique inasmuch as every member of the department probably is an expert in the field. However, if the book would be used by only a few instructors in a somewhat more advanced course that forms the basis of still other courses that other instructors teach, then the decision is somewhat more complex. Should all those who would ultimately be affected be involved? Should only those who are teaching that particular course be involved? Again, the chairperson's decision will influence the respect that he or she will receive from the other members of the group and will affect the discipline with which the group works toward the achievement of future goals or changes that may be desirable.

Summary of Participation Guidelines: This discussion has not pinpointed the *exact* level of participation that would be best in any one situation. However, going through the following process can help one better determine the proper level of participation:

1.   Before making a decision or discussing a goal, always ask the question, "What level of participation will lead to greatest success?" This automatically ensures that the choice of participation level will receive serious consideration. Just asking the question, therefore, will lead to a better choice of level.
2.   As a useful next step, look at the technical quality requirements as well as the acceptance quality requirement of the decision or goal. This helps to narrow the choice of participation level and provides a few other ideas about how to approach the goal or decision.
3.   Once this question has been resolved, look at the capabilities and other factors related to the subordinate or subordinates to help zero in even closer on the best level of participation. These include (a) emotional maturity and attitudes, (b) willingness to participate, and (c) knowledge of subject matter.

When the steps in this thought process have been completed, you must make the final choice. Nevertheless, going quickly through these steps should bring a more rational choice of participation level than you would select if you gave less thought to this crucial question. While the process is complicated, it need not be time consuming. Learning to stop before making a decision—to ask the proper question—is the difficult part. The rest goes quickly after some practice. When you can decide on the appropriate level of participation in a fairly factual manner and can follow through on your conclusion, you are practicing a wide range of leadership styles. You will select from the many dimensions of leadership style those aspects which fit the needs of the situation and of the subordinate. At one moment with respect to one situation you may rely on others to supply answers and decisions, and in a different situation you may merely announce the decisions you have made. In one area you may be highly supportive and provide help, while elsewhere you may insist on strict compliance with previous requests without offering any additional resources.

Such flexibility to adapt to the needs of the situation can easily be mistaken for erratic, unreliable behavior if it is not based on careful thinking and practice and on a sound framework that allows you to communicate, at all times, the reasons for your choice of style. Such explanations are of utmost importance. Consistency and reliability of leadership do not mean rigidity, however; nor do they mean restriction to a limited number of leadership approaches. Instead, they are based on the soundness of the underlying principles that guide your actions and on your ability to explain these principles adequately.

Performance Evaluation and the Goals Process

Most individuals are concerned with what their supervisors think of them and of the quality of their work. They want to know how they are progressing in relation to their own future and in terms of their contribution to the overall success of the organizational unit. Information about performance or specific assignments should be made available to subordinates on a regular basis and should cover both positive and negative aspects of the subordinate's progress. From time to time, however, there should be a formal review that (1) clarifies how the manager perceives the subordinate's overall performance, (2) suggests ways in which the subordinate's performance can be improved, and (3) explains how the manager can help the subordinate reach personal work and career goals. Such reviews are usually called *performance appraisals* or *performance evaluations*.

At one time, performance appraisals were based primarily on the personal opinion of the superior; they were judgments about the subordinate's ambition, initiative, general reliability, loyalty, and so on. The supervisor also would evaluate quantity and quality of the work, punctuality, and other aspects of the subordinate's work that were somewhat more measurable. Very often, though, these were not based on facts, but mainly on feelings, and therefore, they were heavily influenced by how much the boss liked the subordinate. Gradually there came greater awareness that appraisals of this type were grossly unfair to many people and especially favorable to those who managed to establish a friendly relationship with their bosses. As a result, they often were resented and contributed to poor morale and controversy.

Many voices were raised, therefore, asking that performance appraisal be based on achievement, and the best way to measure achievement, many people felt, was with goal accomplishment. However, this too turned out to leave a lot of freedom to the manager to use personal opinion in deciding whether the subordinate had good and acceptable reasons for missing a goal. Since many difficult goals are not achieved and many easy goals are exceeded, there is still a great deal left to personal feelings and to the opinion that a manager has about any one subordinate. Obviously, there will never be a system that can completely eliminate these defects. However, a performance-appraisal system that is based on the effort that people devote toward the achievement of goals and on the quality of that effort has the greatest chance, at the moment, to be fair to the organization and to the individuals involved.

The most meaningful appraisal/evaluation systems are tied closely to past plans and their specific objectives and to an improvement plan that itself becomes as important as the evaluation. Just as planning itself cannot be carried out in isolation from the realities of the organizational unit, so too, performance appraisals should not be separated from the planning process. The best system of planning and performance appraisal will be achieved if it is possible to fully integrate the planning process and the performance-appraisal system.

Planning and Performance Evaluation: An effective planning and performance appraisal requires a framework within which data for a meaningful evaluation can be collected and an adequate dialogue between manager and subordinate can take place. The process, therefore, might consist of three stages (see figure 4-10): a planning process, a review process, and an evaluation process.

Stage 1. Planning: Establishing goals and plans of action. This is the process in which manager and subordinate meet to see what has to be achieved and how it will be achieved. Specific goals are set and agreed on for the forthcoming period.

Stage 2. Reviewing: Reviewing goals regularly. The goals review provides the data for evaluation and thus becomes the key link between planning and the ultimate performance appraisal.

Stage 3. Evaluating: Conducting the performance appraisal itself. In this part of the process, manager meets with subordinate once or twice a year to evaluate his or her performance and to determine what specific personal development goals should be established for the future. Here specific criteria are used to measure the *manner in which the individual has worked toward the goals that have been established during the previous goals reviews*. Evidence accumulated during these reviews can provide a firm foundation for the discussion of performance. The performance appraisal also can devote time to a discussion of specific knowledge, skills, and other items that the subordinate needs to develop

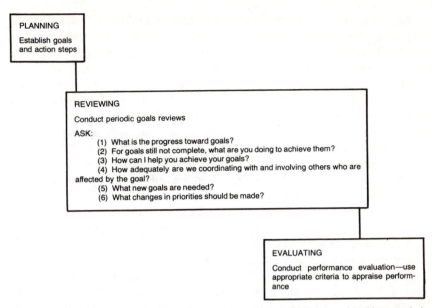

Source: Copyright © 1977 by Didactic Systems, Inc., Cranford, N.J. Reprinted by permission. Artwork courtesy of Bureau of National Affairs.

Figure 4-10. Planning and Performance Appraisal: A Three-Phase Process

in order to become better at his or her present job and to develop the background needed for positions toward which the individual might be aspiring.

Almost every employee and manager wants to know, and has a right to know, how superiors feel about his or her performance, and the manager who must evaluate performance has the obligation to obtain factual and adequate performance data. Similarly, every instructor and professor has a right to know how the department chairperson or dean views his or her performance. Most people want to do the best they can within the limits of their capabilities; therefore, they need to know where they stand. If managers and leaders meet with the people in their departments in a thorough review session on some regular basis, they will become more factual in the way they evaluate performance and will rely less on personal preferences and expectations.

If performance evaluations are to support the organizational unit's plans and goals, they must be as fair and factual as possible; they must be based on controllable accountabilities; and they must provide an opportunity for the subordinate to participate in the process. There are nine specific guidelines that can be used to evaluate performance.

1. Ambitiousness or taking initiative: This guideline measures an individual by how ambitiously he or she sets goals and objectives.
2. Thoroughness: This guideline measures the extent to which all goals have a thorough set of action steps supporting them.
3. Planning: This guideline measures whether the individual is always thorough in keeping all goals in mind and in working on action steps.
4. Quality of effort: Here quality is determined by action steps and is really measured by whether the action steps an individual selects are those which are most likely to achieve the goals most rapidly.
5. Timeliness of results: Here the individual's performance is reviewed against whether or not he or she has achieved the action steps on schedule and according to the plan.
6. Problem solving: This guideline can be used to measure whether the individual takes new action steps when he or she recognizes that those originally planned will not be adequate and new or revised action steps will be needed for goal achievement.
7. Communications: This guideline can be used to measure whether the individual alerts you, as manager, at the earliest possible time that achievement of a goal is in jeopardy and that additional assistance and maybe more resources are needed to attain the goal.
8. Interpersonal relations (with peers, supervisors, and subordinates): This eighth guideline measures the extent to which an individual coordinates with other people who may be affected by the goal or by the action steps needed to achieve it.
9. The number of times that goals have actually been achieved can be an additional criterion if you consider it worthwhile to add. You may find that after a few performance evaluations, it will no longer be necessary.

These criteria provide a meaningful foundation for performance appraisal. They focus on the way the individual works toward achievement of goals. This is the key to effective evaluation and appraisal of performance because it is this aspect of performance that the individual has direct, immediate, and intimate control over and for which, as a result, he or she can and should be held completely accountable.

The best performance appraisals are joint activities in which both the manager and the subordinate complete the required forms and then discuss any differences in the way they perceive the subordinate's performance in each area for which he or she is accountable. Such comparisons, of course, require considerable skill on the part of the manager and, what is even more important, close personal acquaintance with the way the subordinate performs the work.

Performance reviews also serve as an excellent foundation for deciding what knowledge or skills a subordinate needs for better performance and as preparation for possible promotion. These knowledge and skill items can then become the basis for learning goals or for practice goals that the subordinate would strive to achieve. Many competent managers feel that this aspect of performance appraisal is the most important one.

One question that often arises about performance appraisal concerns the similarities and differences with goals reviews. The two are similar because both are detailed contacts between a manager and a subordinate. Both provide an opportunity for the manager to learn more about the interests, views, and aspirations of each subordinate. However, during a performance-appraisal session, the relative position between manager and subordinate is synonymous to their positions: the manager does the evaluating, the subordinate is evaluated. In a well-conducted performance appraisal, the subordinate's views receive a full hearing, and although the subordinate might be encouraged to evaluate his or her own performance on the appropriate appraisal forms, the evaluator/evaluatee relationship remains. The affect on income and career is direct, although possibly not immediate.

During a goals review—if it is conducted in the spirit that will make it most effective—the discussion is between two people, both of whom have something to contribute to the achievement of the goal. The discussion does not center around what was done well and where there were shortcomings. Instead, it concentrates on what else is needed to achieve goals that have been set, what new goals should be set, what goals can be dropped, and most important, how the manager can help with the subordinate's problems.

Performance-appraisal systems also can be used in academic departments, where a modified version of the concepts described in this section may be applied. If a performance-appraisal system exists for use in the academic departments, evaluations should be based on guidelines similar to those used in the administrative departments. Specifically, they should be firmly grounded on the effort that people devote toward the achievement of goals and on the quality of that effort. A chairperson, for instance, might have worked with a colleague to set goals that will help the instructor achieve higher professionalism in the classroom. An effective performance-appraisal system should take into account, for example, the thoroughness of the instructor's planning and the quality of his or her action steps taken to achieve those goals. An improvement plan might identify further steps the professor might take to achieve a higher level of performance and, consequently, obtain better appraisals in the future.

Summary of Performance Evaluation and the Goals Process: The following points are a concise summary of performance evaluation:

1. The most meaningful appraisal/evaluation systems are tied closely to plans and their specific objectives; they evaluate the performance of

each person in terms of how that person works toward the achievement of his or her objectives.

2. An effective performance-appraisal process might consist of three stages: a planning process, a review process, and an evaluation process.

3. Performance appraisals should be as fair and factual as possible, and they should be based on controllable accountabilities.

4. The best performance appraisals are joint activities in which both the manager and the subordinate complete the required forms and jointly discuss the subordinate's performance in each area of accountability.

5. Each performance appraisal must conclude with an improvement plan covering ways the employee can improve so future appraisals can be better.

Operational versus Developmental Goals

As stated earlier in this chapter, operational goals are for people (see subsection entitled Operational Goals). Developmental goals, like operational goals, are also for people, but in a more personal way. Developmental goals are concerned with the professional development of the people who work on the organizational goals.

The professional development of personnel through training is an important concern for all organizations. Such development enables personnel to become more competent in their current jobs and to become better qualified to accept the responsibilities of higher-level positions when openings occur. An organization made up of skilled and competent personnel who are continuing to develop themselves toward even higher levels of competency is more likely to achieve its goals than is the organization that has little or no concern for the professional growth of its personnel.

A manager who attempts to create a workable goals program has many opportunities to determine what the personal needs and aspirations of subordinates are and what specific knowledge or skills would most help them improve their performance. The manager can sometimes discuss these matters during the regular goals review after the work goals have been covered or, what is probably more meaningful, in a formal training and development needs analysis prior to, or in conjunction with, the performance evaluation. Such analysis will be discussed in detail in chapter 5, which covers the linking elements dealing with technical competence.

Developmental goals should become a regular part of the goals program because they provide opportunities for the manager to be totally supportive. Development goals usually can be set by the subordinate, with the manager providing guidance and counseling. In allowing the subordinate to set personal goals, the organization, through the manager or leader, provides evidence that it does not consider the goals program a one-way street aimed at better organizational performance alone; it also sees the program as a way to satisfy the needs of employees at all levels.

Similarly, department chairpersons should encourage all instructors to set developmental goals and provide maximum leeway for colleagues to do this. For example, a marine biologist might be inclined to pursue professional development through a research project that entails studying the behavior of fish in response to environmental stimuli. An effective department chairperson could assist his or her colleague with this project in many ways, including (1) supporting the biologist's efforts to obtain funding, (2) providing space and equipment, (3) arranging for the biologist to present the findings at professional meetings, and (4) supporting the publication of the study's results.

A chairperson also can assist his or her colleagues by providing counseling and guidance. While this may be especially valuable for new instructors, an effective chairperson will also communicate his or her willingness to work with senior colleagues and help them set and achieve developmental goals. The chairperson who communicates such an interest is likely to perform at a high level and earn the respect of his or her colleagues.

Motivational Impact of an Effective Goals Program: Many managers and chairpersons believe that it is their function to "motivate" their people. They are often told by researchers, lecturers, and other experts that if they are good "leaders," they can actually do so. There is some truth to this, of course, but this belief is also somewhat misleading. First of all, there are limits to motivation. Some people find work so distasteful that they can never really gain satisfaction from it. Fortunately, this is true only for a very small minority. Most people, however, cannot be "motivated" artificially, even by a very good leader. Much more is needed than just considerate leadership. A total management approach is required that creates a climate which allows employees to find motivation—the desire to accomplish more or better things. It may be said that all the activities in a well-managed goals program encourage people to find motivation. Clearly, there is no single act, no simple way, that provides an environment in which people will feel strong motivation to do all the things a manager would like them to do. A manager who helps individuals attain greater satisfaction from their work usually finds that motivation increases. Unfortunately, however, it is very difficult to know how people will respond to help or what they would do if the manager behaved differently.

The studies that have been made have consistently shown that those managers who are technically competent and also skilled in providing job satisfaction to their people end up with the best performance. The point here is that it is satisfaction with belonging to the work unit and achieving work-related goals, not just a happier outlook on life or personal liking for the manager, that is important in stimulating motivation. It is equally important to remember that not everyone can be motivated to the same extent and that even in the very best climate there are always some people who do not share the same level of enthusiasm as do others.

Summary of Operational versus Developmental Goals: The following guidelines can be used for setting developmental goals:

1. A goals program that covers only operational goals concerned with performance objectives is not complete; individuals need to see that the goals program includes some goals whose primary purpose is to help them, not the organizational unit.
2. Developmental goals provide opportunities for the manager to be supportive and create a climate that allows people to find motivation.
3. As individuals attain greater satisfaction from their work, their motivation generally increases.

Making a Goals Program Successful

A smoothly operating goals program can help to bring about a climate in which people can find motivation. Such a program can be developed and maintained if the necessary steps are taken to avoid the eight potential problem areas summarized in the acronym EQIFAPPO:

1. If an appropriate number of goals are set, goals properly challenging the subordinate, and if priorities are selected so that they satisfy the desire to accomplish something worthwhile, then there is positive motivational impact.
2. The quality of goals and goal statements contributes to the motivational climate because accuracy and explicitness remove uncertainties and questions about what is really expected and because good quality eliminates much confusion. Good goals give a feeling of direction that anyone can share. Winning the next game is a highly motivating goal for every ball team. In the work environment, goals are rarely as challenging or as motivating as they are in sports, but if they are meaningful and clear, then they have the potential to challenge employees.
3. The level of involvement by the manager is important. The climate of motivation is enhanced if a manager exercises good judgment in providing help when members of the team need help and refrains from becoming involved when they would rather perform the jobs in their own way.

4. A manager who reviews progress on a fairly regular basis and who, during these reviews, explores what help the individual team members need to achieve their goals provides the kind of support and the kind of secure feeling that can add substantially to job satisfaction.

5. The manager who holds people accountable for the things they can achieve and does not muddy the water by blaming them or giving them credit for things over which they have no control adds a feeling of confidence that also contributes to job satisfaction and thereby to a motivational climate.

6. The right amount of participation in goal setting brings many job satisfactions. If a manager allows the proper amount of participation in those matters which affect the members of the team, then team members gain the feeling that they have influence over their work and their future. They know that they have a voice in deciding the way the work is to be done. This knowledge contributes greatly to the feeling of satisfaction they obtain from their work and to the confidence they have in their organization and their managers.

7. Performance evaluations can have a very significant impact on motivational climate if they are appropriately tied to the goals program and are based on accountabilities that consider only matters under the control of the person. Performance evaluations provide the feedback that tells people where they stand and what they have to do to improve. These evaluations do much to enhance the confidence of people in their organization if they are factual and fair; if they are based on criteria that are known, understood, and accepted; and if they are reflected properly in compensation and career decisions.

8. Finally, a goals program can achieve a significant improvement in motivational climate if it is not restricted to operational goals, but also covers developmental goals that help individuals improve performance on their current jobs and prepare them for the next higher jobs or for better jobs to which they may aspire.

Notes

1. Stephen Singular, "Has MBO Failed?" *M.B.A.*, October 1975, p. 48.
2. N.R.F. Maier, "Assets and Liabilities in Group Problem Solving: The Need for an Integrative Function," *Psychological Review*, Vol. 74, No. 4, April 1967, p. 240.
3. Ibid.

5

The Remaining
Linking Elements

Although chapter 4 presented the first linking element, this does not mean that goal setting is most important. When goal setting is a way of life, however, higher levels of performance can be attained. At the same time, when EQIFAPPO is clearly understood and managers are able to satisfy the requirements that EQIFAPPO implies, then that linking element alone provides considerable help toward the creation of an appropriate, work-oriented climate that also satisfies the needs of people. Employees have clear direction, they are constantly informed through regular reviews, and they know that superiors are aware of their contributions. All these and others are matters of considerable help in creating such a climate. They all come from the linking element in which the manager attempts to bring greater alignment between the goals and standards of the organization and the performance standards of individuals.

This shows that all linking elements are interrelated, that they are mutually supportive, and that they all contribute to the climate that exists. It also shows that if one is not working, or is not handled properly, it will detract from the others. This chapter will discuss the remaining linking elements as they can be applied by managers and leaders in higher education. (As in the previous chapters, discussion in this chapter will focus on the manager/subordinate role as it exists in higher education. Parallels will be drawn to clarify the skills and strategies that academic leaders can apply in their relationship with colleagues.)

One organizational objective is to provide a satisfactory quality of work life for the people in the organization. *Quality of work life* consists of those rewards, conditions, and policies an organization offers its people to satisfy their psychological and tangible needs. Some of the elements that make up quality of work life are salary and benefits, appearance, environmental conditions, organizational procedures, and systems that recognize employee performance.

Quality of work life in itself does not bring happiness. However, when an appropriate environment is established and quality of work life is high, then people have an opportunity to find greater satisfaction and greater happiness in their work. The following two segments, which discuss the linking elements that are concerned with satisfying psychological and tangible needs, identify strategies that managers can apply to create high quality of work life.

Satisfying Psychological Needs

The behavioral sciences, as has been discussed previously, provide a major support for the Linking Elements Concept. Of the many researchers whose work contributes to the Linking Elements Concept, it is the work of psychologist Abraham H. Maslow that is representative of what all others are saying. Maslow's work is comprehensive and, therefore, provides an excellent foundation with which to explain the approaches suggested by the Linking Elements Concept.

The Work of Abraham H. Maslow

Psychologist Abraham H. Maslow concerned himself with the total range of human mentality and relationships. His "hierarchy of needs" from *Motivation and Personality*, first widely published in 1954, has had a major influence on the development of current management theory. In simple form, his conceptualization can be diagrammed as shown in figure 5-1. Maslow's basic premise is that people are motivated by the desire to satisfy needs that are not fully satisfied. He identifies five levels of needs and assigns them the following levels of relative importance.

Basic Physiological Needs: These are needs primarily related to bodily survival: the need for food and water to maintain life and the need for clothing and shelter to protect the body from harsh environments.

Safety and Security: These are needs concerned with safety of body and security of provisions: the need for self-preservation and the need to ensure

Source: Adapted from A.H. Maslow, "Hierarchy of Needs," *Motivation and Personality* (New York: Harper and Row, 1954); artwork courtesy National Fire Protection Association.

Figure 5-1. Simplified Diagram of Maslow's Conceptualization of the Five Levels of Basic Human Needs

future security. These needs essentially concern the protection of the basic physiological needs.

Belonging and Social Activity: The need to belong to a group, to have some means of group identification, to receive and give affection, and to participate in some form of social activity constitute this category. These needs should be met at work as well as away from it.

Esteem and Status: The need to have, to receive, and to give esteem and status (both of which are essential to human dignity) make up this category; self-respect and respect for others are important in a modern industrial society because the previous three needs are, to a large degree, satisfied.

Self-Realization and Fulfillment: This is the need to become all that one is capable of becoming; when this need exists, work becomes a challenge and provides greater satisfaction.

To some extent, Maslow portrays a pattern of human growth and suggests a human tendency to continually strive for even higher objectives. To illustrate this, consider as an example the person who is trapped at the lowest level of physiological needs and thus has to devote all thought and energy to the struggle for food, clothing, and shelter. Once these needs have been satisfied, such a person will usually require the assurance that in the future these same needs will continue to be satisfied. Given this assurance, the person will then usually want the society of other people, probably including the pleasures of friendship and group effort. From this stage grows the need for recognition by others and, finally, the need for inner knowledge of personal competence and worth (a quality that Maslow also calls "self-actualization"). This highest level, in particular, represents questions that were largely unexplored in management theory during Maslow's time.

A simplistic visualization of Maslow's theory is to imagine a person climbing up the "pyramid" illustrated in figure 5-1, one step at a time. However, it is also important to visualize *all* the needs represented by the steps of the pyramid as operating to some degree at the same time. For example, a newly hired administrative manager, while still seeking a feeling of "belonging" within his or her department, may simultaneously be looking forward to a time of promotion and to a time when complete self-confidence and personal satisfaction are realized concerning the choice of a career in higher education. In some exceptional circumstances, a person may be seeking higher-level needs while ignoring others. An example of this would be the dedicated artist to whom painting the "right" picture is more important than food and housing.

A Closer Look at Maslow's Hierarchy

Although it has survived for many years as one of the finest explanations of human needs and perhaps still provides the best available foundation for the discussion of motivation, there are a number of questions that Maslow's hierarchy raises. The three most important ones are (1) What exactly is the role of money in motivation? (2) How important are esteem and social needs? (3) What is self-realization?

What Exactly Is the Role of Money? As most managers know, people seem to think that money motivates. There is certainly ample evidence to show that people will come to work when they are paid; however, they also work as volunteers on projects they like when they are not paid. Yet people talk a lot about money needs, and it is common to hear someone say "If you want me to do that, then pay me for it." Maslow's diagram, however, appears to be fairly mute on the question of money and its relationship to employee needs, which may be one of the reasons why managers do not see Maslow's theory as a practical concept to be applied in an organization.

Most behavioral scientists have concluded that although the promise, or the prospect, of a raise seems to have a positive effect on employee motivation, the effect is only temporary. People will most generally revert to their preraise motivations if their job and environment remain essentially unchanged. However, the fact still remains that people respond to money because of the necessities and luxuries purchased by money.

What Is the Relative Importance of Satisfying Esteem and Social Needs? The considerable research that has been done to validate Maslow's hierarchy of needs seems to indicate that the two lower levels—the physiological and security needs—are indeed valid, fundamental needs. There is, however, considerable question about the definition, the meaning, and the relative relationships of esteem and social needs. For example, it would seem that there are many people who place the satisfaction of esteem needs above the satisfaction of social needs. For these people, it is more important to be recognized as individuals and to be valued for particular strengths and characteristics than to be members of a group.

Other people, however, feel that being part of a group is more important. They want to be liked or to feel the security of a group, which is more valuable to them than being esteemed. Wanting to be part of a group may be the result of upbringing and culture, or it may be a natural need for the security that a group provides. Whatever the reason, there are many people who prefer warmth that a group can provide to the recognition of personal worth for outstanding characteristics.

What Is Self-Realization? For those people who clearly understand what they want to do during a part of their lives or with their entire lives, there is no doubt that self-realization is the highest level needed. For other people, however, self-realization is a somewhat nebulous concept. During certain periods of their lives, people seem to gain exceptional joy and satisfaction from doing certain things. These periods have a tendency to change, however, during the course of one's life and one's career.

The many types of self-realization raise questions about what self-realization really is, and how a manager or leader can help individuals in his or her department find some of it or more than they are currently enjoying. If a manager or leader does not know what self-realization is and does not think about it, how can he or she help someone else find more of it?

Despite the questions inherent in Maslow's theories, the basic framework of his hierarchy of needs can be retained because of the evidence available that attests to its validity. Maslow's diagram can become a practical tool for managerial decisions even though it has areas under question, for it places the important needs of individuals into perspective. The following paragraphs will explore the linking elements that are concerned with the satisfying of tangible and psychological needs and will suggest answers to the preceding three questions.

The Role of Money in the Maslow Hierarchy

Physiological Needs: In order to clearly show money's role in the hierarchy of needs, a separation between psychological and physiological needs must be made. Although some physiological needs are free (such as air), most are supplied by one's salary. Clearly, food, clothing, and shelter can be obtained only through purchase.

Safety and Security Needs: Many safety and security needs are satisfied with money, especially those which reflect the physiological needs of food, shelter, and clothing for the future. Safety and security for these items can be obtained through organizational pension programs, hospitalization insurance, and other insurance programs. Other ways of ensuring safety and security needs are through business contracts such as a union contract or a tenure agreement. Both ensure the safety of an individual's job and the security of knowing that a salary will be received for an agreed period of time.

However, there are psychological matters that also contribute to a feeling of security on the part of employees. These are primarily the attitudes and beliefs about an organization and its managers. People who work for an effective institution that has competent administrators and trustworthy supervisors feel secure. However, people cannot feel secure when they work for an institution that is unstable or for a manager who is unreliable or untrustworthy. Therefore, a manager or leader who is competent and at the same time honest with employees is more likely to create a positive motivational climate than one who has shortcomings in either area.

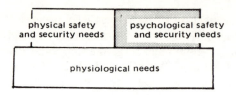

Source: Courtesy of National Fire Protection Association.

Figure 5-2. Modification of the Maslow Diagram, which Shows the Separation of Safety and Security Needs into Tangible Areas (White) and Psychological Areas (Shaded)

Figure 5-2 shows the separation of safety and security needs into physiological and psychological ones. If this analysis is correct, then a manager's personal competence and ability to earn the confidence of subordinates can have a major influence on motivational climate.

Esteem and Social Needs: Although Maslow diagrammed esteem and social needs as two separate entities, there seems to be mixed feeling (as stated earlier in this section) as to which need is more important. Therefore, for the purposes of this text, both will be shown together as one step in a hierarchy of needs (see figure 5-3). Although these two needs are depicted in figure 5-3 as psychological, there is also another side to these needs. Many people obtain gratification of social and esteem needs by mimicking someone whose lifestyle they admire. "Keeping up with the Joneses," however, requires monetary reward in order to obtain their (the Joneses) particular view of social and esteem needs.

Even though many people obtain some measure of esteem and social satisfaction from the things that money buys, segments of these needs still remain that must be satisfied in other ways. Policies and procedures of an organization that evoke greater cooperation and assistance between people create more social and esteem needs satisfaction than policies and procedures that lead to friction and conflict. Anything that managers can do to stimulate mutual support among the members of their unit, such as group assistance for personal emergencies or work sharing when someone is overloaded, can help satisfy esteem and social needs. There are many ways to involve the group in work activities that strengthen the bonds between group members.

Opportunities to satisfy esteem needs are even more widespread. Few managers go out of their way to find things for which subordinates can be commended or seek out different ways to commend them. One of the greatest tools for creating a better motivational climate—the use of praise—is one of the least utilized ones. The result is that few employees and lower-level managers receive much individual recognition from their superiors.

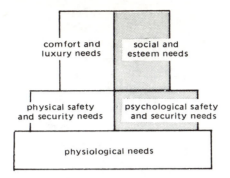

Source: Courtesy of National Fire Protection Association.

Figure 5-3. Modification of the Maslow Diagram, which Shows Social and
Esteem Needs as One Psychological Entity and Comfort and
Luxury as a Complementary Tangible Entity

There are, of course, many perfectly legitimate reasons why few
managers use praise as much as they could, for their own and their team's
benefit. First of all, nobody wants praise to appear contrived or false, and it
is usually difficult to find many things for which sincere praise can be given
easily. Nonetheless, much more praise could be given honestly and would be
well received. Most people hear in a word of praise the desire to be friendly;
therefore, even if praise is recognized as being less than fully sincere, it still
has favorable impact.

There are many other means besides using praise that can bring to
employees feelings of greater esteem. They include such things as asking for
an individual's advice or giving a few words of commendation of an
employee to a higher-level manager. In addition, there are written commen-
dations and many forms of formal recognition, among which may be found
monetary awards for suggestions, for good safety records, for completion
of training programs, and sometimes even for good attendance.

From an understanding of social and esteem needs come many opportunities for managers to provide greater satisfaction of these employee
needs. Managers can create an environment that provides more job-related
satisfaction, even if they cannot add to the luxury and comfort needs of the
employees. Creating a climate that satisfies social and esteem needs is
especially important when considering the psychology of self-realization
(see figure 5-4).

Self-Realization: Self-realization is a concept that is difficult to define
because few people recognize early in life that they have a strong professional preference for their work. Some artists, scientists, and renowned individuals have always had strong inclinations toward their work. However,

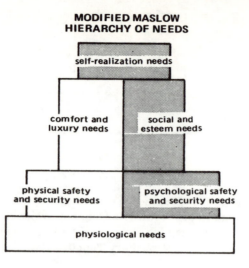

**MODIFIED MASLOW
HIERARCHY OF NEEDS**

self-realization needs

comfort and
luxury needs

social and
esteem needs

physical safety
and security needs

psychological safety
and security needs

physiological needs

Source: Courtesy of National Fire Protection Association.

Figure 5-4. Modification of the Maslow Diagram, which Shows the Relationship of Self-Actualization Needs to Tangible and Psychological Needs

people in other fields of activity also have achieved self-realization in their work. There is a true case about a pot washer in a New York City hospital who apparently was so devoted to his job that one could say that he had found his self-realization. He reported to his kitchen happily every morning and continued to be content as long as his pots and pans were not mishandled by others. On the few occasions when he was absent from work and another individual took care of the pots, he was clearly disturbed when he returned to work to find the pots neglected.

While this individual may be a rarity, there are other people from all walks of life and jobs who are happy with their work because they enjoy it. Their days pass quickly with interesting things to do. They enjoy going to work in the morning, and they often leave with the feeling of accomplishment. Even when unpleasant events occur during a day, they have the feeling that the next day will be better—and it usually is.

People who find such enjoyment in their work are fortunate because it makes for a much more pleasant life to find satisfaction in work. Not every individual who works long hours is a "workaholic." Some enjoy their work as well as, if not more than, socializing or watching television. People who feel joy in striving for the difficult and attaining it are compensated for the extra hours they have to devote to what other people call "work." They regularly gain the same exhilarating sensation from seeing projects near completion that scientists or artists experience when, after strenuous effort, their work finally meets their own exacting standards.

Other people rarely find pleasure in their work. Their work may be dull or strenuous or their supervisors may be lacking in competence, both of which contribute little pleasure to their work. For most people, however, the enjoyment of work comes despite the fact that they have no special preference for their particular occupations. They may have drifted into their jobs because their first real jobs gave them the necessary experience, or a college professor may have told them that enjoyable careers existed in a particular field. However, these people would know little about self-realization in work. They would know that there may be activities that they prefer, such as hobbies, sports, or social activities. Yet they may have difficulty in indicating the work activities that would retain their interest or effort for the majority of the time.

Something akin to self-realization undoubtedly exists for most people. A person who works apathetically on the job may work enthusiastically, without pay, during off-hours in a community or social organization. What is it, then, that makes one person find greater satisfaction from work than another? What conditions must be met by employer or employee in order for work to be more rewarding?

Small teams of participants in hundreds of seminars were asked the following question about their motivation: "If you think back to positions you have held in the past, or if you look at your current position, what actions could your superiors take, or have taken, and especially your direct supervisor, without spending any money, that would bring, or have brought, additional job satisfaction to you?"

Whether people work in the public or private sector or in the professions or the trades, the answers are always very similar. The statements that come up, almost invariably, are the following. Individuals want

More information about what is happening on the job.

More freedom to do the job.

To be brought into decisions at an earlier time.

More guidance.

More recognition.

Honest feedback about performance.

No promises that cannot be kept.

More awareness by the boss about the work they are doing.

More interesting assignments.

Less over-the-shoulder supervision.

More support when needed.

More confidence from superior.

This list is interesting in that all items do not refer to any specific type of work. If people found self-realization in specific tasks, there would be such requests as "Let me do exactly this," or "Let me do exactly that." However, this does not occur. People are not asking for more technical work, more supervisory duties, or more specialized assignments. Even the general statement "more interesting assignments" is exceedingly rare. To some extent, people are in jobs that appeal to them more than other jobs; nevertheless, one would expect many statements about the specific work that the boss could give them or has given them.

The picture that emerges from these answers is that people believe they could obtain much greater satisfaction from their existing jobs if their managers treated them differently. They want to know more about what is happening in the organization, and they want a bigger voice in decisions that affect them. They want to be freer to do their jobs the way they believe they can best be done, but they do want guidance and training to ensure successful completion. Most important of all, it seems, people want to be recognized for their accomplishments. The fascinating part of these results is that self-realization lies not so much in specific work, but rather comes from the environment. People are, in effect, saying "The work may not be the greatest, but it can come much closer to giving me some self-realization if the boss would provide more safety and security [by being honest, fair, and open] and more esteem satisfaction [by providing recognition and participation in decisions]." Even though self-realization is a nebulous concept, the supervisor, manager, or officer can indeed do a great deal to help subordinates find a larger amount of self-realization in their jobs.

Helping People Find More
Self-Realization in Their Work

There are two approaches to helping employees find more self-realization. One of the approaches has already been touched on and discussed in previous chapters. It concerns the impact of regular, though semiformal, goals reviews, which may even be conducted by managers who regularly work closely with their subordinates. The other approach involves three strategies for improving the motivational climate through planned managerial action.

Three Strategies for Improving the Motivational Climate: There are many specific steps that managers can take in addition to holding regular goals review sessions and annual or semiannual performance reviews. These steps require considerable effort, but they can gradually create a climate in which there is substantially more motivation because they help to bring more satisfaction of psychological needs.

The steps are grouped into the three strategies to improve motivational climate—short-run, intermediate, and long-run—as shown in figure 5-5. All three strategies start with the recognition that few managers or leaders commend their people for as many actions as they could. Apparently, managers rarely see the picture from the point of view of their subordinates. Even though they themselves feel the large number of negative and unpleasant impulses that reach every person in today's complex world, they rarely give much thought to any responsibilities they might have to do something about them. The increasing complexity of the world with which it is so difficult to cope sometimes, the reports that are becoming more detailed, the many different ways in which machinery or gadgets can fail to operate properly, the large amount of routine paperwork—all these contribute to unpleasant moments or unpleasant sensations. Several unpleasant minor incidents can fully offset some important matter that is proceeding smoothly.

If there were less tension and less frustration in a working environment, people could accept a work environment in which there are only a few pleasant events. In the modern world, though, a manager has an important responsibility to balance the negative impulses by providing satisfying moments or pleasant impulses. Some of the balance can come from people, but much comes from the work, from success, from doing things well, and from pride in an accomplishment. To achieve this balance, a manager or leader can apply the three strategies mentioned earlier.

Short-run strategy, which is the left column in figure 5-5, concerns the steps that a manager can take by spending a few minutes, several times each week, thinking about and listing the actions for which individuals could receive recognition and the ways that recognition could be shown. Managers who have tried this have found that with practice and experience, the lists usually become long. There are many ways that a manager can commend a job well done to all people in the unit, not only the outstanding individuals. For example, a manager can commend individuals in his or her department for an infinite number of actions. For every specific job that is done well—helping others, making worthwhile contributions during a planning session, or taking initiative with something that needs to be done—some form of recognition can be given. It is important, however, that recognition goes not only to a few outstanding people, but also to others who contributed to the best of their own abilities. Commendation for even minor improvements in an individual serves to elevate motivation. It

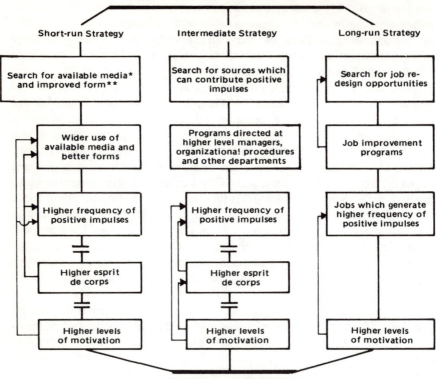

CLIMATE IMPROVEMENT STRATEGIES

Short-run Strategy	Intermediate Strategy	Long-run Strategy
Search for available media* and improved form**	Search for sources which can contribute positive impulses	Search for job re-design opportunities
Wider use of available media and better forms	Programs directed at higher level managers, organizational procedures and other departments	Job improvement programs
Higher frequency of positive impulses	Higher frequency of positive impulses	Jobs which generate higher frequency of positive impulses
Higher esprit de corps	Higher esprit de corps	
Higher levels of motivation	Higher levels of motivation	Higher levels of motivation

GREATER ACHIEVEMENT

*Media are the ways in which motivational impulses can appear. Positive ones include such things as challenging assignments, supportive statements, routine reports, tie pins, certificates, etc. Negative ones are reprimands, reject notices, mistakes, etc.

**Form is the style that influences the impact of the motivational impulse. It can be the way the award is presented, the words which are said during the telephone call, or facial expression, place, timing, etc.

Source: Copyright © 1974 by Recognition Systems, Inc., Cranford, N.J. All rights reserved. Reprinted by permission; artwork courtesy National Fire Protection Association.

Figure 5-5. A Representation of the Three Strategies Used by Management for Improving the Motivational Climate for Employees

is important that the manager or leader provide all members of a unit with positive moments that are related to the work.

The short-run strategy is based solely on the manager personally providing more recognition and other pleasant work-related events for an employee. The emphasis here is on "work-related" because compliments or other non-work-related friendly words are not likely to have the same impact on the motivational climate. They lead more toward the "country club" atmosphere than to the desire to achieve.

Figure 5-5 shows that a manager who wishes to take full advantage of the opportunities the short-run strategy can give will begin to use more media (newspapers, bulletins, letters, informal notes, various verbal forms, and so on) to bring more frequent instances of pleasant experiences for staff members. This, in turn, may lead to a higher job interest and greater *esprit de corps*—the common spirit existing in the members of a group and inspiring enthusiasm, devotion, and strong regard for the honor of the group. There is a limit, however, to the effect that this short-run strategy can have because there are just so many times in the course of a week or month that a manager can give direct recognition. This is why there is a break in the line between "higher frequency of positive impulses" and "higher *esprit de corps*," and again before "higher levels of motivation." More is needed than just the short-run strategies to increase pleasant work-related occurrences.

The intermediate and long-run strategies can bring the additional positive impulses that are needed. To carry out the intermediate strategies, the manager must involve other managers at his or her level and at higher levels to provide pleasant work-related experiences. To implement these strategies, the manager can, among other things, send a reminder to the next higher level manager to commend someone for something that has occurred recently. Or the manager can commend people in other departments whose managers might respond in kind. Steps taken to anticipate and prevent friction and differences between members of the team and with other teams also can help create a more pleasant job-related environment by increasing the satisfaction of social needs or, at least, by preventing them from being decreased. Anything that brings recognition or other positive impulses and does not come directly from the immediate superior is part of the intermediate strategy.

As long as all the pleasant experiences come from people, they must, of necessity, be greatly limited. The average person will not receive too many in any time period. To greatly increase motivation, a long-run strategy is needed. The long-run strategy is the most likely to help a person reach the higher levels of motivation, because positive impulses come directly from the job itself and reinforce its positive aspects without dependence on other people. If jobs can be shifted or changed in such a way that the job itself provides satisfying sensations, then there is a much more continuous flow of pleasant experiences; and from these will undoubtedly come a higher motivation to achieve job-related goals. As you will note in figure 5-5, there is no longer a broken connection between action and result. If the job provides the satisfaction directly, then there is little question about the job's potential impact on motivation.

This is where the three strategies for climate improvement come together with goals reviews and performance appraisals in helping to improve the overall motivational climate. If a manager keeps in mind the list of things that will bring more fulfilling jobs, then he or she can easily practice job enrichment. By trying to develop a satisfying work atmosphere, the manager reinforces directly the other actions he or she must take to guarantee a smoothly operating goals program, one that makes goal achievement a way of life.

These climate-improvement strategies also can be applied to some extent by chairpersons in academic departments. It has to be recognized, however, that most academicians are highly motivated toward achievement in their respective fields. Recognition of their achievements will not necessarily bring greater motivation for achievement in their respective disciplines. It will, however, bring greater motivation to devote effort and attention to the needs of the organization and the needs of goals outside the direct discipline. For example, recognition might help instructors develop a greater willingness to think in terms of goals related to teaching and student relationships, as well as departmental and administrative goals. Therefore, any direct recognition related to the discipline itself (unless coming from a chairperson, who is a recognized authority in that particular field) should be directed more at things that are being done to achieve goals related to student needs and administrative aspects of their work.

The short-run strategy of looking for additional ways and forms through which colleagues can be given recognition is, of course, the easiest one for a department chairperson to implement. For example, a chairperson might compliment a professor who has designed an attractive arrangement of student ceramics projects in a library display case. A professor who covers a few classes for an ailing colleague might be commended at a department meeting, while a professor who has coordinated the appearance of a guest lecturer might be thanked publicly in a letter posted on the faculty bulletin board.

The intermediate strategy also might lead professors to be more willing to work toward goals related to student departmental needs. A chairperson might involve people from the entire school community—other departments and administrative units, students, and possibly deans—to provide recognition to a colleague for his or her work with students. Local newspapers and the campus newspaper might be encouraged to publish articles describing a professor's accomplishments, or a chairperson might even inform the President or the Board of Trustees of an exceptional achievement by a colleague. Recognition from outside sources such as these can help to create an appropriate climate of morale within a department.

While there is very little need to redesign the job of a professor in an institution of higher learning, still there are ways of bringing greater satisfaction from the work out of the peripherals of the job over which the chairperson has some control and where his or her influence can be used. For example, the assignment of research projects for which a chairperson has direct control may present an opportunity to provide greater job satisfaction to a colleague, or when the privilege of teaching an upper-level or graduate-level seminar enriches a professorial position. Finally, a professor who is inclined toward administrative work might be assigned coordination responsibilities in an interdepartmental program. In each of these instances, certain aspects of the professor's work—the ones most rewarding to the individual—can be emphasized.

The Role of Goals Reviews and the Planning Process: Regular goals reviews, discussed in chapter 4, also provide managers with opportunities to help create a more positive climate in which people can find higher levels of motivation. In these discussions, subordinates can become deeply involved in the total planning process, from the beginning through plan revisions. If the involvement is extensive, it brings the satisfactions that stem from participation in decisions affecting the work environment. Higher involvement, of course, tells subordinates that the manager has confidence in them. This, in turn, gives them an opportunity to increase their confidence in the manager.

A periodic goals review gives a manager many chances to provide recognition and to tell staff members in what ways he or she is satisfied with their work. If the manager is careful to stress that he or she is not evaluating performance during a goals review, and if he or she remains fully supportive, the factual feedback provided in a goals review tells people where they stand. Even if the manager shows them what could be done better with respect to a particularly difficult goal, in most instances, he or she also provides assurance and support for continuing efforts.

Regular goals reviews help a manager to know more about what individual subordinates are doing and what they are thinking. Subordinates can provide insights about what they consider interesting assignments, and the manager can help them develop the skills and knowledge to perform these assignments successfully. Without question, properly conducted goals reviews provide subordinates with frequent evidence that their manager stands ready to back them up with the support they need when they need it.

Similarly, regular goals reviews are opportune moments for academic leaders to involve members of their departments in the planning process. At such an informal meeting, the staff member might provide suggestions with respect to departmental and student needs. This can be an excellent opportunity to provide recognition for these suggestions and for all other actions the instructor has taken to help the department reach the goals that have been outlined. Higher involvement, therefore, may bring additional opportunities to commend colleagues and acknowledge the importance of their contributions.

Summary

This section had identified the skills and strategies that managers can apply to align psychological rewards provided by an organization with the psychological needs of people. These strategies include

1. Providing employees with balanced and regular feedback on their performance, both during goals review discussions and at other times.
2. Using the three climate-improvement strategies to provide recognition and facilitate greater employee involvement in decisions.

Satisfying Tangible Needs of Employees

Along with providing employees with psychological rewards, an organization also provides them with various tangible rewards. As was previously discussed, these rewards may include not only salary, bonuses, and incentive payments, but also fringe benefits, which do so much to add to the tangible feeling of safety and security, and promotions, which have wider implications.

Most managers and leaders have very little opportunity to influence the extent to which the institution satisfies some of the tangible needs of its people. Decisions about overall pay and benefit levels are usually made only at the highest level. However, there are basically three ways in which a manager can help to support the climate that is created through the other linking elements. These are

1. Administering salaries, commissions, bonuses, and incentives equitably
2. Obtaining maximum advantage from the fringes that are available
3. Helping employees reach the highest income level of which they are capable and attain more rewarding positions through appropriate career guidance and promotion management

The linking element dealing with tangible rewards is very important. Tangible rewards are likely to be dissatisfying when they are inadequate. However, when they are adequate, they are rarely satisfying or stimulating. People work harder when they know they are going to get an increase in pay, but this usually does not mean that the pay raise has given them a higher level of motivation. Several factors contribute to their higher enthusiasm for their work. If a merit increase is involved, the recognition it brings frequently acts as a temporary motivator. Even if the reward is more of a routine adjustment, the anticipation can reflect favorably on performance. More important, the promise of a raise tied to a specific performance improvement can exert a strong influence on most people. During the time that people are being observed to determine whether or not they will receive the increase, work performance usually is superior to the normal level. Shortly after they have received the increase, however, there often is a gradual return to old ways.

What is true of salary is even more applicable to fringe benefits. A highly adequate fringe package rarely stimulates people to work harder or better or pay more serious attention to important aspects of their work. However, the failure of an organization to provide adequate fringes does have a negative impact that helps people justify to themselves why they do not care, why they do not do their work the way they themselves are sometimes aware it should be done. Because pay raises and fringe benefits do not affect motivation directly, the manager's work in administration of pay raises and fringe benefits involves a rather passive role. The opportunities in career guidance and promotion management are more extensive.

Administration of Salaries and Other Payments

The functions of managers, except those who determine salary structure, lie in three areas: pay administration, administration of fringes, and promotion management. Most managers have tightly prescribed rules governing pay increases or bonuses. Very often their task mainly concerns distributing a specific allowance among staff members in an equitable way that gives due consideration to merit, longevity, and the potentially unfavorable impact of increases that are considered to be inadequate. So that the distribution of pay raises has as much positive effect as possible, a manager should be articulate in explaining the reasons for the size of the increase to each staff member.

Managers who do not have influence over salary should be aware that there are few compensation systems that all employees see as "fair." Salary administration demands balancing the following considerations:

Pay increases that reflect the performance record of the individual

Equal pay for equal work

Appropriate pay differentials for work requiring different levels of knowledge, skills, and physical exertion

Reasonable pay level in comparison with pay levels for similar work in other organizations

Pay ranges wide enough to allow for differentials based on merit

Capabilities of the incumbent that are beyond the requirements of the position and therefore not given great weight

Differentials based on longevity that become very small or disappear after several years

Total earnings that reflect in some way the individual's contribution to the mission of the organization

Pay scales that are known to members of the organization and not hidden

Fairness in application of pay principles

Clearly defined salary review dates at which increases are given (these review periods or increments should occur more frequently during early employement)

As may be apparent, several of these principles do not apply fully in an institution of higher education. For example, it is obvious that the contributions of professors are directly related to the mission of the organization, while those who perform maintenance functions serve in a supportive capacity. However, it is not uncommon for the total earnings of a professor to be lower than those of maintenance employees, especially those who have the opportunity to be paid considerable overtime. The professor may be working the same hours, but without extra pay.

Managers who do have influence on the design of the compensation system or who can influence modifications in it can consider other concepts in addition to these principles. The compensation system should reward continued competent and stable performance through regular salary increments. Moreover, it should reward outstanding performance or effort during the past period. Unfortunately, not all compensation systems do so. An equitable system, however, should provide some rewards for exceptional performance. Where they exist and are administered carefully, bonuses can provide these special payments for superior-level performance during a limited period of time. The compensation system also should reward people who have been reliable *and* who have produced at a high level. In this situation there is a need for higher increases or merit-type increases that are retained only for a limited number of years. Maintenance of this spread between the standard-salaries scale and the special-performance scale would be dependent on continued reliable performance way beyond the average. Salary level would gradually decrease if that high level of performance were not sustained.

People who perform consistently above the average are rewarded in some systems with promotions. However, promotion opportunities are often limited. For example, a professor who is a consistently exceptional performer may reach the top of the existing salary framework; promotion to a higher-paying position is no longer possible. Further, such an individual may be unwilling to accept a promotion into an administrative position, preferring instead to continue working in his or her respective discipline.

In most colleges and universities, department chairpersons have limited or no authority to recommend salary increments for people in their departments. A chairperson who has influence over compensation may find it useful to use the principles identified in this section to ensure that salaries are apportioned on a fair basis.

Clearly, it is the responsibility of all managers to help create a healthy climate with respect to tangible rewards. A positive climate requires absolute fairness in income decisions and clear communications to staff members of the principles that guide these decisions. Open communications can dispel the common belief that pay is based much more on the personal preferences of the manager than it really is.

Administration of Fringe Benefits

In administering the fringe-benefits program within their respective areas of responsibility, managers have three primary principles to keep in mind. Fringes will be least likely to lead to dissatisfaction if the manager (1) makes sure that employees clearly understand their fringe benefits; (2) shows a sincere interest in helping employees gain all the fringe benefits to which they are entitled; and (3) devotes the necessary effort, when required, to help overcome any problems that staff members encounter in promptly obtaining any of the fringe benefits due them.

Managers who can influence fringe-benefits packages must see to it that benefits are equivalent to those offered by other institutions. Some fringes concern time off, such as vacations and holidays. Here the manager's role is an obvious one—to plan and arrange schedules in such a way that they will satisfy the special needs of staff members as much as the demands of the job permit.

Career Guidance and Promotion Management

Career guidance and promotion management are linked to the manager's responsibilities for satisfying both the tangible and psychological needs of employees. In one sense, the manager's objective is to help the employee gain the greatest possible satisfaction from work and career and at the same time gain greater financial rewards. Among the manager's responsibilities in career guidance are (1) providing help in defining possible career paths; (2) making realistic evaluations of the strengths and weaknesses of the individual in relation to positions along these paths; (3) helping the individual set developmental goals that are challenging, but still achievable in light of the individual's capabilities; (4) providing fair performance evaluations so that the individual will receive proper consideration in the selection of the candidates for a position that has either opened up or that is otherwise available; and (5) adhering to an openly communicated system that helps to ensure fairness in selection of individuals for promotion.

Summary

Among the skills a manager must exercise in aligning the tangible needs of people with the rewards an organizational unit can provide are

1. Distributing increases fairly and equitably, in keeping with salary administration principles, budget, the relationship of salaries and jobs, and especially the performance record
2. Distributing incentives and bonuses available to the organizational unit fairly and equitably, on the basis of contributions to the unit's performance
3. Obtaining the greatest benefits for the staff members from available fringes
4. Providing career guidance and help in career development
5. Selecting candidates for promotions fairly
6. Maintaining open communications to ensure that members of the unit can express concerns and dissatisfactions so that they become aware of the realities of the situation and develop or maintain confidence that the manager is doing the best the environment permits.

Achieving Technical Competence

Development of human resources is one of the most important tasks of a manager, if not *the* most important. The linking element aligning the technical competence requirements of the organizational unit with the technical competence that people bring to the organization is concerned with human resource development.

Behavioral scientists and managers often speak of aligning goals of people and goals of the organization. Although this may appear to be achievable, the Linking Elements Concept quickly shows that it is not. The goals of an organizational unit are aimed primarily at improving control—for example, the achieving of higher production goals, better coordination, and better adherence to rules—as well as at developing higher levels of technical competence. The goals of individuals, however, are aimed at achieving higher levels of satisfaction for the time and effort spent at work. Tradeoffs do exist, of course, between the organization and the individual. In effect, the organization provides higher levels of satisfaction for employees directly through its people and policies and indirectly through the work itself; in exchange, it receives greater employee acceptance of organizational goals and a greater desire to achieve them.

One place where the requirements of individuals and those of the organizational unit are directly connected is in the linking element pertaining to development of adequate competence. This is especially true for people who have accepted specific positions because they are interested in acquiring experience as well as the knowledge and skills required for the positions. The achievement and development of the skills and knowledge provide great personal satisfaction, while at the same time assuring a higher level of performance for the organizational unit.

While most managers recognize that employee development is one of their most important responsibilities, in the course of day-to-day operations it is often not given the priority it deserves. Competent managers recognize that they must keep the process of developing their people constantly in mind if they do not want it to be managed haphazardly. This means regular reviews to see what each person needs in order to become more competent in the current job and to develop knowledge and skills for other jobs along the career path. While opportunities for diagnosing specific development needs occur regularly, there are several formal occasions when managers can obtain a more comprehensive insight into the development needs of the people reporting to them. These formal occasions include goals reviews and, especially, performance appraisals.

Because of the pressures of daily business, managers tend to avoid the detailed diagnosis necessary to attack a specific knowledge or skill deficiency directly. Emergencies often bring needs to their attention. When they do attempt to deal with development needs, they often use a buckshot approach. Employees are sent off to enroll in a course, or the personnel department is called in to develop a program to deal with a problem on a general basis. A systematic approach to development is required, and development must be carried on in an environment that supports what is learned. It must be based on individual needs, capabilities, the job, and the atmosphere in the department or section. Outside training can rarely cope with these inferences.

In order to ensure effective education and training, several basic conditions must be satisfied:

Individual deficiencies must be correctly identified.

A program to eliminate deficiencies must consider the relative importance of the individual's shortcomings.

Provisions must exist for continued surveillance of learning.

Learning goals must be revised regularly to reflect changing conditions.

Study materials and expected level of achievement must be geared to the individual so that they are neither too easy nor too difficult.

As much as possible, learning should be immediately applied on the job.

These objectives can best be satisfied with individualized knowledge/skill analyses and then with study and practice assignments geared to the specific situation. A needs analysis, to be of most value, must be very specific in identifying for each individual those knowledge areas and skills which will help improve performance.

The two people who can best develop such a needs analysis are the individual and his or her direct superior. A joint effort involving both supervisor and subordinate is therefore desirable in the production of an accurate analysis with priorities based on the expected effects or benefits to the organizational unit and to the individual. People must assume responsibility for their own education and training, but managers must be thoroughly involved and supportive for full effectiveness.

Besides providing for the development of administrative personnel, institutions of higher education also support professional development for people in the academic departments. Often the chief academic officer allots developmental funding to department chairpersons for distribution. Besides providing financial support, the chairperson might help an instructor obtain facilities, equipment, or even the services of typists to prepare manuscripts.

In some institutions, the chairperson does have a responsiblity to provide some guidance to colleagues, particularly junior ones, with respect to professional growth. Suggestions might be given during informal goals review discussions; in some institutions, the chairperson might provide guidance during a performance appraisal so that the instructor can achieve higher evaluations in the future.

Overview

Development activities will bring much better results if the people in the organizational unit are capable of learning and have the desire to perform well in their jobs. Elimination of deficiencies in knowledge and skills therefore starts with the *selection* of new employees. It continues with appropriate *position* management, so that people will be in jobs that make best use of their abilities and where they will find the greatest amount of personal satisfaction in their work.

Selection, position management, training, and education and development are so intertwined and dependent on each other that they really should almost be seen as one function. While, on the one hand, the way positions are structured in the organizational unit affects the choice of candidates, on the other hand, the people who are hired often determine how the work will be assigned so that the greatest benefit, for both employees and for the unit, will result. Training, education, and development depend entirely on that mixture of people and jobs which the manager creates, and they must be handled well if they are to support an appropriate motivational climate.

Selection: The road to higher levels of technical competence starts with the selection of new employees and with careful decisions when people are chosen for promotion. Ability to learn and interest in learning the whole job should be an important selection criterion. When people lack these characteristics, it is difficult, if not impossible, for them to develop high technical competence. This applies whether their skills are highly specialized, as in engineering, or of a more general nature, as in many areas of management.

Many managers, in looking at qualifications of applicants, look primarily at past experience and accomplishments. These *can* be excellent indicators of success, of ability to adapt to a new environment, and of motivation to gain additional knowledge and skills, but frequently they are not. Many people who are highly motivated to achieve success in their current jobs just will not devote the additional effort that would properly prepare them for advancement. The result is described in *The Peter Principle*, by Dr. Lawrence Peter, which says, in effect, that people usually get promoted to a job they are no longer able to do right. This is why there is so much incompetence, claims Dr. Peter. The Peter Principle is a tongue-in-cheek argument, but there is considerable truth to it. Few people will devote the effort to self-development, once they have received the degrees they sought, to thoroughly prepare themselves for the more demanding positions they often achieve. Many do not even put enough effort into learning what they need to know to keep up with the changes in their own jobs.

Careful initial selection and equally careful observation of new or recently promoted employees during their probational periods will therefore do more good than training and other developmental efforts at a later time.

Position Management: Once employees have remained on a job long enough to exhibit their performance strengths and weaknesses, the manager is then able to explore how to improve strengths for the organization's effectiveness and how to correct weaknesses. A manager may rearrange work schedules or delegations of tasks to incorporate a new member. If the new member is part of a unit, such as a keypunching unit, the workload for the entire unit may be rearranged to some extent. The changes can simply concern minor rearrangements to accommodate work preferences of the new person, or they can be more extensive and involve the desires of several team members. Such changes do not have to take place immediately; they can evolve gradually as members discuss with each other the adjustments they would prefer. However, the leader can consciously guide changes to take into account the needs of the organizational unit as well as those of its members.

Whatever changes occur within an organizational unit—by the manager or by employee suggestions—the needs of the organization and its members guide the formation of a change. The work that has to be done should be analyzed and broken into clearly definable tasks. These tasks must then be arranged into positions that fit the capabilities and interests of people who have to follow them. The new arrangement of tasks can lead to (1) high productivity, (2) good-quality work, (3) the ability of the team to quickly and effectively respond to changing demands of the school community, and (4) the highest possible level of needs satisfaction for the team members.

If the arrangement does not result in achievement of these four requirements, tasks must then be arranged until the requirements are adequately satisfied. Even though, in an existing organization, workloads and delegations have always been completed, rearrangement of workloads and trial periods for these arrangements constituted a continuous process that is especially important whenever a new person joins an organization. A competent manager will usually look at the positions of members in an organization in the same way a football coach would look at the players to decide who should do what during the next play for the best performance. The same thing occurs in any organization; the manager assigns the tasks on the basis of the capabilities of the individuals.

However, an organizational unit also must have backup members capable of handling each task that may come along. This requires cross-training, so that most people can do more than one job, although, in a situation that must be handled expediently, it is best to use people in positions that will take advantage of their greatest strengths.

The appropriate selection of people for tasks and assignments in keeping with their strengths can contribute to the highest technical competence of the team, but only for the moment. For the long run, it is an error to use particular individuals over and over again on those tasks which they can do best; this may make the entire unit heavily dependent on that group. In the absence of a few people, the entire unit may become incapable of performing tasks normally delegated to a small group of individuals. Good technical competence means flexibility and the ability to adapt to many different environments.

Careful assignment of tasks on the basis of strengths and weaknesses, as well as on interest, are as important with outside candidates as they are with current employees. In selecting from current employees, the manager usually has access to the employment records and can get additional information from the people with whom the employee has worked in the past. This information can help the organizational unit plan the way it will adapt to the new member.

If the person selected for the job is a competent employee, it would seem wise, in the interest of the unit's technical competency and its ability to achieve a high level of performance, to rearrange positions. If this is done jointly with the members of the unit, an arrangement can usually be found that leaves everyone at least as satisfied with their respective jobs as they were before, and some no doubt will be more satisfied.

Training and Development: Good selection and position management are not enough to bring high technical competence in an organization. Continuing training and development is essential even if experienced, competent people are selected and job assignments take full advantage of their strengths. There are many reasons why this is necessary, among them

1. Continuing changes in technology bring the need for frequent updating of knowledge and skills.
2. Employees and their managers usually can achieve smoother communications with other departments from learning more about the work of the departments with whom they are in contact.
3. All employees and managers are more knowledgeable and skilled in some areas than in others. Considerable education and training is needed to eliminate or at least reduce deficiencies as much as possible.
4. Career development for those who aspire to higher-level or more specialized jobs requires continuous developmental activities.
5. Knowledge and skills that are not in continuous use begin to fade; refreshers from time to time help to avoid surprises when knowledge or skills are suddenly needed.

Before deciding on training as a way to resolve a knowledge or skill deficiency, it is worthwhile to look at whether a training need really exists or whether other problems stand in the way of a particular achievement. Figure 5-6 can be used to help identify whether training is really the solution or even part of the solution.

PERFORMANCE ANALYSIS MODEL

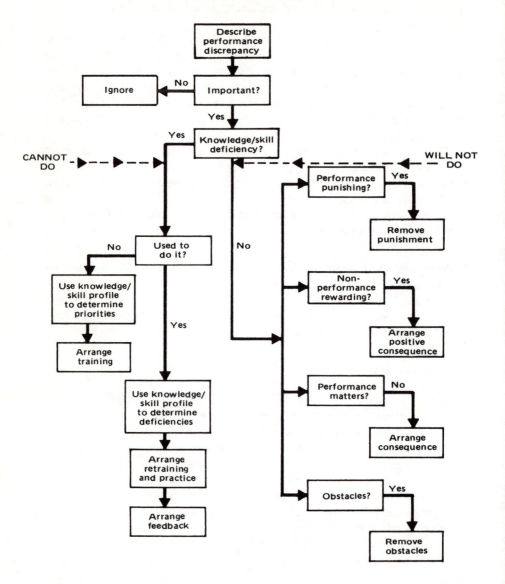

Source: Adapted from Robert F. Mager and Peter Pipe, *Analyzing Performance Problems* (Belmont, Calif.:) Fearon-Pitman Publishers. Copyright © 1970; reprinted by permission; artwork courtesy National Fire Protection Association.

Figure 5-6. Performance Analysis Model that Aids a Manager in Determining Whether an Individual's Lack of Performance Is Related to Training or to Performance Problems

Analyzing Performance Problems: In order to investigate the cause of a performance problem, managers should recognize first that an individual comes into an organization with personal performance standards, which are measured by (1) a willingness to work and (2) abilities, which are reflected by an individual's knowledge and skill. The individual's personal performance standards must be able to coincide and unite with the organization's performance needs in order for an employee's work to be satisfactory. Many times an employee requires a small amount of training in order to fulfill organizational performance standards. However, some individuals may require more extensive training, and others may need a solution to a particular performance problem that training cannot solve. Figure 5-6 diagrams several questions that should be asked by a manager when employee performance standards must be rectified. These questions and their answers may lead to possible avenues of solutions that will help to link the individual with the organization.

Training time should be devoted to those matters which deserve highest priority at the moment. It is therefore important to distinguish between those performance problems which can be rectified by training and those which are the result of causes other than lack of knowledge or skill.

Following figure 5-6 down from the top, if an employee has a performance problem and it is an important one, then the first question that a manager should ask is whether or not a knowledge/skill deficiency is involved. If this appears to be the case, then the next question is whether the employee used to be able to do the work involved. If the answer is no, then training should definitely be arranged. If, however, the employee was able to perform the task in the past, then it is more likely that a knowledge/skill deficiency is not the primary problem but may contribute to it. Retraining should be arranged to see whether it can solve the problem or whether other causes requiring other corrective measures must be found.

If in figure 5-6 the manager must answer the question "Knowledge/skill deficiency?" with a *no* because the employee knows how to do the task, then the problem is not one that can be solved by training. Following the line labeled *no* down from the box denoting knowledge/skill deficiencies leads to four other causes that could be the source of the performance problem. (1) Performance may be punishing. (2) Nonperformance may be rewarding. (3) Performance may not appear to matter. (4) Other obstacles to performance besides skill deficiencies may exist.

Punishing Performance: Tasks may be performed poorly if an employee views these performance tasks as "punishing." For example, inventory taking may be performed poorly by employees in the administrative offices. This could, of course, be due to inadequate training, but it also could be due to the fact that inventories are not announced sufficiently far in advance and employees are told at the last minute that they have to have their records in order. Lack of notification could thus be the major cause of problems and could contribute to a negative attitude.

Inadequate knowledge also can make performance punishing. For instance, if a new financial aid counselor was insufficiently prepared to inform students of newly enacted governmental regulations, the counselor might avoid discussing these topics because his or her inability to answer some questions would be embarrassing and punishing. Lack of training, therefore, can be part of the problem.

Other situations occur in which doing something quickly and well leads to undesirable assignments to fill available time. In all the situations described here, training alone is not the answer and will not help until the punishment has been removed.

Rewarding Nonperformance: Another obstacle to good performance lies in situations in which nonperformance is rewarding. This can be a very important source of problems, particularly in organizations with weak supervisors. Sometimes a supervisor requires less work when employees object or allows more time for duties when they are being ignored. Higher level managers sometimes do similar things with their direct subordinates. In all these cases, nonperformance is clearly rewarding, and training is not likely to solve the problem. Instead, it is important to recognize that a problem exists and then to arrange for some specific consequences for achieving, and for nonachieving. Training can then support any required effort where knowledge or skill deficiencies exist.

Unimportance of Performance: A third source of performance problems is lack of attention on the part of superiors to some aspect of the work. This gives the impression that performance does not matter. Employees come to believe that their superiors do not care whether a specific job or task is completed properly or not. If someone is asked to help prepare a report and no one asks whether that report has been prepared, or if a goal is to conduct a certain number of reviews and no one ever checks whether they have indeed been made, then subordinates may ignore parts or all of these assignments. The message from above appears to be that it really does not make any difference whether the task is performed or avoided. More training will not solve this problem either; managers must provide evidence that performance is, indeed, important.

Other Obstacles to Performance: Obstacles to performance can take many forms, such as physical illness, inadequate funding, improper or insufficient tools or materials, inadequate instructions, and so forth. Obviously, to make training sessions count, all these obstacles must be removed beforehand.

The previous sections described the strategies that administrative managers can apply with respect to technical competence. Chairpersons also can apply these strategies to create an improved alignment in their departments. For example, the department chairperson plays an important role in the selection of a new instructor, but the role may vary greatly according to institutional hiring procedures. In some institutions of higher education, the chairperson is basically responsible for the hiring; in others, he or she recommends. In the latter situation, the chairperson might screen the resumés, conduct initial interviews, and present several candidates to a faculty committee with a recommendation. Depending on the institution and the character of the department chairperson, this recommendation will carry varying degrees of weight with the faculty.

While people in the academic departments are generally chosen to teach courses in a specifically defined area, the chairperson might need to apply position-management strategies for those courses which are institutional requirements and for which not enough volunteers are available. In this type of situation, the department, under the leadership of the chairperson, has to make decisions with respect to the assignments. The qualifications of instructors, their interests, and departmental needs are among the important considerations that have impact on these decisions.

The department chairperson's role in helping a colleague set developmental goals was discussed in chapter 4 and earlier in this chapter. As part of an evaluation, or during an informal goals-review discussion, the chairperson might identify areas in which knowledge/skill deficiencies exist, particularly with respect to administrative matters and those which pertain to student relations. The effective chairperson will work with the instructor to set goals and plan action steps that will lead the instructor to higher competency. At the same time, the chairperson might suggest, for example, specific learning experiences or specific courses.

Summary

Achieving the highest possible technical competence in an organizational unit involves several skills and activities which the competent manager constantly strives to improve. These include

1. Good selection of new staff members
2. Careful monitoring of positions to ensure that they constitute the best arrangement for achieving high levels of productivity, quality of service, response flexibility, and needs satisfaction
3. Review of performance problems to ensure that all obstacles to improved performance are removed
4. Appropriate education, training, and development

Improving Coordination and Cooperation

According to the Linking Elements Concept, the manager has two primary responsibilities for linking coordination and cooperation: setting up coordination procedures and making them work. An urgent project may require that several teams, units, or departments complete their respective assignments on time and have them in the proper place in the form most useful for the next activity. This involves coordination procedures and illustrates the three elements of coordination: time, place, and form. An item presented in proper form and on time, but submitted to the wrong place may cause as much delay as an item submitted on time in the wrong form to the right place.

Coordination, therefore, requires many skills from the competent manager. One necessary skill is scheduling, which, like financial analysis or Electronic Data Processing (EDP), flowcharting, or programming, involves specific technical knowledge and skills a manager may need to function efficiently in certain situations. Since this book concentrates on the management of people, scheduling procedures such as network diagrams (for example, PERT and CPM), or Gantt charts are beyond its scope.

Not only is it necessary to schedule carefully and to communicate the schedules appropriately, but the manager, also must keep an ear carefully tuned to any indications of unhealthy friction between various members of the subunit or others in the department. However, it is not always easy to distinguish when conflict is potentially troublesome and when it is not. Competition for best performance is a form of conflict, yet one would not consider it undesirable until the competition becomes so intense that one team obstructs the work of another team rather than concentrating solely on perfecting its own activities. Similarly, it is not easy for a manager to recognize what statements are gripes or when subordinates air their dissatisfactions. At one time or another, every organization has dissatisfied an employee in some small way. Gripes are then aired and work continues as before. It is important to distinguish these from the more serious indications of conflict with other people or units that may lead to detrimental actions, such as open or hidden refusals to cooperate.

Creating an Open Communications Climate

Managers who wish to ensure good cooperation have to distinguish between major complaints and minor gripes. Once they have identified complaints that require their attention, they must apply counseling skills to resolve such problems. Many managers have not had training in counseling and therefore may be reluctant to start a private discussion with a staff member when trying to resolve a conflict. Some may step in too abruptly or bluntly and accomplish more harm than good. A good counselor, for the purpose of achieving coordination, need not be a trained psychologist, but a manager can easily become a good counselor by sharpening a few basic skills. These same skills, incidentally, are also useful during goals reviews (discussed in chapter 4), for grievance handling, and for dealing with other matters that relate to employee achievement and motivation. The basic skills include creating an open climate where communications can proceed smoothly, providing feedback, employing therapeutic and empathetic listening, and using Transactional Analysis concepts and questions.

The Johari Window: Figure 5-7 is a depiction of the Johari window, developed by Joseph Luft and Harry Ingham (*Johari* is an acronym combining the first names of the inventors). This diagram can be useful in

	Known to Self	Not Known to Self
Known to others	1. Area of Free Activity ARENA	2. Blind Area (knowledge/awarenes gap) BLIND SPOT
Not known to others	3. Area of yet Undisclosed or Confidential Matters (possibly avoided matters - private self) CLOSED MOUTH	4. Area of Unknown Activity UNKNOWN

Source: From Joseph Luft, *Group Processes: An Introduction to Group Dynamics*, by permission of Mayfield Publishing Company. Copyright © 1963, 1970 by Joseph Luft.

Figure 5-7. The Johari Window

increasing one's skill at achieving more open communications between two people. In the past, the Johari window has been presented as an intensely personal method for achieving self-awareness. It has, however, a much broader application when used to create a climate of open communications in a work situation. The concept can be used by the manager to open area 1 and lead to more meaningful discussions.

While the Johari window applies to both parties, it is assumed that the manager will take the initiative to ensure that the discussion will lead to the most useful conclusions. The manager's purpose in any communications process is to increase the area of free activity. The manager can achieve this by

1. Making sure that he or she knows as much about the topic as possible. In doing this, the "Blind Spot" is reduced.
2. Identifying what the other person does not know and helping that person to have greater knowledge. This helps to reduce the "Closed Mouth" area.

For example, by seeking information from the other person, asking appropriate questions, listening carefully, and seeking feedback (see figure 5-8A), a manager learns about the topic and reduces area 2. Likewise, by providing the other person with information, making sure that the other person has the necessary information, and providing self-disclosure (see figure 5-8B), a manager helps to fill in the things the subordinate does not know and, thereby, decreases area 3.

The manager who accepts responsibility for the communication, therefore, can effectively bring about the largest area of free activity that can be achieved (see figure 5-8C). The arena opens and an open climate where communications can proceed smoothly is more likely to develop.

Providing Feedback: Providing feedback is not easy. If it is too abrupt or too blunt, it will not achieve its purpose because it intimidates or hurts the other person. If it is too subtle, it may be unclear and easily misunderstood. Here are some useful rules on providing feedback:

1. Feedback should be as factual as possible. This means that it should be based on specific occurrences.
2. Feedback should be timely. It is not much good to say to somebody, "Three months ago you did such and such, and that was not the best way to go about this thing." Feedback should, if possible, be given immediately, since then it will have more impact and more meaning to the person receiving it.
3. Feedback should concern only those things which are under the control of the other person. Telling a young man that he is not smart enough is not going to help him very much. However, suggesting that he study some specific subjects or specific chapters in a book or practice a specific way of doing something could be very helpful to him.

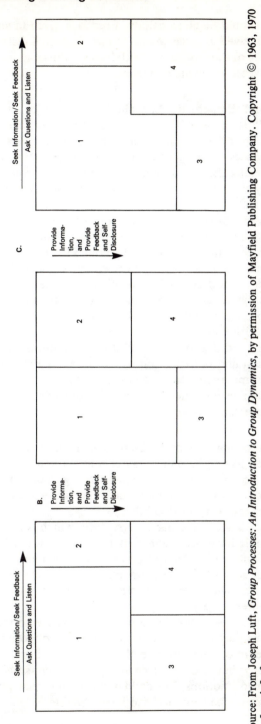

Figure 5-8. The Johari Window under Various Conditions

4. Feedback should be given calmly. Feedback given in an excited way is usually perceived as a reprimand or criticism. In a discussion, criticism may put one of the parties on the defensive, thus making the person less willing to share thoughts or feelings.

Therapeutic and Empathetic Listening: Therapeutic listening helps the other person "get things off the chest" and thereby relieves burdensome feelings so that the discussion about a problem can proceed with fewer emotional interferences. During effective counseling sessions, the counselor does more listening than speaking, for persons being counseled must have an opportunity to open up feelings to someone who can and is willing to understand them.

A good counselor must keep tight control over individual conclusions until the other person has completed the verbalization of feelings. After the opening-up process, questioning by the counselor interspersed with a few direct statements will usually be far more effective than telling the other person what to do. Good counseling requires that the person who is being counseled sees the advantages of looking at the situation from an entirely different perspective with the aid of the counselor.

Empathetic listening shows the other person that there is a genuine desire to understand that person's point of view and therefore encourages open explanation and participation by the speaker. Empathy can be combined with a sympathetic attitude for the other person's point of view; however, one can be empathetic and wish to fully understand the other person without necessarily agreeing.

Use of Transactional Analysis Concepts: Transactional Analysis is a technique for analyzing human behavior and communications. It is an excellent way to see emotional involvement in the transmittal of messages. The Transactional Analysis theory states that a person has, at all times, three ego states that vary in strength.

The first ego state is the parent ego state, which is made up of all the things that people have been taught by their parents, teachers, and others they have encountered in life. The parent is the righteous segment of one's personality that says work hard, stay pure, and follow the rules and laws that have been set. The parent is usually stuffy, self-righteous, knows it all, and has an answer for everything.

The second state—the child ego state—is the emotional, happy-go-lucky, rebellious part in people that is almost the opposite of the parent. The child rushes into things; likes to play, explore, and create; likes to enjoy life and be happy; but also feels free to express anger as well as many other generally subdued emotions. The child in a person is relatively weak and insecure, but also can be stubborn and unreasonable.

The third ego state—the adult ego state—is the rational and factual part of the individual. The adult ego state makes decisions based on information it receives from the child, the parent, and the world in general. The adult is logical, reasoning, helpful, understanding, and responsive. These three ego states are often depicted as shown in figure 5-9.

Although the adult state appears to be, and is, the more appropriate one for most work-related situations, to be "adult" at all times is not necessarily a desirable goal. A natural, open individual often displays the child, and even the parent, in his or her personality—because to be natural means to be one's self, and a complete self contains all three ego states.

Transactional Analysis starts by defining each communication between people as a transaction. If one person says "hello" to another person, this is a transaction. If the other person answers, this is another transaction. If the other person does not respond, this is also a transaction, although of an entirely different kind. The friendly greeting is a positive transaction; a refusal to return the greeting is a negative transaction.

Transactions, of course, have to start from some ego state. If at any one moment the parent ego state is dominant in a person, then the parent ego will be heard when that person speaks. If the child ego state is dominant at the moment, it will be the child that is speaking when that person says something. Sets of transactions can come in three different ways: a set can be complementary, or it can be crossed. There also can be a double set, with one set hidden.

Complementary Transactions: Complementary transactions occur when a message from an ego state of one person is responded to by a message from the ego state that it addressed in the other person. An example of this transaction is shown in figure 5-10. The figure could represent a manager jokingly

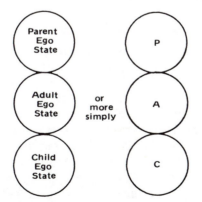

Source: Courtesy of National Fire Protection Association.

Figure 5-9. A Representation of Transactional Analysis Ego States

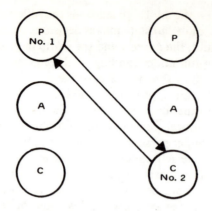

Source: Courtesy of National Fire Protection Association

Figure 5-10. A Representation of a Complementary Transaction

saying, from a parent ego state, to a subordinate who is struggling with a specific task: "Why don't you stop playing with that thing and get started on the project you should be working on?" The subordinate might reply from the child ego state, "But that wouldn't be as much fun."

Of course, transactions occur between equivalent ego states at work; the most effective transactions are complementary adult-adult ones, although there are appropriate times when it is desirable for the child or the parent to be dominant.

Crossed Transactions: Crossed transactions are the result of an unexpected response made to a statement. Take, for example, the following exchange, represented in figure 5-11:

Manager: "What did you do with that report?" (Adult addressing adult.)

Staff member: "I gave it to you. Did you lose it?" (Parent addressing child.)

It is obvious that a crossed transaction does not often lead to easier and friendlier communications. At the extreme, this kind of transaction could almost immediately lead to a heated exchange that could only be rectified by a better communication between complementary ego states.

Crossed transactions can occur easily because either the child or parent ego states are often the dominant ones. The manager who must get something done often starts a conversation from the adult state and receives

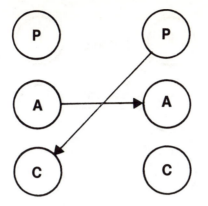

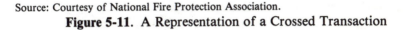

Source: Courtesy of National Fire Protection Association.

Figure 5-11. A Representation of a Crossed Transaction

a reply from either the child or the parent in the other person. The result is a minor crossing of transactions, and if that is recognized, it becomes easier to lead communications to complementary transactions. More work, of course, is accomplished by adult-to-adult complementary transactions. By communicating on an adult level, managers and employees can review situations, and the actions that should be taken can be discussed in a calm and factual manner.

Hidden Transactions: Hidden transactions have an unspoken meaning that is somewhat like a double message. When such a message is sent, it is usually disguised behind a socially acceptable transaction. For example, a manager in the Registrar's Office might say to a subordinate, "Steve, those semester grade printouts for the psychology department must be finished today. We've got to get them done one way or another." While this seems to be an adult-adult transaction, the hidden message really is parent to child: "You will complete all those printouts today" (see figure 5-12).

Recognizing ego states and understanding transactions are the most important Transactional Analysis skills for a manager or leader to master. They can help maintain calm when the other person is temporarily dominated by the child or the parent. Remaining in the adult state is the more mature course of action; awareness of this helps considerably in maintaining one's own equilibrium and thus helps to gradually bring the other person to the adult ego state.

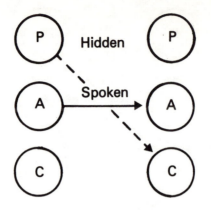

Source: Courtesy of National Fire Protection Association.
Figure 5-12. A Representation of a Hidden Transaction

There are three other concepts in Transactional Analysis that are of value to managers. They are (1) life positions, (2) strokes, and (3) stamp collecting.

Life Positions: The four life positions come from Dr. Thomas A. Harris' book, *I'm OK—You're OK*:

1. I'm OK, you're not OK. In a general way, this is the position of the parent who has to tell the other person what is right and what is wrong.
2. I'm not OK, you are OK. This shows the position of the child who understands that full maturity has not yet been reached. This position, however, also could indicate a mental health problem that is more serious than just a temporary child ego state.
3. I'm not OK, you're not OK. This position is definitely one that is assumed by people who have moderate to serious mental health problems.
4. I'm OK, you're OK. This is a position that the adult person assumes. The adult sees that every individual has certain strengths and weaknesses, but is otherwise fundamentally sound. The I'm OK, you're OK position includes the three ego states and concludes that any of these ego states can be the dominant one at the moment; however, this life position also acknowledges that in every person there is a strong adult. There are times when the child ego should be allowed to enjoy itself, and there are times when it is necessary for the parent ego to show itself. In the I'm OK, you're OK position, however, the adult ego is always in control.

An understanding of these life positions may help managers recognize a subordinate's view of the world and help that person see the life positions clearly and, therefore, help him or her remain more continuously in the appropriate one.

Strokes: In every transaction there is a stroke. If what is said or done gives the other person a pleasant feeling, then it is a positive stroke; if what happens gives a negative feeling, then it is a negative stroke. A friendly greeting is a positive stroke; an unfriendly greeting is a negative stroke. A failure to return a greeting is a negative stroke; unfair criticism is a negative stroke. Commendation or praise is a positive stroke. In general, what was discussed as positive impulses in the three climate-improvement strategies are positive strokes when they come from people or even when they come from the work.

Stamp Collecting: Stamp collecting is based on strokes. In a relationship between two people, or between a person and work, no stamps are collected if the positive and negative strokes are balanced. If, however, one person provides a series of positive strokes to the other person, the latter person is collecting positive stamps; sooner or later, these stamps are likely to be "cashed in" by reciprocation on the part of the collector. However, if one person collects many negative strokes from another person, sooner or later, some argument or negative reaction will take place.

The Use of Questions: Questions can be excellent tools in helping to achieve agreement on an issue when they are used properly and in moderation. Three types of questions can be used in obtaining information about an issue: (1) open questions, (2) reflective questions and statements, and (3) directive questions. All three types of questions serve to open areas for discussion because they cannot be answered with a simple "yes" or "no."

Open questions are intended to start the other person talking and generally begin with phrases like "How do you feel about . . . ?" or "What do you think of . . . ?" Often a moment of silence can serve as an open question.

Reflective questions and statements, however, merely repeat the last point the other person has made without adding anything significant. Instead, they reflect what has been said in different words in order to encourage further explanation and lead to new information. For example, in a performance-appraisal session, a manager may ask, "What you think, then, is that I have not been fair in distributing assignments to members of the department?"

Directive questions are questions that help expand the area of agreement by leading to further explanation of a particular point. Directive questions could start with phrases like "May I ask why you like . . . ?" or "How would you respond if I say that you agree . . . ?"

In addition to these questions and statements which are designed to bring a detailed response form the other person, are closed questions which can easily be answered with single words. Closed questions can bring specific pieces of information and can be used to confirm a point of agreement or disagreement.

There are many benefits that good questioning and listening skills can bring. For example, they can bring more accurate knowledge about the other person's needs, more information about the problem, greater opportunity to recognize potential areas of agreement, and greater confidence that the counselor is handling the situation correctly.

It is important to recognize the differences between a meaningful interview and an interrogation. An uninterrupted series of questions (including reflective statements, which are often viewed as questions) can form an interrogation. The best way to prevent an interrogation or an impression of one is to allow enough time between questions for the other person to answer at length and to restate or summarize, from time to time, to show that the other person's position has been understood. In this fashion, a steady stream of questions is interrupted and a more meaningful two-way communication is established.

The skills and strategies described in this subsection for use in administrative units also can be used by academic leaders. While many department chairpersons have a smaller role with respect to the counseling function (discussed in chapter 4 and earlier in this chapter), they do find themselves in this situation. For instance, since a chairperson is frequently the most respected member of the department, he or she may find that junior members will come for advice and guidance. In these situations, the Johari window, as well as the Transactional Analysis and feedback concepts described earlier, can be very helpful.

Summary

To align the coordination requirements of the organization with the willingness of people to cooperate, a manager should continue to develop technical skills such as scheduling, programming, and flowcharting. These are needed to ensure that good coordination procedures exist and are appropriately communicated, thus allowing people to work as smoothly with each other as they are willing to. A manager also should (1) monitor procedures to ensure that they are adequate for the required level of coordination; (2) be alert to signs of cooperation problems; (3) intervene when necessary, but not at the first sign of minor complaints; and (4) counsel and open up communications by applying techniques such as those described in the Johari window concept, by applying Transactional Analysis, or by using feedback and questions properly.

Aligning Rules and Personal Behavior Codes

The third linking element involves aligning the organization's behavior rules with the employee's personal behavior code, philosophy, and morality. A simple example of the alignment of an organization's rules with employee behavior codes concerns working hours. When an employee joins an organization, it is the employee's responsibility to work during the designated business hours. Although an employee may personally be accustomed to waking at 10 A.M., if the job begins at 9 A.M., the employee will have to meet organizational rules by conforming to the starting time.

However, alignment of organizational rules to employee codes is not solely an employee responsibility. Management also is responsible for "rules-to-code" alignment. A manager's responsibilities with respect to rules fall into five categories:

1. Communicating the rules and making sure that everyone clearly understands them. This, of course, includes personal adherence to the rules since violation of rules by the manager sends the message that the rule may not be very important
2. Ensuring that all necessary rules are in writing, but that the "rule book" does not grow to unwieldy proportions
3. Enforcing rules with compassion for the needs of individuals, but at all times keeping in mind that every privilege granted can become a precedent other people may demand as a matter of right
4. Reviewing rules regularly to see whether the rules are right for the organizational unit, changing those which can be changed directly, and working toward changing those which require the agreement of higher levels of management
5. Maintaining a balanced view on rule enforcement and on granting privileges during periods of organizational stress

Communicating Rules

Rules exist so that every person in an organization knows the correct and incorrect forms of behavior that are required for the effectiveness of the organization. In order to ascertain that all organizational members conform to a set of rules, managers must ensure that all rules are explained and understood by either oral or written communication. Until people are aware of rules, they cannot abide by them; therefore, it is important that everyone clearly understands the rules.

Written Rules

Many small organizations communicate their rules orally to their small staffs. Larger organizations commonly issue a written set of rules and regulations—a guidebook or a handbook—detailed to reach their large numbers of employees. However, a guidebook sometimes creates more problems than it solves. Individuals may associate a written set of rules as a complete set of requirements for an organization; therefore, any rule that is not clearly spelled out may be open to individual interpretation. Employees may feel that they can do what they believe is right in an unwritten situation because if there had been a rule for that particular situation, it would have been in the guidebook. Therefore, attempting to obtain control by trying to compile a strict, written set of rules may be self-defeating.

Nevertheless, a small number of written rules on the most important policies applicable to a particular organization can be highly desirable, for they set the tone and provide the background for everyone to visualize the rules of reasonable behavior. Beyond that, maintaining an open climate in which problems can be discussed and decisions can be made in fairness to all concerned is the best policy. The manager will set the overall motivational climate by either adhering fairly strictly to a minimum set of rules or by allowing frequent privileges with the rules that exist.

Enforcing Rules

Every manager knows that once privileges are granted, they are difficult to take away. As soon as others learn that one person has been granted a privilege, they expect the same benefit. Granting privileges to one person and not to others is a situation that any leader does not want to create, for such an action can give a leader a reputation for playing favorites or of discriminating against some people. Similarly, failure to enforce rules that most members of the unit consider appropriate can bring a manager the reputation of soft-heartedness or, worse, lack of backbone and lack of ability to make difficult decisions. If employees are unionized, this situation becomes even more important. If one person is granted certain privileges, the union can use this as a reason to demand that the same privileges be extended to all employees, either informally or through a change in the contract.

Managers can avoid problems of special privileges and their consequences by employing wise decision making and constructive discipline. Many managers do not realize how wide the range of choices is for resolving rule problems or problems related to requests for privileges. Decision making in such situations may seem to be a matter of saying either yes or no. However, a manager can say yes to a request in such a way that it clearly makes it very difficult, or impossible, for the person making the request to ask for another privilege in the future; that is, "I will make an exception in this instance, but only in this instance." Or a manager can deny a request in such a way that the person requesting the privilege feels that the manager has been very fair and has given the request the most favorable consideration; that is, "After much thought, I've come to the conclusion that I cannot allow you to do such and such. I'm sorry that this could not be possible." Wise decision making means that before making a final decision on a request, a manager carefully analyzes all the choices that are available to make a decision while keeping in mind that granted privileges are difficult to take away.

A manager also can use constructive discipline in a situation in which an exceptional privilege is requested. An approval of the request could be given in exchange for some sacrifice. This would allow the organization to offer the same privilege to others who request it, provided they are willing to accept the same sacrificial consequences. A brief story may illustrate this strategy. In a southeastern university, building maintenance personnel worked 8-hour shifts, with night-crew personnel earning slightly higher rates of pay. Despite the pay differential, few people liked the night shifts.

One of the night-shift employees requested a change to the day shift because of an invalid mother who required full-time care. The employee's relatives and neighbors helped to care for the mother during the day, but the employee could not afford to hire someone to stay with her at night. Despite the employee's circumstances, the director of grounds and maintenance felt that the university could not allow the transfer because others who were not fond of the night shift might request a similar privilege. However, because of the employee's circumstances, the director did suggest that the employee find someone to exchange shifts.

When the employee could not find anyone to change shifts, the employee again appealed to the director for help. After lengthy deliberation and discussion, the director came up with a solution that employed constructive discipline, that is, compassion for the employee, respect for the rules, and granting of a major privilege in such a way that it would not set a precedent for others. The director offered the employee an open position on the day shift, which was available at significantly lower pay and gave the employee no assurances that another opening at the employee's current salary would be available in the foreseeable future. The employee made the sacrifice, and both the institution and the employee benefited from the method of privilege. Six months later a position at the employee's previous wage opened up for which the employee was qualified; thus the entire matter was resolved to everyone's satisfaction.

Review of Rules

A manager who wishes to create the positive motivational climate that the Linking Elements Concept fosters must keep in mind that rules that are considered unreasonable or arbitrary will not receive unquestionable employee support. Because of this, the manager should review existing rules for their applicability and relevance to organizational needs and goals. Innumerable instances exist where unreasonable or obsolete rules are either being maintained or ignored at a high cost to an organization's chance to heighten the existing *esprit de corps*. A regular review of rules would give the manager the ability to change poor rules as soon as possible or work to have them changed. Appropriate participation of team members is essential in any rules change, of course, since such changes require a high degree of acceptance.

Rules in Times of Stress

One frequently recurring problem with respect to rules and the granting of privileges lies in the lack of flexibility with which managers adapt to changing situations. During times of stress, even managers who normally are people-oriented will frequently become more autocratic or less gentle in their relationships with their people. Managers commonly pass on to their people any pressures they receive from above. When demands are high, rarely will managers be as free with granting privileges as they are when demands are low. They may enforce rules more rigidly than at other times and in general pass along the tension that the work pressures impose on them. Usually this is just the reverse of the type of behavior that is needed for the situation. When there is considerable pressure in an organization because of the demands that quotas, schedules, or problems place on it, people usually sense the pressure. For managers to increase the pressure through their own behavior will often fluster people and lead to less careful work. If managers become less willing to grant privileges at the same time or become more inclined to demand strict adherence to existing rules, the work climate can rapidly deteriorate, and efforts in other areas to improve the motivational climate will be hurt.

When the work pressures are high or problems exist, managers should not change their normal behavior. The extent to which they grant privileges or insist on adherence to rules should remain consistent with their actions in the past. If anything, to the extent possible, rules should be relaxed slightly to compensate for the extra pressure that the work schedules or work problems have created.

Although they have the same basic responsibilities, academic leaders, for the most part, have fewer requirements for achieving adherence to rules. However, the need for ensuring adherence to rules still exists. For instance, an instructor who fails to ensure that an adequate number of classes are held during the semester with respect to his or her course violates the course requirements and institutional rules relating to that. The chairperson has the responsibility to achieve both an understanding and compliance with those requirements. Obviously, the chairperson has to follow the same steps to ensure that the department member is treated fairly.

Summary

Several things have to be done in order to align organization rules with the behavior of staff members. First, rules must be clearly communicated. Second, written rule books must be limited in size in order not to be self-defeating. Third, rules must be enforced to avoid precedents, but enforced with compassion in special situations. Fourth, rules must be reviewed regularly to ensure that they are appropriate to changing situations. Fifth, rules that are no longer appropriate should be changed as quickly as possible. Sixth, team members should have as much of a voice as possible in deciding on rule changes. And finally, during times of stress, enforcement of rules and granting of privileges require even more careful thought to avoid damage to the motivational climate.

Conclusion: Links between Linking Elements

Before closing this chapter, it would be beneficial to discuss the interrelationships of the linking elements. As was pointed out previously, the linking elements support each other in creating a climate in which people can find motivation not only to do better work, but also to prepare themselves for greater achievement in the future. Most of the "linkages" between the linking elements are fairly obvious and do not require elaboration. However, a brief review of some might be useful here.

Goals/Performance Standards
and Coordination/Cooperation

1. Goals reviews provide considerable information about where coordination problems may exist.
2. When working to eliminate coordination/cooperation problems, goals may have to be set if important matters are involved.
3. Self-development goals for staff members (in the areas of scheduling, planning, organizing, and coordinating) may have to be set to improve unit performance and cooperation.

Goals/Performance Standards and Rules

1. Goals reviews can provide information about rules that are, or are becoming, inappropriate.
2. Goals can be set pertaining to the way a staff member adheres to rules.

Goals/Performance Standards
and Technical Competence

1. Goals reviews and performance evaluations provide information about developmental needs of subordinates.
2. Goals should be set to eliminate deficiencies.

Goals/Performance Standards and Satisfaction
of Tangible Needs

1. Career goals can lead to satisfying tangible needs; guidance in setting career goals occurs during goals reviews and performance evaluation.
2. Competent goal setting on the part of staff members can lead to greater respect by superiors and thus help with the achievement of career plans.

Goals/Performance Standards
and Psychological Needs

1. Through effective goal setting, the subordinate gains information about what occurs in the organization and has an opportunity to influence the shape of the work.
2. The open communications that comes from meaningful joint goal setting leads to a much more open working climate in all areas.
3. Effective goal setting and performance evaluation provide several levels of meaningful factual feedback on performance.
4. When goal setting is done properly, the subordinate knows that superiors are aware of his or her contributions to the organization.
5. With proper goal setting, performance appraisals are factual and fair, and subordinates are not held responsible for matters over which they have little control.

Governance in Higher Education

Forward: The Evolution of University Governance
Bernhard W. Scholz

University governance means the exercise of authority over university matters, such as conferring degrees, setting tuition and fees, appointing faculty and staff, designing programs, or carrying out business activities. University governance comprises general governance and academic governance. Although ultimately vested, by charter or statute, in a board of governors or a ministry of education, many of the powers of university governance are delegated—powers of general governance to presidents, rectors, chancellors, and their subordinate officers; and academic matters, that is, programs, courses, degree requirements, faculty appointments, promotion and grievance matters, to faculties. Today's patterns of university governance were shaped by the special needs and circumstances of the societies that the universities serve. However, university governance, as much as all other aspects of the modern university, also mirrors the medieval archetypes of the university and the political forces and intellectual developments that transformed them in the course of the centuries.

The model of university governance generally followed in the United States has its precedents in English and continental patterns. The continuity in university governance from the twelfth to the twentieth century is amazing and is witness to the continuity of the university's mission—the preservation, generation, and dissemination of knowledge—and to the fundamental conflict resulting from it—the need for autonomy, on the one hand, and the responsibility to the society the university serves and on whose support it depends, on the other.

The university as it developed in the West was from the beginning a community of teachers and students. The students submitted to a prescribed course of studies and aspired to obtaining a degree. The medieval university began as an educational guild of teachers and/or students, in the tradition of guilds formed earlier by artisans and merchants. Guilds organized themselves into "nations," and "nations" had as their heads an officer called the *rector*, perhaps the first official in the history of the university and still the head of many continental universities.

In the eleventh century at the University of Bologna, where law was the major course of studies and where students therefore tended to be educated and older, the guild of students was dominant in all matters except determining the requirements for degrees; masters (teachers) there swore obedience to the rectors of the student guild and were subject to their authority in matters such as appointments, time and length of lectures, and leaves of absence. However, governance by students, the Bologna model, did not become a lasting pattern in Europe. By the fourteenth century, students at Bologna and other Italian universities had to share control of university affairs with their professors and with municipal governments.

A much more influential model of university governance was set by the University of Paris, namely, university governance by the teaching faculty under the supervision of episcopal authority. The University of Paris had its origin in the cathedral school of Notre Dame. The chancellor, an official of the cathedral chapter, supervised the cathedral school and, as a consequence, exercised considerable authority. He granted the license to teach, which was in fact the first degree granted, and could withdraw the privilege of teaching from the masters. Friction between masters and chancellor was frequent, and the masters eventually formed a guild. In the year 1200, the king issued a charter that confirmed certain privileges to masters and students. Early in the thirteenth century, a university official named the *proctor* appeared as head of each of the four nations into which the faculty of arts was then divided. By the middle of the thirteenth century, there was a rector, who functioned as the elected head of all masters of arts. The other faculties—theology, medicine, and canon law—were each headed by a dean. Arts being the largest faculty, the rector claimed to be and eventually became the chief officer of the university.

The Oxford model followed that of the University of Paris. However, from the beginning there was greater emphasis on collegiality and less outside interference. There were students at Oxford as early as the late twelfth century. An official called the *chancellor* held office by the early thirteenth century. For a while, the masters were divided into two nations headed by proctors. The nations eventually disappeared, but the two proctors remained. Faculties other than the arts faculty were weak. The chancellor and the proctors constituted the only officials of the university, but the assemblies of masters made policies and executed the functions of university governance.

Paris and Oxford shared many features, especially the struggle to become independent from church and secular authorities. The heads of the universities gained secular authority by royal or papal grant. The chancellor at Oxford and the rector at Paris had jurisdiction over masters, students, and their servants and laid down rules when conflicts erupted between "town" and "gown." The Paris rector supervised the guilds of suppliers of books, ink, and paper and determined the price of food and lodging. Eventually, ecclesiastical jurisdiction shifted from the bishop of Paris to the rector of the university and from the archdeacon of Oxford to the chancellor. At Paris, degrees were at first granted by the chancellor and cathedral chapter, but in practice this power soon was in the hands of the faculty.

As early as the thirteenth century, concerned patrons of students founded houses at Paris, Oxford, and other budding centers of higher learning, where poor students could find lodging and take their meals. Usually there was provision for one or two masters to live with the students. Students therefore learned with resident masters (Sorbonne, Merton), and the colleges took over the task of teaching and examinations. Oxford and Cambridge had an uninterrupted history of self-government. The universities there were held together by conventions rather than structures. The constituent colleges enjoyed great autonomy, and universitywide structures of governance were weak. Oxford and Cambridge were run as self-governing guilds of scholars until, in recent decades, the demand for social justice and public accountability began to question the ancient arrangements. Even today, the colleges and universities remain discrete legal corporations; the university sets standards for degrees and provides lectures, and the college provides tutorial instruction.

The spontaneous and haphazard appearance of "universities" in the half-century before and after 1200 eventually gave way to the deliberate creation of universities by princes and, especially in Italy, municipalities. Emperor Frederick II, for instance, founded the first royal university at Naples in 1224. As princely foundations, these universities were subject to increasing control by royal, princely, or municipal governments, although the same fate also befell most of the ancient foundations, such as Paris and Bologna. They had to accommodate national, regional, or municipal interests. Therefore, they became agents of secular governments in the new sovereign states. Their professors acted as state officials and considered it their task to train servants of the sovereign. The Reformation in Germany reinforced this trend, and for a while, Protestant and Catholic universities were instruments in the hands of rulers and their respective churches. Even Oxford and Cambridge, although their internal government arrangements were not changed, came under greater royal control; the heads of the colleges functioned as a board of governors responsible to the crown.

Yet another model of university governance developed after the Reformation in several Protestant countries. In Geneva, Leiden, and Edinburgh, the universities were placed under the supervision of external, nonacademic boards. Martin Luther already had argued that the universities in states of the new persuasion should be responsive to the needs and interests of the reformed communities. At the University of Leiden, founded in 1575, there was a university senate that included the rector as well as professors, doctors, and masters. The rector was appointed by the crown, acted as chief executive officer, and was assisted by four assessors, one from each of the faculties of arts, theology, law, and medicine. Two permanent curators chosen by the states of Holland had responsibility for the development of the university and had the right to attend meetings of the senate. Administrators thus became representatives of lay boards (in Oxford they were the servants of the academic community). The important precedent set was that outsiders now had a share in running the government of colleges and universities.

Governance of colleges in colonial America borrowed from both the Oxford and Geneva models. Harvard had a governing council consisting of the president and teaching fellows as well as a board of external overseers, which had the right of visitation and final approval. Its charter of 1650 changed the original arrangement. The Board of Overseers was charged "to safeguard the interests of the Commonwealth and churches, and to prevent the President and Fellows from doing anything unwise." The corporation consisting of the president, the treasurer, and senior fellows was the actual governing agency. President and professors later constituted an informal body, the "immediate government." Its purpose was to manage the business affairs of the college, to supervise student discipline, or to rule on expulsion. Eventually this body was superseded by the "faculty," which had no formal legal power, but a great deal of internal authority.

The Harvard model was not followed; Yale set the pattern instead. Its charter of 1701 gave sole authority to a governing board consisting of outsiders, a group of ministers charged to "erect, form, direct, order, establish, improve and at all times in all suitable ways for the future to encourage the said school." The state universities followed this model. In continental Europe, public universities were agencies of the state under the control of ministries of education. In the United States, they became public corporations similar in their organization to private colleges. State legislatures placed governing authority into the hands of boards of trustees, that is, boards of external lay members. They had authority over finances and property as well as the university's relationship with faculty, students, and administrative personnel. Lay boards had a tendency to involve themselves in administrative minutiae, down to the classroom observation of teachers. University governance was authoritarian, if not autocratic. Modifications in the direction of greater faculty participation in decision making were slow to come. Here again Yale set the pattern, and by the later nineteenth century, its faculty participated in the hiring of new faculty. Even such academic matters as educational policy and student discipline, however, remained for decades in hands other than those of the faculty. Businessmen increasingly replaced clergy on boards of trustees; they carried their authoritarian practices into the university and looked on professors as employees. Professors, on the other hand, saw the board as fit only to take care of financial affairs and unqualified to meddle in academic matters.

Boards of trustees dominated by men who looked on university governance from the perspective of business leaders selected men of similar outlook as presidents, individuals whose strength lay in organization, administration, and public relations and who surrounded themselves with subordinate agents devoted to the management of the university. The "administration" made its appearance, and it was a body of people not primarily concerned with education, but with the managerial and organizational side of the university, clearly distinct from, if not in an adversary role to, the faculty. Concessions were made to faculty as a result of competition among the great universities and the growth of departments, which sprang from the professionalization of knowledge in the nineteenth century, and this signaled the rise of greater faculty autonomy. However, up to the First World War, power remained with boards and presidents. Major changes in the direction of decentralization occurred only in the last half-century. Boards increasingly withdrew from interfering in the internal operation of the university; presidents functioned less as educational leaders than as links between the university and the public and became mainly concerned with matters of finances; and faculty gained control over educational policy and the appointment and promotion of its own membership. Perhaps the most notable fact was that by the 1950s, faculty autonomy in academic matters was a reality in a large number of American universities.

The process of democratization, however, did not stop there. In the late sixties and early seventies, a large number of American colleges and universities established university senates, usually consisting of representatives of faculty, students, and administration, but often including representatives of other constituencies as well. These bodies were designed to make decisions on policies affecting all units or personnel of the university or, at least, to advise presidents or boards on such matters. While this was seen by many as a step toward university self-government, others believed the principle of "what affects all should be controlled by all" could not be applied to university governance. Certainly the creation of such universitywide representative bodies meant an erosion of faculty authority. More than ever, faculty members sought support in affiliation with associations representing their respective disciplines and, as far as their rights and economic security were concerned, with national organizations that would support collective-bargaining efforts. The latter meant increasing submission to external controls. Meanwhile, the growing role of government, especially some states and, of course, the federal government, in university affairs not only spawned a new generation of university administrators, but increasingly subjected university governance to governmental controls. The big question at the moment, then, is what measure of self-governance the university will be able to retain in the face of growing pressure for external control, especially from its paymaster, the state.

University Governance
Nathan Weiss

Before embarking on a discussion of governance, it is necessary to clarify what is meant by the term. *Governance* is used here as it was elegantly stated by John D. Millet: "a structure and process of decision making, within a college or university, about purposes, policies, programs and procedures."[1] It is essentially analogous to the process of governing within the political system at large and, to a lesser extent, comparable to management in business organizations. Just as governmental levels have constitutions or charters to guide this process, so do institutions of higher education have statutes or charters. These documents spell out the major framework within which the organic process of day-to-day decision making takes place. Within this framework, rules and regulations develop over the years that adapt the decision-making process to the realities of the external environment and the political forces within the institution. Influencing these changes are the major constituencies that serve and/or are served by the institution.

There are several theories that attempt to explain the process of governance in higher education. How valid these theories of governance are is a matter of judgment. No doubt there is some truth in the idea that in each of the theories there is an element of considerable validity, and indeed, it is likely that any existing system of governance reflects elements of all the particular theories. In any event, it will be useful to look at some of these theories as foundations for the discussion on how the Linking Elements Concept can provide further insights.

The Collegial Concept

One of the earliest concepts has been called the *collegial concept*. Essentially, this is the idea of a community of scholars, including administrators and faculty, that arrives at decisions collectively. It is largely a process of reaching concensus, as distinguished from the purely political majority rule. Based on the idea of a community of scholars, the collegial concept is reminiscent of the platonic concept of the Philosopher State—the rule of the wise men (and women).

In terms of the Linking Elements Concept and its foundations, as described in earlier chapters, the collegial model of governance can be effective only if its assumptions are satisfied.

1. Most, if not all, members of the collegiate community have reached the left extreme in their life-cycle development (see chapter 4, "Life-Cycle Theory of Leadership") and are thus highly responsible in their approach to

problems concerning the allocation of resources and the resolution of differences and conflicts of interest.

2. Managers are rarely needed, because decisions are made collectively. The managerial style of those in positions of organizational authority, such as deans, the chief academic officer, and the president, is usually at the extreme right of the Tannenbaum and Schmidt continuum (see figure 4-8). This means that professionals, other than the authority figures, make decisions without limits on most matters. Partly excluded from this concept of governance are the clerical and secretarial staff members, as well as new instructors, who are considered less self-reliant and need more directive leadership.

3. Since everyone has, in this model, an equal voice in every decision, individuals will selectively disqualify themselves or selectively assume a stronger voice as is appropriate in light of their personal technical competence with respect to the issue under discussion. This means, in light of the Maier diagram (see figure 4-9), that those who do not possess the technical knowledge necessary for a resource-allocation decision, for instance, or any other major decision will voluntarily defer to others who have greater knowledge. Thus consensus can be reached, in each case, by those who possess the technical knowledge required for that decision, and acceptance will then be given freely by those others who have voluntarily abstained from participation.

The conclusions that emerge from analysis of the collegial concept indicate that it can have only limited application. It can serve as a useful guide to governance only in those rare situations in which the assumptions approximate the reality of the situation. For instance, the collegial concept can have considerable application at the department level, where it often can be an appropriate guide for the "managerial" style of the department chairperson, especially if the members of the department are mature individuals in the sense the word is used here.

Many faculty members tend to see the collegial model as the ideal that should be followed by administration and boards. Therefore, it is often necessary for high-level managers in colleges and universities to create awareness that although the collegial model is not universally applicable, it is being applied whenever it promises to bring consensus.

The collegial model will not work when there are very strong conflicts of interest among the constituents within the institution. Competent managers will therefore lean toward using other governance concepts in such situations. Inappropriate or broad-scale application of the collegial concept, therefore, will most likely lead to failure to make any decisions. It will bring splintering of the constituents, with resultant frustrations, feelings of impotence, and paralysis. Generally, these are worse than any dissatisfactions that failure to adhere to the collegial model would bring. Furthermore, there is one other shortcoming of the collegial model as a practical guide to governance as distinct from a philosophy, and that is its failure to provide an appropriate place for the student body and student organizations. Thus the collegial governance model represents more an ideal philosophy than a practical model for institutionwide use. In fact, J.V. Baldridge, the noted theorist, called it a revolutionary ideology and a utopian projection rather than a description of the reality of governance in higher education.[2]

The Collective-Bargaining Concept

In almost direct contrast to the collegial model, at the other end of the spectrum figuratively, is the *collective-bargaining model*. This model recognizes the dichotomy inherent in the conflicts of interest between those who provide the resources or who are charged with the responsibility for apportioning them and those who use the resources directly. In the collective-bargaining model, the chief academic officer and the president, as well as the managers in the administrative departments, are considered management, while all others are organized into one or several bargaining units. By the very nature of the relationships that are established in the bargaining model, some of the personal freedoms of the individual may be sacrificed. As a result, management functions move closer to those in other organizations. Management and employee "rights" are spelled out in the institution's collective agreements with the respective bargaining units. Paradoxically, the collective-bargaining model imposes on those who sit on the management side not only the role of managers, but also its responsibilities. As a result, practical management principles apply. In effect, the faculty and other members of bargaining units say to the management people who sit at the bargaining table across from them something like this: "We are spelling out here, in this bargaining process, our rights and yours, and our obligations and yours. Within the limits of that collective-bargaining agreement, we thereafter expect you to manage the institution in such a way that the greatest benefits will accrue to those who have established the institution, as well as to those who serve in it, and to those who are served by it."

As a matter of fact, many agreements contain management clauses which specifically state that it is the right and responsibility of management to make the necessary decisions so as to achieve high-level performance, whatever that may mean, for the institution. In practice, the bargaining philosophy of governance usually concerns itself primarily with terms and conditions of employment, leaving the academic concerns to be resolved some other way—possibly on the basis of the collegial model. Since collective bargaining in institutions of higher learning has a relatively short history, having become widespread only since the sixties, it is still hard to predict whether it will expand the same way as it has in government and private organizations. There, the terms and conditions that once covered only a limited number of personnel decisions have broadened to encompass more and more decisions that once were management prerogatives.

The decision process in government and private industry is different from that in educational institutions, however, in that the individual member of the bargaining unit rarely has the same strong desire to protect personal interests as an employee while at the same time seeking a strong voice in managerial decisions pertaining to the direction that the institution should take. Nor are there, outside the educational institutions, managerial decision-making bodies staffed by employees that are equivalent to the faculty senate or faculty councils that are so widespread in higher education. Because the collective-bargaining model is a far more practical and stable one than the collegial model, the competent manager has access to, and should appropriately use, the entire range of management styles depicted in the Tannenbaum and Schmidt leadership continuum (figure 4-8). To avoid continuing expansion of the scope of decisions that are subject to collective bargaining, it is essential for management, in that environment, to firmly make decisions and to set goals that are within its scope under the agreement. This does not mean, however, that such decisions have to be made unilaterally or autocratically, but rather that considerably more care has to be devoted to deciding which issues should involve the faculty senate or faculty body and which should be made by administration alone. The freedom the collective bargaining model of governance gives to the administration to make those decisions allows managers considerably greater control over the major decisions than the pure theoretical appearance of the model would suggest. In fact, collective bargaining, rather than restricting those who govern institutions of higher learning in the way they can approach major issues, may sometimes have a tendency to clarify those issues and thereby make governance a less ambiguous process.

While the collective-bargaining process still exists chiefly in the northeastern and midwestern public colleges in the United States, it appears likely that its application will spread geographically, particularly as states establish laws that legitimize the process in public institutions and as competition increases within the institutions for limited resources. The recent Yeshiva case will probably retard the spread of collective bargaining in the private college sector (*Yeshiva University Faculty Association* v. *Yeshiva University*, U.S. Supreme Court, February 20, 1979).

The Political Governance Concept

A political system, according to David Easton, is a system of interactions on the part of individuals or groups to influence the authoritative decision makers (in higher education these are faculty senates, presidents, boards of trustees, vice-presidents, and so on) to render decisions in accordance with their value systems or preferences, particularly as they relate to the allocation of resources.[3] In a sense, this is similar to the wider American political society in which any group who wishes to achieve a certain objective rallies support for that objective and thus tries to influence decision-making bodies to allocate the necessary resources.

The political governance concept is really a conglomeration of many that can be seen as a continuum. At one extreme is organized anarchy, in which the various interests or political groups pursue their own roads, with little regard for the needs and situations of others or of the institution as a whole. They do so within the overall institutional framework of laissez faire, where neither interferes with the activities of the other. For a decision to achieve acceptance, however, it must be of such a nature that it does not seriously offend or hurt the interests of any one of these groups, since each of them can effectively obstruct or limit the implementation of the decision. While they have little power to achieve a positive decision in their favor, each can effectively veto any actions they oppose. In such an environment, the manager or administrator is primarily a catalyst who seeks to stimulate those ideas with which he or she identifies. Otherwise he or she passively participates in the process by selecting or generating ideas that appear appropriate for the institution and then stimulates interest among those who can benefit from these ideas. Thus, enough support can sometimes be developed, so an idea may avoid being blocked by one of the interest group.

At the other extreme of the political governance concept is what could be referred to as "the institutionalized governance process," where highly formalized governance bodies have emerged with codes spelling out their powers and limitations. These generally are faculty senates and student governing bodies, as well as administrative councils. In an institutionalized governance process, these well-defined bodies provide the steps and the environment in which decisions are made on issues that are submitted either by members of any of the constituencies or by the administration itself.

Viewed from this broad definition of the term, the political model as a guide to governance in higher education has considerable merit. It represents a pluralistic situation involving student councils representing all kinds of students—part-time or full-time students, evening students, graduate students, and other kinds of student organizations. It also, of course, involves administration and faculty organizations, such as faculty senate and faculty unions (AAUP, NEA, or AFT, and so on), using influence and pressure to affect decisions. There are other kinds of employee organizations representing administrative/clerical people, security and maintenance staff, cafeteria workers or housing people, and so on. All these groups obviously have values and needs for which they seek satisfaction.

College governance systems are analogous, in many ways, to those of a municipal government. However, a campus political system may not be as fully developed and structured. Larger institutions, whether they are private or public, and older ones usually have the more fully developed systems, approaching those of actual governments.

It should be noted that the word *political* is not used here in a negative sense. It is merely used as a term to describe what some believe to be reality. The collegiate decision-making process is a highly fluid one in which decisions are made largely as a result of the ebb and flow of political groups as they compete with each other for scarce resources. Economists, in describing what they refer to as the economizing problem that all societies face, often refer to the fact that there are unlimited demands and limited resources. Indeed, that is certainly true of the collegiate scene.

In the world of academia, the scarce resources include such things as academic status, budget, personnel, and students. Getting published can be a political process, as can be obtaining tenure or a larger share of the line positions for the department, funding for a new program, or acceptance of a course as a prerequisite. Deciding the ground rules under which decisions will be made is the fundamental political process in which exercising power, consolidating power, or affecting a change in the power relationships can help an individual or group obtain satisfaction of its claim or demand.

Coalition Management

To manage effectively in a political environment requires not only the managerial skills discussed in the Linking Elements Concept, but also those of a political leader or, more specifically, those of coalition management. Coalition management can gradually help an institution move from some form of organized anarchy toward an efficiently working institutional governance process. When used effectively, coalition management can provide a fertile environment for goal setting and decision making, with appropriate consideration for the long-term benefits of the institution, as well as for satisfaction of the immediate, major legitimate needs of the various groups.

Coalition management refers to a process in which the manager, who has accepted responsibility for the achievement of one or several goals, proceeds to develop the political strength that will make the achievement of those goals possible or will lead the institution to adopt the goal as one of its own. For instance, a dean may feel that the institution could gain from offering a new bachelor of science degree in nursing that might utilize biology and health science courses offered in the biology department and chemistry courses offered in the chemistry department. Coalition management in this situation would, first of all, mean identifying those groups—departments, student groups, administration officials and others—who are likely to see sufficient benefit in the idea that they will endorse and support it in the respective decision-making bodies that will gradually consider it. After identifying individuals and groups who are likely to favor the idea, the dean would then consult with them to develop the program in greater detail, in such a way that it obtains as much enthusiastic support by the respective groups as can be achieved. At the same time, the dean would identify those groups who might oppose the new academic program on various grounds, such as that better use of the resources may exist elsewhere, that the concept itself is philosophically not desirable for the institution, that it does not fit the mission sufficiently to deserve consideration, or that it may cause obstacles in other areas that would detract from the benefits it can offer.

The dean would then meet with these people or groups to identify areas of concern and to either acknowledge them by making changes in the contemplated program or correcting any misunderstandings about the impact of the program on the institution at the present as well as in the future. Some institutions have formalized this process by requiring impact statements on new programs or on major changes that must be developed by those who are sponsoring them. In this case, the dean is apparently the sponsor of the idea as well as the coalition manager. The process works best when an idea has both. The sponsor usually is the visible champion who appears to carry the idea through the system until it is either accepted or temporarily rejected. The coalition manager often works behind the scenes, quietly seeking common ground whenever conflict erupts.

While temporary rejection of an idea occurs frequently, permanent rejection in the political system is unlikely, since changes in environment, as well as within the institution itself, may present opportunities to persistent sponsors and/or coalition managers to rejuvenate the idea and present it in a new form that may be acceptable to the new coalitions that may emerge.

In coalition building, it is mutually understood that the various members of a coalition have to refrain from interfering with those aspects of the decision about which other members of the coalition feel strongly. If the members of the coalition fail to adhere to these unspoken limits on their freedom to affect the ultimate shape of the program, then the coalition is in danger of falling apart. It is, of course, the coalition manager's function to step in whenever a group or individual thus threatens the survival of the idea.

With respect to the Tannenbaum and Schmidt continuum (see figure 4-8), even though the coalition manager usually lacks authority over most, if not all, members of the coalition, there is nevertheless clear delegation of decision-making freedom through the mutual support that members of the coalition and the coalition manager give each other.

The competent coalition manager is also aware that an idea will achieve the highest likelihood for success and become a firm institutional decision if, in Maier's terms, he or she approaches two groups: (1) those who have the technical knowledge to make an effective decision in the first place and who can present it in such a way that it is understood to be an appropriate decision, and (2) those whose acceptance is most important for appropriate implementation of that decision. Keeping Maier's model in mind, therefore, will help a coalition manager build the strongest coalition and thereby greatly enhance his or her chances for acceptance of the concept.

Besides approaching existing groups in the shaping of a coalition, a coalition manager has other options. Sometimes it can be shown that an idea has intrinsic merit, which means that people can be convinced that the long-run benefits clearly outweigh the short-run disadvantages. In such a situation, the coalition manager can sometimes significantly enhance the chances for acceptance of the idea through suggesting that a new group be formed that will have influence over the more traditional, existing groups or by creating a new group if it is within his or her power to do so. Such bodies could be commissions, committees, or task forces. If properly chosen so that they are made up of prestigious or highly respected members of those constituencies who are most effected or who may be negatively affected by the contemplated change, such new groups can frequently give the coalition the necessary additional strength to achieve acceptance of the idea.

Coalitions are issue-oriented. This means that new coalitions will shape themselves and old ones will disband as issues arise or as they lose significance in the environment. Creating new bodies can therefore have several effects:

1. They can influence any existing, opposing coalition to be more receptive to the new idea.
2. They can prevent the formation of new groups that might tend to strengthen an existing opposing coalition.
3. They can directly influence the attitudes of an existing coalition.
4. They sometimes can have the effect of preventing the formation of an effective opposing coalition so that the opposition to the idea is divided. While this does not always help to lessen opposition, it does bring such a result at times.

Coalition management can bring success for an idea with long-run benefits even when the short-run disadvantages may present significant hardship on some groups or individuals. The competent coalition manager therefore analyzes the environment carefully during the initial (consultation) stages, when meeting with the strongest coalition members that are most favorable to the new idea, and when assessing the likely opposition to the idea. He or she will then develop a strategy that will strengthen the coalition relative to expected opposing interests. As every administrator in institutions of higher learning knows, this process of coalition management requires considerable restraint and great patience. Hasty attempts to speed the process frequently can tear the coalition apart or polarize the community and may make it practically impossible to create a favorable environment for the decision until the constituencies have reshaped, one or possibly several years later. There are some interesting examples of the failure of appropriate coalition management. Two of these are fairly typical.

In one college, rather than taking the time to achieve a strong coalition to deal with the matter of changing the procedures for retention of faculty, the administration moved somewhat too quickly in suggesting that the rules should be modified. These were immediately opposed by the faculty union, and in order to achieve the strongest possible bargaining position, the union took an extreme stand in the opposite direction. The result is that both sides considered the other unreasonable. Considerable hostility characterized the futile attempts to resolve the problem, and the entire educational process suffered for years.

The second example is at the other extreme. It concerns a college with a disproportionately large school of education. The process of building a coalition toward new directions in noneducational professions seemed so difficult to achieve that the effort was abandoned after a feeble start. The result was that once educational job opportunities declined sharply, enrollments dropped precipitously. The college was faced with crisis reductions in staff and in resources; it had difficulty maintaining the facilities, and it had to cope with all the problems associated with sudden decline. Greater skill in coalition management on the president's part could have avoided the hardships that accompanied the crisis.

Conflict Managment

Coalition management requires more than average competence in conflict-management skills for those who hope to be successful as managers at all levels in institutions of higher learning. These conflict-resolution skills are especially important because the conflicts of interest between various individuals and groups in and outside the coalition must be resolved in such a way as to achieve, or obtain, the greatest possible support for the issue around which the coalition has been built.

Not all conflict, of course, is unhealthy. Conflict of ideas that leads to the emergence of creative new combinations of ideas can be very beneficial. An example might be the conflict that usually exists when members of a coalition meet to shape strategy and plan tactical steps. Such conflict leads to better approaches. Similarly, competitive conflict can be a healthy form of conflict. It can lead to greater willingness of people to subordinate their personal interests to those of the group. It thus sometimes brings additional effort with benefit of greater achievement and at the same time greater satisfaction for those who participate in the effort. In these healthy conflict manifestations, there is considerable energy generated that is channeled into positive directions.

In contrast with beneficial conflict, the destructive conflict types detract from the potential for achieving goals or prevent people from devoting effort. In such conflict, groups will polarize or will feel and possibly act on their desire to obstruct the efforts of another group. Since conflict management is so important to management in an academic environment, a brief discussion of conflict resolution is provided in appendix B.

Mission Statement

One of the primary areas that can lay the foundation for avoiding excessive conflict lies with the definition of the mission of an institution and its segments. Since this is a transition chapter, its emphasis is primarily on the mission statement itself. How a mission statement is translated into specific goals has already been discussed. A specific example is provided in the section of chapter 7 entitled Achieving Academic Goals.

Defining the mission of an institution has become increasingly important as a result of the greater competition for a declining student population and the resulting reduction in the resources available to institutions of higher education. To a degree this has never before been necessary, but today, each institution has to define the "business" it is in so that it can channel its resources to achieve maximum marginal productivity or, in Peter Drucker's words, so that the resources are allocated in such a way that the 80 percent of benefits that can be achieved with 20 percent of the resources are obtained in all areas. In today's environment, an institution that attempts to provide more detailed course offerings or more programs than its resources can properly support obviously is courting disaster. Similarly, an institution that has not adequately evaluated its situation and the strengths and weaknesses of the environment that it serves or the strengths and weaknesses of its own resources will not shape programs that will find widespread acceptance.

For all these reasons, the clarification of an organization's mission has become increasingly more important in providing direction for the various elements of that institution in shaping their own mission statements and broad strategic goals. A mission no longer is a luxury or the attractive generality that it once was. Today's mission statements can be relatively precise and, therefore, have significant impact on the ultimate use of resources once the mission has been accepted and has become established in an institution. Nowhere are the skills of coalition building more important than in shaping a meaningful, fully accepted, and reasonably precise mission statement or groups of statements. The extent to which the individual segments of the organization will fully accept that mission statement depends on the breadth of the concensus that can be achieved, and this in turn means that the coalition must be as widespread as possible, attempting to reach unanimity. An example of how a modern, fairly detailed mission statement could serve to provide a framework for appropriate goal setting in the various segments of an institution is given in the next two sections of this chapter. This particular example goes somewhat beyond the conceptual limits of a mission statement as defined earlier, but it illustrates clearly how the search for a definition of mission can lead to a document that explains and details direction for specific strategic and operational goals for all segments of the institution.

XYZ College-Mission Statement

As a major state institution of higher education, *XYZ* College recognizes as part of its inherent responsibilities the need to offer academic programs of recognized excellence, to promote research and scholarship, and to function as a cultural and social service center for its region.

The college has established as its multipurpose mission the education of undergraduate and graduate students in traditional liberal arts and sciences, professional education, and applied disciplines. *XYZ* will continue to offer programs in these three academic areas that are of greatest interest to the students that the institution serves and of salient need to the citizens of the state. Within these broad areas, the college will increasingly strengthen existing programs and will develop a few new carefully selected ones, both graduate and undergraduate, that will support the institution's developing emphasis on allied health disciplines, human and social service programs, and administrative sciences.

Liberal Arts and Sciences

XYZ College over the past 10 years has developed strong undergraduate programs in liberal arts and sciences such as biology, psychology, and political science. Approximately one-third of the students are now pursuing majors in seventeen of these disciplines. Additionally, the liberal arts and sciences provide the general educational component of every program in the college and serve students specializing in the applied disciplines and professional education with courses supporting their major programs; these disciplines also provide a challenging array of elective offerings. The integration of the liberal arts and sciences with other programs of the college is considered essential to a sound undergraduate education, a policy that will manifest itself throughout this statement.

Career Disciplines

The college has made a strong effort, with marked success, to develop baccalaureate programs in the career disciplines and has placed most of these in the School of Arts and Sciences. The practice of offering career programs in academic departments with corresponding liberal disciplines provides students with opportunities to integrate theoretical and applied elements of learning and to better understand the interrelationships between closely allied fields of knowledge. This arrangement helps to ensure that the students enrolled in the career disciplines will receive and understand the value of liberal education.

The college will continue to develop this career focus. It will propose, after careful studies of feasibility and needs, new majors that will complement the already operational programs in medical technology, occupational therapy, and physical therapy. These majors, along with other health-related programs in the School of Education, such as those in learning disabilities and speech pathology, will distinguish *XYZ* College as an institution emphasizing programs in allied health.

Additionally, the college plans to develop further its existing programs in administrative sciences, stressing particularly management in the public sector and quantitative methods of management. Already strong in these specialties with majors in public administration and management science, as well as the complementary major in computer science, *XYZ* College will continue to improve these programs by adding full-time faculty, library holdings, and educational equipment; by developing internship components; and by rigorously reviewing and revising curricula. In the year ahead, the college will propose the offering of a program in professional accounting and will explore the offering of one in health care administration, a specialization compatible with both the emphasis on management and that on allied health.

The major in social work, the first new career program to be offered at *XYZ* College, has been fully accredited for two years and is exemplary in all its aspects. In the School of Arts and Sciences it stands as an undergraduate curriculum representative of the college's interest in offering strong programs in the general area of human and social services. Other programs in this area and interest in further developments in this direction are to be found in the School of Education.

New Directions in the School of Education

The college is aware of the changing demand for new public school teachers and the necessity to assess its resource dedication and programs accordingly. It also recognizes the importance of maintaining its acknowledged reputation and leadership in selected areas of teacher education. It is *XYZ*'s intention to continue to offer quality programs in professional education and to maintain its recognized strength and reputation in selected fields.

Schools of education have a long tradition of preparing professionals to work in agencies that respond to human service needs. Teaching in schools is the most common occupation. However, school personnel have become prepared to provide other human services: health education, recreation, guidance and counseling, social and vocational development, and rehabilitation for special populations, are a few.

If schools of education are to maintain and develop a responsible and constructive contribution to our society, they must continue to broaden their role beyond traditional K-12 instruction. In addition to the complementary human services already provided in school settings by professional educators, schools of education should begin to develop alternative preparations for education personnel who can function in nonschool settings as human service educators.

The School of Education has already established a number of human service programs that have proven successful in terms of both appealing to students and providing subsequent employment opportunities. The undergraduate program in recreation has attracted a large number of majors who have become successfully employed; the undergraduate and continuing-education courses in gerontology are considered models in the state; and the graduate guidance and counseling program is attracting professionals from corrections and various other social service agencies. The undergraduate and graduate programs in speech and hearing have always prepared clinical personnel for a variety of agencies.

During the academic year 1979-1980, the School of Education will begin a reorganization and expansion of the Institute of Child Study into a Center for Human Services. The center will assume a dual mission. First, it will coordinate existing programs for the training of human service educators, and second, it will initiate new emphasis, within appropriate existing majors, for service as educators in the fields of community health, family studies, gerontology, vocational rehabilitation, and corrections and alternative settings for education.

Graduate Education

In graduate education, the college hopes to realize over the next two or three years the multipurpose mission for state colleges envisioned by the Higher

Education Act. Graduate studies must be expanded beyond the already firmly established programs in professional education to include the liberal arts and sciences and the career disciplines. A plan for graduate studies is in the process of being developed, and it identifies those programs where need exists and where *XYZ* College has the undergraduate and graduate resources and potential resources to mount these programs.

In the area of professional education, major programs have been developed to meet the in-service requirements of practicing teachers. Furthermore, certain of the existing professional education programs are being changed to satisfy emerging societal needs and requirements; modification of graduate programs in special education and individualized services and in early childhood education are examples.

XYZ College is continuing to strengthen the program leading to the degree of Master of Arts in Liberal Studies, which was approved by the Board of Higher Education in April of 1978. Development will proceed along the lines indicated in the program document. Good progress was made in 1978-1979 with the use of Program Improvement funds.

The major effort of the college in graduate education through the academic year 1980-1981 will be the development of two or three professional programs in the general areas of allied health disciplines, human and social service programs, and administrative sciences. Although a number are under consideration, the following three are emerging as those of high priority. In May of 1978, after conducting an extensive feasibility study that yielded very favorable results, *XYZ* College submitted a preliminary proposal for a program leading to the degree of Master of Social Work. Further study for preparation of the program and development is proceeding on schedule, and the final proposal, subject to local approval, should be submitted early in 1980 for implementation as early as the academic year 1980-1981. Building on its undergraduate strength in administrative sciences, *XYZ* College plans to propose, again, subject to local approval, a masters program in public administration. In 1979-1980, a thorough feasibility study and other groundwork planning will be undertaken. The college also will further explore the need and design of a masters program in management, emphasizing the unique strengths of this institution in computational science and quantitative methods of management. (In addition, the statement/report includes segments on major programs concerning alternative modes of instruction, basic and applied research, and cultural and community-related matters.)

XYZ College Strategic Goals

The mission statement can then lead to strategic goals such as ones outlined below for health care programs.

A. Mission Statement (Reference): The college will continue to develop this career focus. It will propose, after careful studies of feasibility and needs, new majors that will complement the already operational programs in medical technology, occupational therapy, and physical therapy. These majors, along with other health-related programs in the School of Education, such as those in learning disabilities and speech pathology, will distinguish *XYZ* College as an institution emphasizing programs in allied health.

B. Goals and Objectives for Health Care Programs (for 1979-1980, Using Program Improvement Funds):

Goal	*Objectives*
1. Creating an administrative structure for health care programs that will permit these programs to function as effectively as possible.	Completing a thorough study of the current structures of allied health offerings; identifying strengths and weaknesses in the programs and in supporting services; beginning the design of a structure that will provide the best possible mechanism for developing and maintaining programs of high quality.
2. Developing a coordinated approach to student advisement for the health-care professions.	Systematically identifying the advisement needs of students interested in the health professions; developing a structure and procedures for the best use of faculty, staff, and other resources in meeting those needs.
3. Developing an undergraduate program in health care administration.	Planning the structure of the program and securing concept approval at the college and state levels.
4. Developing an undergraduate program in medical records administration.	Planning the structure of the program and securing concept approval at the college and state levels; initiation of implementation steps for the program.

Goal	*Objectives*
5. Developing an upper-division program leading to the Bachelor of Science in Nursing (BSN).	Defining and planning for the type of BSN program that would serve the needs of the county and its immediate area and that would complement other nursing programs in the county; designing a mechanism for a cooperative approach to nursing education with other institutions; securing concept approval at the college and cooperating institutions.

While this chapter has taken the perspective of broad institutionwide issues, the following three chapters, covering academic affairs, student life, and administration, will explore in greater detail the issues that are of concern to those respective areas and thus impact on the governance process.

Notes

1. John D. Millet, *New Structures of Campus Power* (San Francisco: Jossey-Bass, 1978), p. 9.

2. J. Victor Baldridge, David V. Curtis, George Ecker, and Gary L. Riley, *Policy Making and Effective Leadership* (San Francisco: Jossey-Bass, 1978), p. 33.

3. David Easton, *A Systems Analysis of Political Life* (New York: Wiley, 1967).

7

Academic Affairs

Richard J. Nichols

Introduction and Overview: The Melange that is Academic Affairs

The term *academic affairs* in most institutions covers an exceedingly broad range of duties and responsibilities. The extent of this range was graphically illustrated at a 1978 workshop for chief academic officers conducted by the Resource Center for Planned Change of the American Association of State Colleges and Universities. On the cover of one packet of working materials someone had cleverly superimposed a number of advertisements requesting applicants for this crucial position (by whatever title: Vice President, Dean, Vice Chancellor, and so forth). An excerpt from one of these advertisements will serve to point out the expectations a college or university is likely to have:

> The college is accepting applications for the position of Vice President for Academic Affairs. The Vice President is the senior academic officer of the college and reports directly to the President. Responsibilities include: planning, development, administration and evaluation of all academic programs, faculty evaluation, budget preparation, and supervision of academic service areas.[1]

Other similar advertisements, with yet additional responsibilities, also were listed on that cover page. If these advertisements can be taken as at all representative of what academic affairs is all about, then it seems perfectly appropriate to label it as a melange, which according to Websters is "a medley or mixture, a hodgepodge."

In this chapter, an attempt will be made to bring some sense of order to this melange, by examining the interrelated roles and responsibilities of those individuals who might be considered academic managers. Attention will first be given to the chief academic affairs officer and then to significant others involved in academic management, including deans and directors, department chairpersons, committees, and individual experts. Discussion in each of these sections will focus on planning, policy, and procedures regarding budgeting, academic personnel, academic support systems, and curriculum and instruction.

The first of the remaining three sections of this chapter will focus on the achievement of academic goals and the employment of the UQIFAPPO concept to do that. The next section will provide a case study reviewing the Linking Elements Concept as employed in academic affairs. A brief summary concludes the chapter.

The Chief Academic Officer

Regardless of the particular title, the individual who is the highest-ranking academic officer is expected to have credentials, characteristics, and competencies that are as broad as the responsibilities assigned. Returning to the advertisement cited earlier, the person desirous of accepting the challenges of that list of responsibilities would need to conduct a self-evaluation to determine if he or she meets the following criteria:

> Candidates must possess: an earned doctorate; an exemplary record of achievement and recognition as a scholar, teacher, and several years of successful academic and administrative experience in higher education. Knowledge and experience in developing academic policies, curriculum development, research, and effective communication skills are essential.[2]

In effect, institutions of higher education appear to want their chief academic officers to be exemplary models of twentieth century Renaissance persons with all the additional positive attributes of successful modern managers. This view seemingly is shared by individuals serving as academic officers. For example, at the 1978 conference previously noted, a group of chief academic officers was asked to arrive at statements defining a chief academic officer and what they perceived as that individual's principal mission. It took only a matter of moments for them to agree that this officer is "symbolically, the academic conscience of the institution," whose principal mission is the "enhancement of the intellectual climate of the institution."

Both these statements seem to reflect a felt need that the chief academic officer must demonstrate a proper concern for the intellect in his or her work. Yet, when asked to provide a one-word description of what they did with their time, many of the terms listed by this group were those of management literature. Five or ten minutes of brainstorming generated the following list:

Plan	Persuade	Decide
Communicate	Negotiate	Count
Organize	Lead	Consult
Evaluate	Catalyze	Monitor
Substitute	Deliberate	Coordinate
Listen	Observe	Generate
Inform	Initiate	Question
Refer	Politic	Worry

This does not suggest that concern for management is necessarily in conflict with concern for the intellect—quite the contrary. Rather it appears to suggest that among this group it was accepted that one was more likely to enjoy a modicum of success in "enhancing the intellectual climate" if one enjoyed success in managing availiable resources toward that end.

Where reservations might be expressed is in the amount of time and energy one may have to spend in "managing" problems and issues perceived as having little directly to do with enhancing intellectual climate. The caution to be exercised by a chief academic officer, therefore, is to avoid being perceived as so engrossed in managing that he or she loses sight of the ends toward which the work is leading. It might be hypothesized that those chief academic officers who become perceived as only managers, to the detriment of their roles as "the academic conscience," have lost sight of the principal mission or have failed in their efforts to help others retain sight of that mission.

Given the caution just noted, it seems reasonable to suggest that the prime responsibility of the chief academic officer of an institution of higher education is to ensure that all the elements of the academic community maintain sight of the principal mission. Maintaining sight, however, is not enough—the chief academic officer must see to it that there is movement toward that end. This is done principally through close attention to the management of available resources.

The "resources" over which the chief academic officer is likely to exercise a modicum of control and influence may be defined broadly and, for the purposes of this discussion, have been grouped into four categories: budget, academic personnel, academic support systems, and curriculum and instruction. The control and influence the chief academic officer enjoys in each of these areas is limited by his or her ability to work with others on planning; to work within the constraints of policies, change them, or create new policies; and to work with, change, or create procedures.

Budget

Planning: In many institutions of higher education, the preparation of the budget provides the principal vehicle for institutionwide planning, for it has become a reasonable expectation that the budget requested should reflect the goals and priorities of the institution in the years immediately ahead. A well-prepared budget request should address these questions: "Where is growth wanted and expected?" "What is absolutely crucial to maintain and/or strengthen?" "What areas should be diminished?" Unless serious attention has been given to the planning process, these questions will not have been answered adequately. It is the contention here that budget-request preparation is an area of academic management in which chief academic affairs officers should exercise particularly great influence. They should be key figures in the planning process and be particularly able to reflect the results of that planning process in the budget preparation.

Allocation of Resources: An especially crucial aspect of the budget preparation is the establishment of goals and priorities to be met by the budget. Determination must be made as to the resource requirements necessary for satisfying each goal and priority. The extent to which these requirements can be accurately determined and satisfied should provide a reasonable predictor of potential resource-allocation problems. Unfortunately, requirements cannot always be fully determined, and frequently priorities may be changed by forces over which the institution has little control. Escalating fuel prices, for example, have forced many institutions to alter priorities in order to pay fuel bills. One also suspects that full funding of a budget request is indeed a rare occurrence, so rare in some instances that it may lead to manipulative budget preparations rather than competent budget-request preparation. When this is the situation, "game playing" is likely to occur, and this is rarely conducive to good academic management. Game playing can be prevented, or at least contained, however, if there is an appropriate atmosphere of openness, honesty, and trust, an atmosphere in which as much information as possible is made available and shared by all responsible for budget preparations.

In any event, the chief academic officer not only has the task of overseeing a competent budget request based on goals, priorities, and shared information, but also must then take the responsibility for allocating the resources that are available in a manner that will permit the greatest movement toward the major goals and priorities established through the planning process. Needless to say, this latter responsibility becomes a particularly difficult task, made doubly difficult by the fact that there are so many areas within the institution desiring increased (or at least maintained) levels of support. In addition, no matter how logical the arguments for reduction may be that the chief academic officer can muster, the institutionwide goals and priorities, determined through the planning process, may be quickly forgotten, or at least overlooked, by the institutional area whose priorities are placed somewhere toward the bottom when the resources are finally allocated. Charles Perrow, in a speech made in March 1978 at a conference entitled "Can We Renew Our Educational Organizations," made this point especially clear. He stated:

> . . . Announced goals are one of the least important constraints on organizational behavior; organizations can be rational instruments of announced goals only to a very limited extent. They have more important things to do. Instead, organizations are resources for a variety of group interests within and without the organization; they are used by a multitude of interests, and the announced purposes, while they must be met to some limited degree in most cases, largely serve as a legitimating device for these interests, or even as a mystification of reality.[3]

Coping with Perrow's "variety of group interests," while moving toward the general mission of "enhancing the intellectual climate" through determining which goals and priorities are worthy of greatest resource support can be especially "draining" of the academic manager. Knowledge and utilization of the Linking Elements Concept (see chapter 4), especially in goals management, may be a particularly useful tool for the academic manager who must cope. Employment of this concept is discussed in a later portion of this chapter.

Academic Personnel

A resource over which the chief academic affairs officer may exercise especially great influence is that of academic personnel. In many instances, this influence is to some extent predetermined by existing policies and procedures, and very often a good portion of an academic manager's time may be taken up with questions and problems that arise relative to the interpretation of a particular policy and/or the use of (or failure to use) a particular procedure.

In a time of growth, the chief academic affairs officer can be especially effective in working toward institutionwide goals through the assignment of *new* personnel lines or positions in the budget to areas established as priorities. The recent history of many institutions will reveal, one suspects, that it was in this capacity, "assigner of *new* positions," that the academic manager probably exercised greatest influence on an institution's movement toward its goals. Once the *new* positions were assigned, however, the academic manager may have played little part in the eventual recruitment, hiring, and so forth of the actual personnel.

Growth, for most institutions, is now a thing of the past, and while the chief academic officer still may have the opportunity to assign new positions, such assignment takes on even greater importance for the achievement of goals. The academic manager of today is much more likely to be concerned with what happens after the assignment of the *new* position and with what might be done to move toward major goals by effective utilization of existing personnel and positions.

Recruitment: When one reads the statistics on the unemployment—or underemployment—of recent doctoral graduates, one is tempted to leap to the conclusion that academic managers now enjoy a "buyer's market," where the principal recruitment effort must be that of carefully "sifting through" all the candidates for a position in order to "select out" the most qualified individual who is most likely to assist in achieving movement toward a major goal. In some disciplines this is the case. By now everyone surely has heard horror stories of trying to deal with 200 applications for a single assistant professorship. Yet this general picture does not fit all situations. In an effort to become "more attractive" to a more diverse clientele, some institutions develop programs in areas in which there is likely to be a limited number of candidates for a position. Some institutions also attempt to satisfy more than one need through a particular position and thus seek candidates with expertise in two or more areas—sometimes areas that are not particularly complementary. Again, in these circumstances, finding qualified candidates is not as easy as it would appear at first glance. Academic managers are finding that they must take a more active role in recruitment if recruitment is to be used to move toward desired goals.

In this process, the chief academic officer must be fully aware of (1) the goals of recruiting for a particular position; (2) the qualifications and experience that are crucial; (3) ways to evaluate a candidate's resumé and conduct an interview; (4) the policies and procedures (both institutional and otherwise) that must be followed. The academic manager should carefully communicate these details to personnel involved in the recruitment process.

Assignment and Deployment: While the number of new positions today's chief academic officer is privileged to assign is likely to be limited, opportunity to assign positions vacated through resignations, retirements, and other means will periodically occur. Indeed, reassignment of vacated positions and/or reassignment of personnel to other areas may prove to be the principal vehicle available to today's academic manager for use in moving toward institutionwide goals. However, it is likely to prove a rather unwieldy vehicle depending on the policies and procedures that exist or the ones that are likely to be developed.

In the situation in which a vacated position occurs, there may be somewhat more freedom for movement; yet even here there are likely to be restrictions. The department or division to which the position was originally assigned is not, in all likelihood, going to be particularly anxious to lose a position it has come to regard as rightfully its own. While the department in question may have had no immediate particular plans for the position, undoubtedly it can come up with some rather quickly if threatened with the loss of the position. However, if the department involved has accepted the institutionwide goals and recognizes the importance of this "transfer" flexibility for moving toward those goals, the academic manager will probably encounter less resistance to the position reassignment than might otherwise be the case.

In the case of reassignment or transfer of personnel (as opposed to vacated positions) from one department or division to another, the academic manager not only has to deal with the "sending" department, but also with the "receiving" department and, of course, with the individual(s) involved. This situation is likely to be much more "emotion laden" and, in all probability, much more subject to questions of policy and procedure. Questions of seniority, rank, qualifications, status, and privileges are but a few of the many that are likely to be raised in any attempt to reassign personnel unless the institution has in place an already agreed upon set of policies and procedures for such reassignments. Most institutions probably do not have clear policies in place, having previously preferred to make any such reassignments out of personal convenience and professional courtesy rather than a sense of institutional need. It would appear, then, that a major task facing many chief academic officers is to develop and achieve an acceptance for reassignment policies and procedures that permits movement toward institutionwide goals, as smoothly as possible. An understanding of the Linking Elements Concept may well make this task easier.

Professional Development: In the past, the chief academic officer's principal responsibility for professional development was likely to be that of assigning resources for travel, study, or research to the departments and divisions and then "getting out of the way," leaving each area to manage its developmental resources as it saw fit. In many institutions, this still remains the responsibility. However, in many instances, this responsibility is now taking on a somewhat different configuration as "development monies" are now being seen as a resource to be used more directly to move toward institutionwide goals. It is not unusual now to see the term *professional development* coupled with the term *retraining*. Many institutions, in their efforts to make best use of available personnel, are encouraging personnel in declining areas to secure professional development funds for retraining in areas of demand. While, in the past, professional development generally meant increasing one's expertise in one's area of specialization, it is as likely now to be used to mean the development of a whole new area of specialization and expertise.

Accordingly, the academic manager's role in the disbursement of development funds is changing and, in many ways, is becoming more complex. Historically, the chief academic officer could sleep with a clear conscience, knowing that the available developmental resources had been fairly and justly divided and disbursed to the departments and divisions, and that it was now the responsibility of the academic managers of those areas to see that these resources were properly and appropriately expended. Now, however, the chief academic officer must frequently also determine that at least a portion of those resources can be identified and accounted for as having been spent on professional development that specifically points toward institutional goals and needs. Where this is occurring, whole new sets of policies and procedures are being developed, and previously unthought of committees are being structured, for example, the newly created Career Development Committee, which was born of legislation and the negotiated contract for state colleges in the New Jersey higher education system. Within a goals management plan, new policies and procedures may well be appropriate, but for the chief academic officer, they represent one more responsibility for which he or she must find a successful means of coping.

Rewards and Sanctions: One of the principal resources for academic personnel over which the chief academic affairs officer is likely to have a degree of control and influence is in the area of rewards and sanctions. Through use of the institution's reward system, the academic manager is able to address the problem of satisfying individual personal and psychological needs, which are such important components of the Linking Elements Concept. Many of the rewards available in most institutions also are used as part of the professional development program discussed earlier and may include such items as travel to conferences and workshops, reimbursement for study, sabbatical leaves, and released time for research and/or creative activity. These are all tangible rewards, and most colleges and universities have relatively well-established policies and procedures for granting them. The chief academic officer is likely to have influence with respect to these rewards through his or her participation on committees and through the interpretation of policies and procedures. The chief academic officer's ability to secure and disburse funds designated for these purposes is likely to be the chief control available.

In addition to the rewards associated with professional development, other tangible personnel rewards may include reappointments, promotions, salary increases, and benefits. Salary and benefits are, in all likelihood, part of a contract package over which the chief academic officer may have little influence except as an informed resource. He or she may have more influence with respect to reappointments and promotions, depending on the policies and procedures of the particular institution.

Unfortunately, as fiscal resources diminish, the availability of tangible rewards also decreases. Furthermore, the items previously listed are becoming perceived less and less as rewards and more and more as perquisites that are due the individual. As a consequence, competition for these "perquisites" is often intense, and rather than achieving the desired morale for which a reward system is designed, the exact opposite may occur. Those who entered the profession at a time when promotions seemed practically automatic (that is, a perquisite) should realize how fortunate they are when they witness the fallout that occurs each year when promotions are announced and perhaps 4 out of 40 eligible people receive them. The 4 may have their morale boosted, but the remaining 36 are likely to see their non-promotion as some sort of intended sanction or punishment; so for everyone whose morale is boosted, there are 9 people whose morale, self-esteem, and perceived social esteem may be considerably lowered. Tangible personal rewards for the few are bringing with them perceived undesirable psychological punishments or sanctions for the many.

In the instances just noted, the sanctions were unintended, but their impact is still great. The question that arises is whether there is justification for using tangible, intended sanctions, and if so, what are some sanctions one might employ? Sanctions, when used, are usually justified as necessary for achieving or moving toward organizational goals, and in institutions of higher education, tangible sanctions are relatively few. Discussing the use of sanctions in organizations generally, Perrow, who was cited earlier, has stated:

> When there is conflict between the uses to which the employees wish to put the organization and those the executive wishes—and there will be some—the executive does his or her best to manipulate, threaten and punish. She or he can manipulate more effectively than punish or threaten. Civil service regulations (and political patronage positions where there is no civil service) effectively remove the threat of dismissal for cause. The lack of power the executive has over the daily running of the organization . . . makes threats of poorer jobs, harder work, no raises, no promotions, and so on fairly ineffective. Anger—direct, personal anger or hostility—is the best she or he can do, and while it works for awhile, as with one's children, it invites retaliation and loses its effect after a time.[4]

If Perrow's analysis of sanctions is at all accurate, and if the prior discussion on rewards has any merit, the chief academic officer has a particularly perplexing problem. The available reward system is in reality too often an unintended sanctioning system, and where sanctions might be wanted, there are few if any available. Obviously, one approach to this problem is to devise other reward systems that can be established, made operative, and can be *perceived as rewarding*. The key, one would suggest, is to find ways for personnel to find more self-realization in their work. Use of regular, semiformal goals reviews is one approach. The academic manager at whatever level (vice president, dean, director, department chairperson) who meets regularly with those individuals who report to him or her, to review the status of goals accomplishment and to reinforce, modify, or revise goals as circumstances dictate, is saying to those individuals that what they are doing is important, has meaning, and enjoys support.

A second approach is to employ strategies for improving motivational climate through *planned* managerial action. Key to this approach is the recognition that few managers commend their people for as many actions as they could. Strategies that employ a variety of techniques to commend positive actions can gradually create a climate in which there is substantially more motivation (that is, the climate is perceived as rewarding because it helps bring greater satisfaction of psychological needs).

These strategies as well as the goals-review approach are discussed in chapters 4 and 5 and should be carefully studied by the academic manager seeking to deal with the issue of rewards and sanctions. The point to be made here is that it is not sufficient to rely on existing tangible reward and sanction mechanisms. If one wishes to be successful in "enhancing the intellectual climate," one also must develop and maintain new systems.

Contract Interpretation: It was suggested earlier that the chief academic officer was likely to have little influence on matters of salary and benefits, since these were likely to be part of a contract package negotiated without his or her input. However, today's contracts ordinarily address much more than just salary and benefits, and in many instances, the options available to the chief academic officer for dealing with academic personnel are likely to have been predetermined through a contract that the academic manager may have had little if any knowledge about until its actual signing. This may be especially true in colleges and universities where a contract is negotiated at the state level for an entire system of higher education.[5] Such contracts may address teaching loads, scheduling, nonteaching assignments, procedures and policies for disbursement of special funds (such as funds for professional development), and any number of other academic issues for which the chief academic officer is nominally responsible.

Contract interpretation, therefore, is becoming an increasingly important responsibility of many chief academic officers. While it is often the case that the academic manager is not involved in negotiations or in the settlement of disputes, the very nature of the position requires that the chief academic officer be well versed on what is permitted by the contract, what is not permitted, and what is not addressed. Chief academic officers who fail to be so well versed, and who fail to find ways to function within the boundaries of the contract, are likely to find themselves spending a great deal of their time trying to manage problems these failures have created rather than addressing their intended responsibilities: enhancing the intellectual climate and providing the "academic conscience."

One may ask whether it is indeed possible to maintain a concern for the intellectual climate within the "labor-management" context that contracts appear to be creating and whether it is not more reasonable to devote one's energies essentially to management, forgetting the intellectual mission. No doubt this is reasonable; yet, as was pointed out earlier in this chapter, individuals who presently hold positions as chief academic officers seemed to readily accept this dual responsibility and felt that successful management increased their chances for success in enhancing the intellectual climate. The question that might better be asked is: "If the chief academic officer does not choose to serve as the academic conscience of an institution, then why have a chief academic officer, why not simply have a foreman?'' Unlike managers in most other settings, the academic manager has a particularly unique role because of the concern with being an academic conscience. Removal of that concern robs the position of its uniqueness. A recent example of this concern at work was in the 1979-1981 contract negotiations between the New Jersey Federation of Teachers (state colleges) and the state. One item proposed involved the selection of texts and how this was to be done. This was perceived by many as an academic-freedom issue and not something that should be an item for negotiations. While the item was eventually removed, its original inclusion and ensuing discussions certainly served to highlight the challenge of being both an academic conscience and an academic manager.

While this dual responsibility makes the role perhaps more difficult and challenging than some other managerial roles, it is also one of the things that serves to make the role so rewarding for many. To be successful as the academic conscience, it helps to be successful as a manager, and this involves being successful as an interpreter of the contract.

Academic Support Systems

In most institutions of higher education, the chief academic affairs officer bears responsibility for a number of academic support systems. This number will vary depending on institutional size and the organizational structure of a given college or university. For purposes of this discussion, four academic support systems will be considered: library and instructional resources, grants and foundations, data recall, and evaluation and research services.

Library and Instructional Resources: Perhaps the most visible and crucial academic support system on any campus is the library and accompanying instructional resource centers. Whenever an accreditation visit takes place, this segment of the college receives particularly close scrutiny. Evaluators concern themselves with the number of holdings, the range and variety of holdings, the acquisition process, the distribution of materials, usage made by students, ready availability of personnel and services, fiscal support, and so forth. The chief academic officer who takes the role of "academic conscience" seriously will pay close heed to the management of the library and its accompanying instructional resource centers. This area of the college, perhaps more than any other, symbolizes the importance given to the "enhancement of intellectual mission." However, in times of fiscal constraints, it is also an area particularly vulnerable to reductions in support.

The prudent chief academic officer must therefore be especially cognizant of program priorities, needed instructional resources for those programs, ways of becoming more cost-effective in the provision of library service, and so forth if rational and intelligent decisions are to be made regarding the management of this resource.

Grants and Foundations: The nominal responsibility for procurement and management of funds secured through grants and foundations often may be assigned to someone other than the chief academic affairs officer.[6] However, such funds are very often sought in order to provide additional fiscal resources to directly support the academic mission of the institution, and in those situations (if not all others), the chief academic officer must play a central role. Funds secured through grants and foundations often make possible the development and initiation of new or proposed program areas that the institution could not support fully from its own resources. Such funds also may be used to strengthen existing program areas, to explore the feasibility of developing programs and services, to conduct needed research, to free existing resources for other uses, to purchase instructional resources, and for a variety of other purposes to "enhance the intellectual climate."

As the traditional sources of funding are becoming recognized as insufficient for accomplishment of their institutions' goals, greater numbers of chief academic officers are seeking grant and foundation money. In so doing, they also are learning that securing such funds is not an entirely unmixed blessing. One must commit a minimal amount of internal resources to secure these new external resources; a particular grant may make demands the institution is unprepared to meet; a grant may not always provide exactly what the institution is seeking for a particular development; new collaborations with their accompanying problems may have to occur; and new management practices within the institution may have to be developed. These are some of the considerations that must be made when external funding is sought. If the academic managers of the institution are knowledgeable of existing resources and clear on goals and priorities, decisions regarding what kinds of external funding should be sought and when and where it should be sought will be made with greater dispatch and with improved rationale.

Data Recall: Preparation of grant proposals, development of budgets, completion of evaluation reports, composition of planning documents—these are but a few of many examples that might be cited to illustrate the importance of data recall. The chief academic affairs officer simply cannot perform efficiently some of the expected tasks unless there is available complete and accurate data that can be quickly recalled. Most institutions of any size have a data processing center or have access to some type of data processing service. While there may be institutions in which the director of data processing reports to the chief academic officer, one suspects that this is not a widespread practice—nor is it suggested here that it should be. However, the chief academic affairs officer should have ready access to the institution's data processing service, and the needs of academic affairs should have an established high priority.

The data processing center is an important resource that quite likely serves many areas of the organization—student services, fiscal affairs, and building and plant management. However, it is viewed here as an academic support system because of the crucial role it can play in academic planning and academic program evaluation. Therefore, serious attention must be given to the tasks assigned to data processing, to the priorities assigned, and to the management and efficiency of the center. If varied examples of the adage proposed earlier were to be given (that is, "that one was more likely to enjoy a modicum of success in enhancing the intellectual climate if one enjoyed success in managing available resources toward that end"), management of data recall and the *subsequent appropriate use* of data might well serve as examples of a resource that probably has more potential uses than has yet been realized. For example, apropos of the earlier discussion in this chapter on rewards and sanctions, "Who gets what data, when, and on what basis?" is a series of questions that must be addressed, and if adversarial relationships are the norm in the institution, the answers given will be perceived as rewards or sanctions. A managerial plan for reducing adversarial relationships will ask those questions relative to agreed upon goals and priorities, will insist that there be some complementary connection between data requests and the goals and priorities, and will insist on regularly scheduled open sharing of data. Over time, this should reinforce a positive motivational climate.

Evaluation and Research Services: The chief academic affairs officer who does not give at least a passing thought each day to required evaluations and needed research must surely be a rare individual. One suspects this is especially true of academic managers who serve in public tax-supported institutions. As the demand for accountability (however defined) grows, it seems the number of evaluation and accreditation visits grow. There have long existed certain expected evaluations such as those for regional accreditations, state approvals, or national professional association approvals, but to these have been added approvals by state departments or bureaus, evaluations of proposed programs by state agencies or professional groups, mandated local evaluation schemes, and so forth.[7] These also have been accompanied by increasing demands for data about the institutions that must be collected and reported to various agencies and in varying formats.

Depending on the size, scope, and importance of a particular project, varied commitments of internal resources must be made. To cope with the situation, many colleges and universities have established an office of institutional research and evaluation. The nominal responsibility for such an office is frequently given to the chief academic affairs officer, who calls on this office to conduct such research about the institution as will be needed for preparation of reports, planning, evaluation studies, and so forth. Therefore, it is a major academic support system that should provide the academic manager with needed information, technical assistance, flexibility and prerogatives.

To the extent that the staff members of this office are aware of evaluation and research needs, institutional goals and priorities, and have the technical competence and resources to carry out their tasks, the office will provide a valuable resource to the chief academic affairs officer and relieve him or her of major burdens in evaluation and research studies. In fact, if well enough managed, such an office might at least partially resolve the following complaint, which is heard with some degree of frequency: "Evaluations are coming so fast and furious that I cannot put into effect any of the recommendations from the last team of evaluators before the next team of evaluators arrives." For example, external program evaluators seem to invariably recommend that there should be follow-up studies conducted on a program's graduates and that curriculum revisions should reflect the results of those studies. This is a recommendation of considerable merit and should not be taken lightly. However, as the institution undertakes to respond to this recommendation for Program X, it is likely also to be undertaking the preparation of an evaluation report for Program Y, which assumes priority. Consequently, the recommendations for Program X may not be attended to until Program X is to undergo its next evaluation. However, a well-managed office of instructional research and evaluation can alleviate the situation by putting into place systematic routine follow-up study mechanisms that can be adjusted to fit particular programmatic needs as required.

Curriculum and Instruction

Thus far attention has been given to the importance of planning, policies, and procedures in the management of resources as a means of "enhancing intellectual climate." While one might argue that curriculum and instruction might better be thought of as factors in the intellectual climate rather than resources, they are in one sense the most important resources of the institution. The academic programs an institution offers and the quality of instruction it ensures for those programs, perhaps more than anything else, establishes the reputation of the institution, and reputation can be an important factor in whether the institution thrives, survives, or dies. Chief academic affairs officers are fully cognizant of this, which is no doubt one reason why they look upon themselves as "academic consciences," and why so much of their time is spent with planning, policies, and procedures pertaining to curriculum and instruction.

Development: Development of new academic programs and of faculty to teach in those programs is a constant challenge to academic managers. In present circumstances of fiscal constraints and declining enrollments, it is especially challenging. Since few new fiscal resources are likely to be forthcoming, and since there is no longer a large number of students eagerly awaiting an opportunity to enter any programs the institution can conceive, much more careful attention must be given to the programs selected for development, to the potential clientele, and to the potential faculties of the programs. Chief academic affairs officers have the responsibility of making this message understood by all involved parties.

Implementation: Once a program has been developed and approved, the chief academic officer has a chance to put to use all his or her acumen as a manager of resources in order to implement. So long as this meant securing new positions, securing new clerical and administrative assistance, and securing new educational and/or office equipment, the principal task was that of making certain that the growth budget was sufficient to do all these things. This was no easy task, and the individual who was 100 percent successful in completing that task probably does not exist. However, the situation is further compounded today. Rather than securing all new resources, the academic manager is more likely going to have to transfer existing positions and personnel, negotiate for shared space, borrow temporary clerical assistance, lend administrative assistance, and make do with surplus educational and office equipment. In the best of circumstances for implementation, conflicts are likely to occur, and the basic principle of attaining organizational goals while satisfying individual needs is likely to be difficult. In today's circumstances, however, opportunity for even more conflicts appears likely. Academic managers at all levels must realize this and be prepared to deal with it (see appendix A for a discussion of conflict resolution). The chief academic officer must expedite this understanding.

Evaluation: In today's world it is not enough to develop and implement a program, it also must be evaluated. Documents prepared as proposals for the development of a program ordinarily include a section discussing the who, what, when, and how of evaluation. Such evaluations ordinarily call for assessments of the following: the curriculum, the students, the faculty and quality of instruction, pertinent administrative services, available resources, and any other appropriate considerations. If the chief academic affairs officer has managed through the office of institutional research and evaluation to put into place an evaluation program that has been accepted as a routine operating procedure, the evalution task will be much easier, and the collection of data for such evaluations will be considerably less time consuming.

Acceptance of a positive operating procedure for evaluations is seen as extremely important, for whether a newly developed and implemented program is going to be permitted to continue and to receive its fair share of available resources or whether a faculty member is to be retained depends on the outcome of an evaluation. Consequently, evaluations are not exactly emotion free; but to the degree that they have been accepted as expected routine, the emotional context may be reduced and a sense of proportion maintained.

Results of evaluations are, of course, also extremely important to the chief academic affairs officer, for they provide valuable data and may suggest future directions. They can, for instance, provide indicators as to what impacts a particular program is having on other areas of the college and whether they are desirable given the agreed upon goals and priorities; they can suggest the amount and kind of resources that may be required to further develop, sustain, or revise a particular program and help determine whether those resources should be committed; and they may bring to light unanticipated or unplanned for effects that must be considered in future planning. Evaluation results should be used as an important resource in planning and policy development by the academic manager.

Revision: Evaluations of a program, whether done by internal or external evaluators and whether done of a long-standing or newly implemented program, are likely to conclude with a series of recommendations that calls for some modification or revision of the program. These can be perceived by the chief academic affairs officer and other academic managers as helpful recommendations that provide an opportunity to perhaps revise not only the program directly affected, but complementary programs as well. These recommendations also can be perceived as so much nonsense requiring a lot of busy work that one would rather not address. The chief academic affairs officer's responsibility is to have in place procedures that make revisions possible without undue delay or frustration and to also have in place procedures by which academic managers can determine whether the recommended revisions are indeed worth making—especially when examined in view of institutional missions.

It is often easier to revise an existing program to meet changing needs than it is to develop a new one. The chief academic officer who takes seriously the role of "academic conscience" will no doubt devote a great deal of time to the creation and revision of policies and procedures that bear upon the development, implementation, evaluation, and revision of curriculum and instructional practices, especially as these are likely to impact on the achievement of agreed upon goals and priorities.

Significant Others Involved in Academic Management

The chief academic affairs officer must work with a number of other officers with respect to general affairs of the college or university (for example, chief fiscal officer and student affairs officer), but the greatest portion of time is probably consumed in working with groups and individuals significantly involved in academic management. Depending on the size and organizational complexity of the particular institution, the titles and positions will vary; however, for ease in writing, the discussion here will use the titles deans, directors, and department chairpersons. Attention also will be given to the role of committees and the role of the individual expert in academic management.

Deans and Directors

Individuals who most frequently work closely with the chief academic affairs officer on matters pertaining to academic management are likely to be the academic deans of the various schools or academic divisions within the institution, the directors of the various academic divisions within the institution, and the directors of the various academic support systems. In a line/staff organizational arrangement, most of these individuals probably report directly to the chief academic affairs officer. The responsibilities of these academic managers are not unlike those of the chief academic officer—only the scope of responsibilities is less and is likely to be somewhat more narrowly focused on particular and specific academic areas.

Academic Deans: Academic deans, who bear responsibility for the academic management of their schools or academic divisions, like the chief academic officer, must be concerned with preparation of a budget and its use as a planning tool, and they must determine how best to allocate the resources they receive for their schools or divisions. Their involvement with the academic personnel within their schools is likely to be more direct, intense, and of a more enduring nature than the involvement of the chief academic affairs officer; therefore, they are particularly concerned with policies and procedures pertaining to recruitment, assignment and deployment, development, rewards and sanctions, and contract interpretation.

In most situations, academic deans also are held responsible for the curriculum and instruction within their schools, and they are expected to see to the development, implementation, evaluation, and revision of their curricular programs and instructional practices. Again, their involvement is likely to be more direct, intense, and of a more enduring nature than that of the chief academic affairs officer, who is likely to be concerned with what happens at the school or division level to the extent that it impacts on the total college program.

If the goals and priorities of the college or university in general are relatively clear, this should make the job of the academic deans somewhat easier, for the responsibility now becomes one of setting school goals and priorities that complement those of the institution at large. Once this is done, the dean must then manage the resources available in a fashion that will permit movement toward the school's goals while at the same time satisfying the personal and professional needs of the individuals in the school or division.

As a case in point, assume that development of programs in allied health, human and social services, and administrative sciences has been established and agreed upon as institutional goals. The role of the school dean now becomes one of seeing that programmatic goals that permit movement toward this larger goal are set. A reasonable school goal in this case might be to develop a program in public administration. If this becomes a school goal, then departments and divisions within the school could be expected to set goals that would complement it. Department chairpersons could be expected to work with their faculties to set goals for course development and revision, for staff development as necessary, for allocation of resources, and so forth—all to initiate and implement a program in public administration.

The preceding scenario assumes that there is clarity about the goals, that the various sectors of the college are reasonably clear about their prime areas of responsibility (that is, which schools are to develop which program), and that existing policies and procedures are such that movement may take place without underlying stress. Unfortunately, it is rarely this simple. Few organizations are or can be completely clear about agreed upon goals. Consequently, mixed messages are received that make the process of planning at the school level more difficult and the plans themselves more subject to modification or reversal. When this occurs, especially if the existing policies and procedures are at all rigid, management of available resources becomes particularly subject to "stops and starts" and causes the casual onlooker to wonder if there is any academic management occuring.

For example, let us return to the situation just described. What is human and social service? What is administrative science? Does a program in public administration complement both these areas? Assuming it does, where does prime responsibility for it reside? Which aspects of the program get primary attention—human and social service aspects or administrative science aspects? If a lot of crossover between these aspects seems in order, can this be developed and implemented through existing policies and procedures, or will some new vehicle need to be created? These are but a few of the questions that might be anticipated given the previous scenario. If the chief academic officer, the academic deans, and department chairpersons are all giving different answers then the casual onlooker has real cause to wonder if any academic management is occurring. However, if they have the same answers that have been openly arrived at and agreed upon, the onlooker might question the answers, but not whether management is occurring.

Directors of Academic Support Systems: Directors of academic support systems bear the responsibility for the management of their divisions in a fashion that will provide support services effectively and efficiently when and where needed. Like deans, they are concerned with the preparation of a budget and the allocation of resources. Each also has responsibility for a professional staff and is naturally concerned with policies and procedures likely to affect working with that staff in ways that permit satisfaction of personal and professional needs while working toward organizational goals.

These policies and procedures will vary depending on whether an institution is in the public or private sector; but in the public sector, with which this writer is most familiar, non teaching professional staff appear to have a very limited tangible reward system designed to satisfy personal and professional needs. There is no promotion system comparable to that for the teaching faculty; promotion as such comes about through position reclassification, which may mean rather dramatic changes in functions performed. Available promotions may be difficult to secure; bitter competition often occurs between applicants for an open position of higher classification. No sabbatical-leave system comparable to that for faculty exists for directors of support units, and there is no system for overload comparable to that provided for faculty. (Nonteaching professionals can be paid overload for teaching, but not for doing overload work in their assigned function.) Since the system itself provides so little in the form of tangible rewards, it becomes crucial for directors of the academic support services to be especially conscious of finding ways for personnel to find more self-realization in their work. The strategies for improving motivational climate that were previously discussed in this chapter and in chapter 5 should particularly be considered.

Overall organizational goals and priorities are particularly important to directors of academic support services, for these provide clues as to how to manage their available resources, particularly in times of peak demand. In a typical organizational structure, directors of academic support systems serve as staff *for* the academic deans, but not as staff *to* the academic deans. Thus it is possible for several demands to be made on a support system by more than one academic dean within the same period. Without some established priorities or some agreed upon system for establishing priorities, a director in this situation may find that (1) services are overused, creating real problems within the division; (2) services are not used at all because of fear of overuse, and the division is not fulfilling its function; and, (3) he or she makes what are considered arbitrary decisions, satisfying no one.

Any director of an academic service is likely to face this, but directors of data processing often seem to find themselves in this dilemma. It was previously noted that the data processing center ordinarily serves many areas of the organization, and as each area makes its demands, the director may find that the center simply cannot always respond in time, creating problems for those it is trying to service and creating problems among the center staff for demanding too much. Consequently, some areas that might have legitimate demands to make of the center may choose not to bother and will instead try to do what they can with their own resources. Thus the center may not be fulfilling its assigned function. However, if these same areas make their demands, this forces the director to make an arbitrary decision about who gets serviced when. Part of this decision might be predicated by the organizational structure, that is, to whom does the director report, and if it is not the chief academic officer, academic management's data needs may receive a lower priority than other management needs. Suggestions for dealing with this dilemma through appropriate goal setting have already been made.

Inasmuch as academic support systems are important resources, meant to be used, academic managers must work out ways for sharing these resources in order that they might be fully utilized. The simpler the sharing system devised, the more likely it will be one that works effectively.

Department Chairpersons

In the typical college or university academic organizational structure, the department chairperson tends to occupy a position having considerable managerial responsibility, but not a great deal of authority. In the matter of managing available resources, it is the chairperson who is perhaps most directly involved in the active management of resources. This is to say, it falls on the shoulders of the department chairperson to make certain that the resources granted the department are deployed in such a way that the daily operation continues at the expected level and that movement toward the goals and objectives of the department and the college takes place. For instance, if given primary responsibility for developing the program in public administration discussed previously, the department chairperson would find it necessary to work with his or her faculty in setting and achieving goals for

1. Determining what a graduate of such a program should "look like" and why
2. Reviewing program standards and requirements, especially as they impact on what is desired of graduates
3. Preparing program documents
4. Determining staff needs for the program
5. Determining student needs
6. Preparing strategies for securing approval of the program

The department's achievement of these goals means that the school will achieve its goal of getting a program in public administration, which is a piece of the broader programmatic goals of the institutions previously noted.

While expediting work on these goals as well as others established by the department, such as goals for departmental staff development and for student enrollment, the department chairperson must still ensure that all classes are covered, that necessary teaching materials and supplies are readily available, that clerical support services for the faculty are provided, and that needed equipment is in a state of good repair. In today's world of stabilized and/or diminishing resources, this is likely to mean that the department chairperson is expected to actually "do more with less." As the academic manager most openly, closely, and directly involved in on-the-line activity, the department chairperson is perhaps the individual most subject to directly receiving complaints and criticism from the staff.

It seems obvious that when decisions have to be made that lend themselves to being seen as rewards for one faculty member and sanctions for another, the department chairperson is going to be seen as "the heavy" by at least one of the parties involved. For the department chairperson, this is inevitably a no-win situation. This situation particularly seems to arise during the preparation of teaching schedules, a major responsibility of the department chairperson. Ordinarily there are a few written policies, such as no one may teach both an 8 A.M. and an 8 P.M. class on the same day, but these are at best the briefest of guides. In addition, and perhaps more important, there are a number of unwritten traditions (these will vary depending on which individual the chairperson is conferring with). These traditions have to do with what hours of the week Professor X teaches, what room is his or hers, and other crucial matters that are to be considered when preparing the schedule. If a chairperson can prepare a schedule that satisfies all the published policies, the individual traditions, particular situational needs, and student demands once in a 5-year span, he or she is probably extremely lucky. Typically, one or all of these things will come into conflict, and it falls on the chairperson to resolve the conflict. In resolving it, someone is not going to receive the desired schedule or at least some piece of the desired schedule. That person is likely to perceive the schedule as a sanction, especially if it occurs repeatedly, and that same person is going to perceive the faculty member who got the desired schedule as being rewarded (even through the "rewarded" faculty may perceive it as a perquisite, not a reward). Obviously, it need not be as bad as described here, especially if some of the suggestions made earlier for handling rewards and sanctions are put into practice.

The chairperson's role as an academic manager is further complicated by the fact that in many, if not most, institutions of higher education, chairpersons are not defined as academic managers, nor do they all necessarily wish to be. As colleges and universities have entered into collective bargaining and negotiated contracts and the distinction between management (academic administration) and labor (faculty and nonteaching professional staff) has been made, the disposition of the chair's role has frequently been especially difficult to resolve. The reason for this, one suspects, is quite simple. Chairpersons are managers because of the many management functions they must perform, but they are also faculty. Most teach and do research, and many are selected (or elected, as determined by the existing traditional practice) as chairpersons more for their academic renown than for any recognized management ability. The chairperson's role, therefore, is a particularly ambiguous one. He or she is expected to perform duties of a manager (administrator), but long-standing traditions and practices identify him or her with labor (faculty). This traditional identification is one that many chairpersons do not wish to relinquish. Consequently, it is not uncommon to find, even in institutions of higher education where collective bargaining has been an established practice for some time, that department chairpersons are considered members of the bargaining unit, that is, faculty/labor and not members of administration/management.

Given this situation, the chairperson who cherishes faculty identification is not likely to relish performing management tasks that may demand making decisions on the allocation of scarce resources, which in turn may have adverse affects on long-time colleagues and friends with whom he or she works daily. As a consequence, decisions that should be made and actions that should be taken at the department level may be "bumped" back up to the dean's level, and the dean may become more involved in the day-to-day management of the school or academic division than is appropriate—particularly if long-range goals are to be accomplished.

Various attempts at finding ways out of this dilemma have been made. One, obviously, is to try, at the time of negotiations, to clearly identify department chairpersons as management by definition, thus removing them from the bargaining unit and to that extent removing identification as faculty. Another is to simply eliminate the position of department chairperson through reorganization and consolidation of various academic units, each new unit to be administered by an academic manager, clearly identified and defined as such, for example, assistant dean, associate director, and so forth. These two solutions may help in defining and distinguishing chairpersons' roles concerning management versus labor, but they may bring with them numerous other problems that are quite delicate: the first because it may be difficult to find and retain chairpersons who wish to be perceived primarily as managers; the second because it may entail organizational restructuring and all its accompanying problems; both because they may be perceived as heavy-handed intrusions. In addition, depending on the context of the situation, these simply may not be viable solutions in many institutions.

Therefore, ways must be found that will permit department chairpersons to fulfill their roles as academic managers, while at the same time retaining their identification as faculty and their credibility with all colleagues (administration and faculty). The chief academic officer faced with finding these ways would be well advised to dedicate resources to managerial development, making it possible for all academic managers, but particularly department chairpersons, to participate in management-development programs that will provide them the skills and knowledge necessary for aiding their faculties to find greater self-realization within the organization and at the same time have more opportunity to find greater self-realization themselves. The chief academic officer also might be well advised to review the Johari window (see chapter 5) and related concepts of self-disclosure and feedback. He or she may find this useful in directly working with chairpersons to resolve the ambiguities in the role.

Department chairpersons want to be good academic managers; they want to see movement toward college goals; and they want to retain their identification as academicians. In essence, this is also what the chief academic affairs officer and the deans desire—the difference is in the degree of emphasis placed on each of these wants and the degree of perceived supervisor, peer, and colleague pressure regarding each want.

One suspects that it may not be possible to completely resolve all these contending wants to everyone's satisfaction, but the contention here is that department chairpersons who are familiar with the Linking Elements Concept will not only come to better understand and deal with their own conflicts, but also will be better able to assist their department members in finding ways to satisfy personal needs while working toward organizational goals.

Committees

It was previously suggested that the control and influence of the chief academic officer is limited by his or her ability to work with others to plan and implement policies and procedures. In present-day college governance systems much of this work can be accomplished through committees. The chief academic officer will likely work with all-college committees, but committees exist at all levels, and academic managers must devote time and attention to them. Committees are not strictly academic managers, for they ordinarily are not held responsible for the management of available resources. Yet they can and do influence the policies and procedures for resource management. Each institution has a committee structure that is unique to its own needs. However, most could be placed within one of the following categories of committees: planning, curriculum, personnel, and support services.

Planning Committee: The committee that has the potential for exerting greatest influence on the future direction of the institution is, in most instances, the planning committee. This body, usually an all-college committee, ordinarily is charged with reviewing mission statements, long- and short-range goals and objectives, and the proposed use of resources. One of the greatest sources of power that this (and for that matter, any other) committee has is likely to be its power to delay and block, depending on how the committee is structured and developed. If the committee is structured to be representative of the various college constituencies and each member perceives herself or himself as a representative of a particular interest group, it may be hard for the committee to be anything other than a blocking agent (see Perrow's analysis of interest groups on page 166), for it will be difficult to reach consensus and agreement on specific objectives and plans that are likely to have negative impacts on any of the interest groups represented. One suspects that this is why the mission statements approved by such a group often tend to be so broad and vague. They are written that way so that no one can disagree with them.

Therefore, it is crucial that academic managers find ways to work with such a committee to make it a mover rather than a blocker. This means that academic managers who work with the planning committee must find ways to reconcile individual and interest-group needs with the needs and goals of the institution at large—not an easy task, but one that must be accomplished. A first step in doing this, one would argue, is that of helping the committee members determine for themselves that they are, when serving on the committee, serving in the role of academic managers who must make recommendations regarding the *best use* of available resources for the *total institution*. This can partially be done by the way the committee is structured at the outset, but it is more likely to be done through the establishment of norms for committee work and the development of a supportive climate within the committee.

If a planning committee is to be a mover rather than a blocker, academic managers responsible for or to that committee must be very concerned with both the content of the task and the process of the group's working. Too much attention to content to the detriment of process is likely to lead to blocking. Too much attention to process to the detriment of content is likely to lead to no work being done. The academic manager can play a crucial role in helping the committee define its role in academic management. That role will be negative or positive, depending on the academic manager's skill.

Curriculum Committees: Curriculum committees play a crucial role as the action committees for moving toward program goals. While the planning committee may exert considerable influence on the actual development of goals, curriculum committees can expedite the movement toward these goals by the way they choose to move, veto, delay, or block. Ordinarily, academic managers serve on these committees—often ex officio, but sometimes as voting members. Depending on the complexity of the organization, the curriculum committee process can present a maze that will challenge even the most ardent of movers. Further, in the instance of curriculum, the opportunity for delay or blocking on behalf of small group interest is even greater than on the planning committee, since curriculum committees tend to exist at all levels. Therefore, everything that has previously been said regarding the crucial role of the academic manager on the planning committee holds equally true in the case of curriculum committees.

Personnel Committees: Personnel committees, like curriculum committees, can play a crucial role as action committees for moving toward program goals. While their function may be somewhat less directly connected in this regard, they can and do exert considerable influence on the appointment, transfer, retention, tenuring, and rewarding of professional personnel. Through involvement in these processes, personnel committees can make the assignment and deployment decisions that will help make the accomplishment of particular goals difficult or easy.

Personnel committees ordinarily exist at more than one level, but when major academic manager appointments are in question, the common practice is to create a committee charged with seeking out and recommending probable appointees. Search committees of this latter type can play a tremendous role in determining future directions of an institution. In these instances, committee members need to understand that they are involved with securing a principal resource, and that they should have some understanding of the role and functions of an academic manager—especially in accomplishing goals. Unfortunately, too often such committees are structured and charged not on the basis of the individual member's understanding of the institution's goals and the skills required for moving toward them, but rather on the basis of satisfying particular, immediate interest-group needs.[8] Such committees can still be successful (and often are), but assurance that search committees or other personnel committees are to be movers rather than blockers can be given only if attention is paid by someone to the content of the task and the process of the group's working, as was suggested earlier.

Support Services Committees: Support services committees may be described as committees established to advise, deliberate, and recommend on matters of particular interest to various academic support groups. Committees on admissions standards, retention of students, library services, and so forth might be viewed as support service committees. Generally, such committees are likely to have less direct influence on the accomplishment of institutional goals then the three committees previously discussed, but they serve an important function in academic management, especially in the day-to-day routine. Often they can serve to assist in the development of policies and procedures that can alleviate managerial problems. Such committees are therefore particularly important to the academic manager. They can provide a vehicle for initiating desired practices, or they can become time- and energy-consuming groups that appear to accomplish little or delay accomplishment. The direction they go is no doubt determined to a great extent by the importance assigned to their function, by the skills of the members, and by the academic manager's skill in working with them.

All committees—support services, personnel, curriculum, and planning—have the potential for making academic management easier. Too often they do not live up to this potential. In most instances, committees are intended to provide a means for constituencies to participate in matters of major import. They are of necessity, however, comprised of proxy delegates from the various constituencies—a role that is not perhaps as well understood as it should be either by the delegates or the constituencies they are presumed to be representing. One concept that seems little understood and rarely discussed is that the delegate to the committee is also a delegate of the committee to his or her constituency. That is to say that the delegate not only is responsible for making known the position of his or her constituency to the committee, but the delegate also has a corresponding responsibility of making known to the constituency institutional positions as reflected by this representative committee.

Committee members are likely to become more effective if this role awareness is developed and if basic procedures are emphasized and acted on. Inasmuch as a great deal of an academic manager's time may be consumed in committee activity, it behooves that manager to provide opportunity for committee members to learn how to work together and to understand the importance of liaison. To the extent that this can be done, the academic manager may be able to begin to reconcile individual and small-interest-group needs within the committee with the needs of the institution at large.

Individuals as Centers of Influence

In the discussion thus far, three impact levels on academic management have been addressed:

1. The full-time managers or academic managers in the definitive sense, that is, the chief academic officer, academic deans, and directors of support services, all of whom identify with and are identified as management
2. The sometime managers, that is, department chairpersons, who perform many management functions but frequently are identified with or as faculty (nonmanagement)
3. The centers of influence, that is, committees that perform no management functions, do not identify with and are not identified as management, but nevertheless work with management and play crucial roles in the accomplishment or nonaccomplishment of institutional objectives

To this third impact level, one final piece should be added—the individual centers of influence, that is, those individuals who are nonmanagers, but who as individuals tend to exert influence for good or ill. If there is not an open climate in the organization, much of this influence is likely to be "ill," for it will be *sub rosa* in nature and perceived as such, unnecessarily adding fuel to any fires of gossip regarding the inexplicable way decisions are made.

However, if an open climate exists in the organization, opportunity for individuals to exert good influence will be enhanced. In essence, what is being suggested here is that the astute academic manager is familiar with all available resources, and these include individuals who have expertise and skills that may be valuable and needed in given circumstances to move toward particular goals. The individual should be able to offer this expertise and the academic manager should be able to accept it or call on it when needed without such action being perceived as an "end run." In an open climate, where the individual's expertise is acknowledged and it is recognized that expertise is being appropriately utilized (that is, where the expert on public relations is asked to work on a public relations activity not arbitrate a dispute between the public information office and an academic department), this can be done.

During the period that the individual's expertise is being utilized, that individual is a center of influence in a particular area, but the influence does not extend beyond that area and ends with the resolution of the problem. The successful academic manager, therefore, will discourage any attempts at *sub rosa* influence by individuals and will make full use of an individual's expertise to move toward institutional goals, openly acknowledging the individual's influence in those circumstances.

Achieving Academic Goals

Throughout the preceding discussion of those involved in academic management, the importance of having clear complementary and congruent goals has certainly been implied, if not made completely explicit. One message was that "enhancement of intellectual climate," an overriding goal for those involved in academic affairs, was sometimes likely to be lost sight of in dealing with day-to-day operations and in trying to reconcile particular needs and goals of interest groups and individuals—especially in times of diminishing resources. It was further suggested that the academic manager who was familiar with the Linking Elements Concept and who had acquired skills in achieving balance between the needs of people and of an organization was likely to encounter fewer difficulties in this regard than might otherwise be the case.

Understanding the concept of a goals hierarchy is a crucial step in working with the linking elements. A thorough discussion of this and other goal concepts was provided in chapter 4, and there is no need to repeat that discussion here. However, a reminder at this point seems in order—especially as it relates to academic goals.

Philosophical Goals: Philosophical, or broad mission, goals play an important function in the life of an institution of higher education. Establishment of and agreement on the institution's philosophical goals serves to set a direction and contribute toward the feeling tone or climate perceived within the institution. "Enhancement of the intellectual climate," as has been noted before, is accepted by academic managers, indeed by most academicians, as a philosophical goal and, in its broadest sense, is generally taken to encompass support of teaching, research, and community services—three terms one is likely to find mentioned in an institution's mission statement. To bring meaning to this philosophical goal, however, entails the development and establishment of programs that contribute toward achieving it.

Strategic Goals: Strategic goals, for purposes of this discussion, are the intermediate and long-range goals that are established to assist in moving toward the broader mission just noted. These further define direction, give meaning to the mission, and are especially useful in planning. Agreement on strategic goals, however, is likely to be much more difficult to achieve than agreement on philosophical goals. At this level, decisions on goal priorities become determiners for the distribution of available resources, which, of course, is a major concern, but it is also at this level that quite justifiably different views among the various groups and individuals of the college surface and must be reconciled. It is also at this level that committees often tend to play a particularly crucial role, especially planning committees, curriculum committees, and academic support service committees. Moreover, the academic manager who has not acquired skills in working with committees in balancing diverse needs and wants may encounter considerable difficulty in establishing and implementing strategic goals.

Operational Goals

Operational goals are those established for the purpose of achieving the agreed upon strategic goals. These, as was pointed out in chapter 4, can be both long- and short-range goals, but describe ends to be achieved. Working with operational goals, and the action steps necessary to accomplish them, is probably where the academic manager (at whatever level) devotes the greatest amount of time and energy. As in the case with strategic goals, it may be very difficult to achieve agreement on the operational goals themselves, not to mention the action steps.

Employing EQIFAPPO: A fairly typical example of the difficulties that can be encountered in an academic goals program is that of resolving the general education question that many institutions have today. General education is a curriculum issue that appears to resurface periodically. Everyone seems to agree that it is important and that college students should be exposed to the broadening experiences a general education is intended to provide, but few seem to agree on what those specific experiences should be or how they should be provided. Those who have spent the last two decades in any particular institution of higher education have quite likely witnessed a major battle on their campuses to reduce the number of highly specific course requirements in general education. If that battle was won by those favoring a reduction of requirements, it was probably then followed by a number of skirmishes to "free up" the remaining course requirements by providing extensive elective options that could be used to meet any given requirement. If the majority of these skirmishes were won by the "free up" advocates, general education tended to become what each individual student chose to make it.

Now we are beginning to witness skirmishes for reinstituting some required common experiences, and if the reader will forgive all these military metaphors, it would appear that a major battle over general education is once again about to take place on many campuses—if it hasn't already. As institutions reexamine their missions and value orientations, attempt to respond to the demands of external agencies and employers of their graduates, evaluate their students' needs, review their staff resources and strengths, and witness what some of the traditional leaders among institutions of higher education are doing about general education, it becomes an issue that cannot be long avoided.

If the issue is not to be avoided, what might be expected to occur as the issue is addressed at each goals level? Obviously, many scenarios are possible, but something similar to the following would not be too unlikely. With respect to a philosophical goal, it is agreed that it should include a statement affirming that the intellectual climate would be enhanced by a strong general education curriculum. There is wide agreement and little conflict. With respect to a strategic goal, it is agreed that a strong general education curriculum should be developed and should include

Experiences in the humanities

Experiences in the natural sciences

Experiences in the behavioral sciences

Experiences in the communication sciences

Using these broad experiences components, agreement is reached, but not without considerable conflict over the components themselves and what is meant by experiences. Great concern is also expressed about experiences that seem to be omitted or underemphasized, such as exposure to a profession, lack of emphasis on the place of physical education, subsuming of the fine arts, and so forth. Nevertheless, the strategic goal becomes that of putting into place a general education curriculum that includes the agreed upon components.

With respect to operational goals, each of the component areas (schools and academic departments) now has the assignment to develop goals for putting into place its component curriculum for the general education program. At this level, still more conflict may occur—not over the strategic goal necessarily, but over the specific operational goals. Lack of agreement and conflicts over definitions and over which component area gets responsibility for which operational goals and to what extent can be predicted to occur almost without fail. If the institution is fortunate enough to have, in place, a school of humanities, a school of natural sciences, a school of behavioral sciences, and a school of communication sciences, there would tend to be natural assignments, each school having responsibility for developing and achieving operational goals consistent with its respective curriculum component. Even in this ideal situation, there might still be some "turf" questions, but not nearly to the extent that is likely to occur if the organizational structure is (as it is likely to be) foreign to this. Clarity of definitions and responsibility for operational goals is therefore crucial, and to the extent that such clarity can be provided from the outset, conflict may be reduced and valuable time saved. Time spent on clarification at the start will be time saved when action is initiated. Such clarification may itself be an important initial operational goal.

Action steps, of course, would fall on those who have accepted responsibility for the various goals—either for achieving them or for leading a team toward their achievement. Once work starts on the actual action steps, conflict is likely to arise only if there was insufficient definition of operational goals.

Each academic manager, regardless of level, is likely to have to see to the development of operational goals and action steps that build toward the broader strategic goals. In the example just cited, certainly the chief academic affairs officer is going to set operational goals and will want to set operational goals with the academic divisions, academic support services, academic departments, and academic committees that relate to the strategic goal of putting into place a strong general education curriculum containing the agreed upon components.

For instance, in the situation being discussed, the chief academic affairs officer may wish to set some of the following operational goals for his or her own purposes:

1. The college curriculum committee will have developed and adopted by January 1981, a list of 25 definitions and guidelines to be used in the preparation of the general education curriculum proposal.
2. By June 1981, each school within the college will have agreed to their general component assignments and will have in place a mechanism for the development of the school's general education proposal.
3. By January 1982, each school will have developed its general education proposal outlining the curriculum experiences for which the school is to be responsible, noting the personnel resources needed to provide those experiences, and providing a plan of action for securing those resources which takes into account as many alternatives as possible given existing resource constraints.
4. By April 1982, each academic support service will have developed and adapted a plan of action for meeting service needs likely to be generated with a newly adopted curriculum (that is, the library will have a plan for increasing holdings, the grants office will have identified appropriate sources of external funding and developed a plan for securing such funding, the office of institutional research and evaluation will have a model in place for securing data about students in the new curriculum and for evaluating the curriculum staff, and so forth).

These and similar operational goals will help maintain a sense of direction and provide the chief academic officer with something to measure progress toward the broader goal of putting a strong general education curriculum in place.

At the next management level, deans and directors, a similar process of goal setting should take place. As complementary goals to the ones just noted, for example, a school dean might set the following:

1. By March 1981, the department chairpersons will have reviewed the curriculum committee's definitions and guidelines, amended the

schools component assignments, agreed on particular departmental assignments, and put in motion vehicles for carrying out departmental assignments.

2. By October 1981, each department will have developed its component proposal and submitted it for review.
3. By October 1981, each department will have completed an analysis of its personnel resources and strengths concerning general education and will have prepared a series of recommendations concerning the deployment of these personnel.
4. By March 1982, working with the various academic support services, each department will have put into place action plans for appropriately utilizing the support services concerning general education needs.

Given this set of goals, the department chairperson, the next managerial level, can work with his or her faculty in developing complementary goals for the department. The following might be some of an academic department's goals:

1. By October 1981, the department curriculum committee, working with other departments' curriculum committees, will have developed a proposal outlining the experiences to be offered by the departments, including new and revised courses.
2. By October 1981, the department personnel committee, working with other available college resources (for example, the office of institutional research and evaluation) will have completed a study on the personnel strengths of the department concerning general education.
3. By March 1982, the departmental liaisons to the academic support service areas (that is, individuals assigned to work with each service area, such as the library liaison, the instructional resource center liaison, the admissions liaison) will have each completed a service needs assessment.
4. By April 1982, each departmental liaison will have developed an action plan with representatives of the support service areas for meeting the department's service needs.

Obviously, many more examples of operational goals development at each managerial level could be provided. However, these should suffice to make the point that goals can be developed at each level that are complementary and that serve to move toward broader strategic goals; such goals also provide a useful basis for determining action steps and measuring progress. Without belaboring the issue, some of the action steps implied in the operational goals of the chief academic officer, for instance, would be to prepare a charge for the curriculum committee, to secure clerical assistance as needed to prepare the reports called for, to convene the deans and work out rules and procedures for making component assignments, and to convene the directors of support services to clarify what is being asked of them.

Implicit in all this, particularly if a sense of direction and progress is to be maintained, is the importance of review. The chief academic officer will want to periodically review with the academic managers their operational goals and the action steps that are being taken or are to be taken, so that responsibility may be identified and assigned or reassigned. Each of these responsible academic managers also will work to do the same with their staffs. The chief academic affairs officer, however, must see that this is all orchestrated so that each sector remains aware that it is not operating in isolation on goals that belong only to that sector, but is operating in concert on goals that are part of a larger scheme.

At this point, that is, "the review with responsible academic managers," the chief academic affairs officer may find the review most productive if EQIFAPPO is used as a means of systematic analysis. EQIFAPPO was discussed in detail in chapter 4, but a reiteration of the major points here to illustrate its use may aid in elucidating its value.

EQIFAPPO, the reader will recall, is an acronym used to summarize eight potential problem areas in a management by objectives/goals program: (1) *E*xtent of goals setting; (2) *Q*uality of goals and goals statements; (3) *I*nvolvement by managers in the way employees and lower-level managers work toward achievement of their goals; (4) *F*requency of goals reviews; (5) *A*ccountability of subordinates, the basis on which performance will be evaluated; (6) *P*articipation by subordinates, the voice that subordinates have in setting goals that affect them; (7) *P*erformance appraisal/evaluation, the relationship between the goals program and the performance-evaluation process; and (8) *O*perational/developmental goals consideration, where developmental goals for individuals fit into the goals program.

Academic managers who use EQIFAPPO will be asking questions of themselves and of those who report to them that will aid in highlighting desired achievements and obstacles to attaining them. In conducting such analysis and in making decision, it is crucial to remember, however, as is pointed out in the earlier discussion, that consideration must be given to the manager's own capabilities, to the capabilities and competence of subordinates, and to the particular situation. Given these three considerations, the chief academic affairs officer wishing to gain full benefit of the systematic analysis that EQIFAPPO makes possible probably will want to devote some resources to a development program for academic managers. Such a program might well be designed to increase the managers' awareness of the differing capabilities and needs of faculty and staff relative to levels of maturity concerning organizational demands and decisions (see discussion of life-cycle theory of leadership in chapter 4) and increase the managers' own competencies and capabilities in goals development and goals analysis.

Linking Elements in Action: A Case History

EQUIFAPPO analysis serves to highlight the importance of the linking elements, and reference to the importance of understanding and using the Linking Elements Concept has been made throughout this chapter. It was suggested earlier in this book that a fundamental truth underlying the Linking Elements Concept is "that an organizational unit will achieve the highest level of performance that its environment permits if the manager can bring a high level of alignment between the characteristics and needs of the unit and the characteristics and needs of the people in it." For the manager, then, linking elements become "the skills and strategies that a manager must apply so that the organization's needs and the rewards it can supply achieve the greatest possible balance with the characteristics and expectations of the employees."

Five assumptions are central to the Linking Elements Concept and are listed in chapter 1. However, they are of such importance as to bear repeating here, particularly since they will be used to analyze the case study that follows. These assumptions are

1. A manager's actions are shaped by three primary influences: the environment, the people who report to him or her, and the manager's personal characteristics.
2. A person cannot motivate other people, but can only create an environment in which the others can find motivation.
3. Decision-making and communication skills are required for all managerial activities; as these skills are improved, it is likely that other skills will improve as well.
4. A major determinant of success for an organizational unit is the extent to which unit needs are aligned with employee needs and characteristics.
5. There is some measure of validity to the findings of all serious, prominent researchers and theorists, and a comprehensive concept must take these findings into consideration.

To illustrate the principles of the Linking Elements Concept, following is a case history of recent actual events that occurred in a state college of roughly 8,000 full-time equivalent undergraduate students and 375 faculty. It is an institution that serves mostly commuter students, many of whom are first-generation college students interested in acquiring a college degree for

enhancement of employment opportunities. In the past decade its enrollment has moved from predominantly students in professional education to
a roughly equal division of students in liberal arts and sciences, professional
programs other than education, and professional education. The faculty
has undergone a similar change. In presenting this case history, a synopsis
of the event will be provided, followed by an analysis based on principles of
the Linking Elements Concept.

Synopsis: A Team Approach to Faculty Development

A real concern in many institutions of higher education in this time of
diminishing resources is how to maintain a fresh, vibrant teaching faculty
when few new faculty members can be hired. Coupled with this concern is
one of how to best deploy teaching faculty when the expertise of the existing
faculty is likely to be in areas of decline and not in areas of need.

To cope with this problem, institutions are creating a variety of development mechanisms that provide faculty with opportunities to enhance existing skills and expertise or develop new skills and expertise. A problem
that must often be faced in the creation of such a program—at least from
the academic manager's view—is that of gaining acceptance of the goal and
of then gaining acceptance for the program itself. In many instances, such a
program might be viewed with distrust and perceived as the possible vehicle
for conducting unwanted evaluations. This latter perception is especially
likely to occur if the development program is seen as "belonging to management." That is to say that if the program is laid down by management, it
may enjoy considerably less success than if it belongs to all.

This possibility always exists and, in fact, occurred to some exent
relative to a developmental program mandated at the state level and "laid
down by state management" at about the same time the program to be
described was getting underway. That problems of gaining acceptance of
the program to be described here did not occur (or were quite limited) was a
result of goals congruence at the institutional level.

To begin with, at the institution in question, quality of instruction has
always been an important component of the broad mission, and enhancement of the quality of instruction is a widely accepted philosophical goal of
both faculty and administration. Concern for this mission is never far
removed from the minds of leaders at the college, and it seemed to surface
from a number of areas in the mid-1970s. It had become a topic of discussion in the faculty senate, which created an ad hoc committee on instruction; participants in an all-college retreat identified this as an important
priority area and created an "action planning team" to address it; and the
central administration, especially the president, had earlier taken a leadership

role in the establishment of a consortial center of teaching excellence, demonstrating the interest and concern at that level.

With this demonstrably widespread agreement on this philosophical goal and the high interest in doing something that was apparent among many groups and individuals, the concern became one of not losing that impetus. The hope was to use it to establish some strategic and operational goals and to design action steps to address these goals. The all-college retreat and a meeting of interested faculty and staff called by the ad hoc senate committee had provided opportunities for discussion and sharing of information on an informal basis, as well as for the germination of some action and ideas on a purely voluntary basis. An academic dean responsible for support services was present at these meetings and took on the responsibility of serving as an administrative liaison.

The result of this arrangement was a request by the ad hoc committee to the president for support of a development program, but without much detail. The administration's response, following up on ideas from the retreat and from experiences with the center for excellence in college teaching, was a request for a full-blown proposal that would set 3-year (strategic) goals, 1-year (operational) goals, and a plan of action (action steps).

Among some of the caveats of the administration were that it was to be a team-managed activity across schools, that there was to be an academic liaison to service the team (but not direct it), that a mechanism for having a revolving and evolving team had to be provided, and that yearly evaluations and plans of action had to be submitted. The administration made it clear, however, that participation in programs sponsored by the team was voluntary; nothing was to go on the individual's record; confidentiality was to be ensured; and the team, not the administration, was responsible for planning and conducting the program bound only by the budget and established guidelines for expenditures.

The proposal submitted provided the goals statements requested within the caveats of the administration. A strategic goal, for example, was that within 3 years there would be a fully established, operative team (unit) capable of initiating faculty development activities and of responding to individual and unit (that is, school, division, department) requests for development activities. Major operational goals for the first year included creating the development unit, establishing credibility of the unit, raising the consciousness level of the faculty regarding instructional quality and development, and devising mechanisms for the unit's continuation that responded to the administration's caveat on membership. Action steps toward these particular goals included selection and approval of the development team (unit) by the chief academic affairs officer, working with the deans and through the faculty senate. Once this was done, the other goals noted required action by the team members themselves. They planned and delivered an extensive program of developmental activities that included many workshops conducted primarily by outside resources during the first year and mostly by internal resources thereafter, opportunities for faculty members to attend outside seminars, periodic reports on the progress of the program to keep it in the minds of faculty, and peer consultations to interested faculty members.

The activities established the credibility of the team members and raised the consciousness level of faculty—all while addressing the broad philosophical goal of improving the quality of instruction. The team members also devised a plan of action for selecting new team members and retiring senior team members on a scheduled basis.

The approach just described provided a nonthreatening development program for individual faculty, while at the same time it satisfied an organizational need for faculty development. Thus two broad general concerns were addressed in a complementary fashion.

The program described is now completing its third year, and the particular strategic goal noted has been achieved. The analysis that follows will indicate how the Linking Elements Concept was employed and will address the achievement just noted, particularly in light of external priorities and changing institutional goals.

Analysis: A Team Approach to
Faculty Development

In analyzing this particular situation, attention is first directed to the axiom of linking elements, "that an organizational unit will achieve the highest level of performance its environment permits if the manager can bring a high level of alignment between the needs of the unit and the characteristics and needs of the people in it." In the first year of the project described, the unit in question was a newly created team of four instructional developers. Each member of this new unit had other units to which he or she belonged and was responsible. The academic manager and fifth member of this new unit was a service dean assigned as administrative liaison to the unit.

The needs of the unit revolved around the operational goals that had been set; that is, how does the unit accomplish the operational goals? The characteristics of the individuals in the unit (including those of the academic manager) differed on many counts, but all shared a common interest in instructional development; and if asked to place themselves on Maslow's "needs hierarchy" (see chapter 5), most would probably have agreed that dominant needs would be within the esteem and status needs level. These were needs that participation on this team could satisfy.

Considering the unit and individual needs as stated, analysis using the Linking Elements Concept will now be done by first viewing the project from the organizational (unit) perspective and then from the individual perspective for year one. A somewhat abbreviated analysis of years two and three will then illustrate the impact of external forces. The analysis will conclude by listing assumptions underlying the Linking Elements Concept and some related assertions that can be made relative to this project.

Year One: From the organizational perspective, the unit required (1) control (that is, direction—goals, standards of performance, discipline), coordination, and adherence to behavior rules; (2) high technical competency; and (3) a high level of morale.

Regarding control, the direction was established early by the administration's request for a proposal that had to address certain stated concerns within stated goals, and the proposal that was written did just that. Coordination both within the team and with other units of the college was also quickly established. Members of the team attended a 2-week laboratory on faculty development designed to assist team members in learning how to work together, to make use of one another's resources, and so forth. Upon the team's return from this laboratory, meetings were scheduled with the school deans so that the team could be made aware of any ongoing developmental activities within the schools and could then coordinate team activities to complement those of the schools.

Behavioral rules for individuals were developed by the team as they were necessary and related to the completion of tasks. Early meetings of the team with the academic manager were devoted to determining who was to do what and by when. Rules also were established regarding meetings, what was expected to occur at meetings, and so forth. Each member of the team was, through this process, made aware of what was expected of him or her by other members of the unit. The academic manager's role during this process was in helping to define the behavioral roles for the unit members within the broader context of the college's needs. When a breakdown occurred (that is, confusion developed over rules and roles), an external consultant was called in to work with the team in redefining rules. The academic manager participated throughout this activity and assumed responsibility for maintenance once the rules were in place.

With respect to high technical competence, each member of the team was selected on the basis of his or her interest in the project, prior involvement in instructional development, and reputation for technical competence in a particular instructional mode or developmental area (for example, one team member was well known for the use of questioning techniques, another for small group techniques, a third for individual consulting techniques with faculty, and a fourth for organizational skills to get things done).

The manager's task was that of seeing that these skills were used, while also providing opportunity for the team members to learn new skills from each other. Much of this was done through discussion and task assignments at team meetings.

Regarding morale, both tangible and psychological rewards were provided. Whether they were always seen as such by team members is open to question, and probably much more could have been done by the academic manager in raising the consciousness level of team members by identifying rewards as rewards, at least in the existing context. In any event, from the organization's perspective, tangible rewards included providing team members with released time from teaching to participate on the team, providing opportunity to attend a 2-week faculty development laboratory at no expense, providing fiscal support for attendance at conferences and workshops of their choice, and providing additional clerical support not ordinarily available to them. Psychological rewards included providing a supportive climate within which to work (belonging and social activity needs), providing opportunity to gain high positive visibility among colleagues (esteem and status needs), and providing opportunity to acquire and employ new knowledges and skills (self-realization and fulfillment needs).

From the individual perspective, each of the team members brought (1) his or her own personal performance standards and willingness to work, (2) a personalized view on cooperation and level of willingness to cooperate, (3) his or her own competencies and capabilities, (4) an awareness of particular deficiencies, and (5) expectations regarding satisfaction of tangible and psychological needs for participation in this project.

The personal performance standards and levels of willingness to work were somewhat uneven from team member to team member, but each would have been classified in the upper category on any high, medium, or low scale. The fact that the individual levels were high should not come as any great surprise given the information that most of the team members were faculty who had been actively involved in instructional-development activities on a voluntary basis from the start. In this situation, particularly at the beginning of the project, one of the academic manager's concerns became that of tracking everything that was being done and seeing that some necessary tasks did not get overlooked in the rush of enthusiasm to accomplish many things.

Coordination and cooperation presented other types of challenges. For the most part, the willingness was there, but often there were blockages. Establishing rules for behavior to get the unit's work done became, therefore, a major agenda item in many early meetings. As was noted earlier, two methods used to create greater coordination and cooperation were implemented: the laboratory in faculty development and the use of an outside consultant to assist in defining rules. The fact that the team members readily sought out and worked with an external consultant on redefining rules is evidence of their willingness to cooperate and coordinate. Cooperation and coordination has, however, remained a constant concern throughout the life of the project and is something that requires the careful and continuing attention of the academic manager.

The competencies and capabilities brought to the unit by the individual members were especially well suited to the unit's needs. Each member had a very accurate perception of his or her particular competencies. Some may have had greater competency in certain areas than they were comfortable admitting, but by and large the personal assessment seemed on target. In fact, most members of the team were anxious to serve on the team because it would provide them a means of employing their particular competencies to a greater extent than their present units did. To permit this to happen, it was agreed from the start that each team member could "stake out" particular goal-directed action steps that required his or her competencies. Once everyone had a particular stake, remaining areas were assigned and agreed upon. It was further agreed that individuals also could be a part of someone else's stake if that person agreed. In this fashion, team members might develop new competencies. Because the team members were aware of each other's competencies and respected these competencies, the academic manager's role primarily became one of seeing that the competencies were being utilized not only for the individual team member's satisfaction, but also to reach unit goals.

Individual deficiencies were not as well addressed as competencies. While opportunity was made available to work on deficiencies by working with a team member who had competence in this area of one's deficiency, this happened only infrequently. Further, some of the deficiencies recognized by individual team members were not particularly deficiencies that impacted on the team's accomplishment of it's goals and therefore received little attention. The principal role performed by the academic manager in this regard was that of distributing information on external seminars, workshops, and so forth to the team members and encouraging attendance at such events as would address particular individual deficiencies.

Finally, considering the individual perspective, tangible and psychological satisfactions were available. Whether these coincided with individual expectations is not recorded. The suspicion is that hopes were not always reached, but some expectations were.

To summarize at this point, what has just been described was a 1-year effort to align the needs of a particular unit with the needs and characteristics of the individual members of that unit in an effort to address a broad philosophical goal of improving instructional quality. It is the description of a project where a conscious effort was made to use the Linking Elements Concept.

Years Two and Three: The reader will recall that a strategic goal of this effort was to have within 3 years a fully established, operative instructional-development team. The reader will further recall that a caveat of the administration was that a mechanism be provided for having a revolving and evolving team and that in response to that caveat, one operational goal established for the first team was devising such a mechanism that would permit the unit's continuation while at the same time addressing the administration's concern.

The agreement ultimately reached was that for year two, four new team members would be added. These members were to be selected from the faculty using several agreed upon criteria, but especially interest and skills in instructional development, since these reflected necessary technical competencies. Thus for year two there would be an eight-person team, and the intent was that all future teams would consist of eight persons. This was to occur by a replacement process in which the four senior members (those who had served 2 years) were to be replaced by four new members. In this fashion, over time, a large number of faculty would have an opportuity to serve on this team and a cadre of faculty skilled in institutional development would have been identified.

The four new members who were added for the second year, like their predecessors, attended a 2-week laboratory on faculty development during the summer and, upon their return, met with the existing team members to develop behavioral roles for this restructured unit that would best utilize all the resources now available to the unit.

Obviously, this change in structure brought new dimensions to the unit and created a challenge for the academic managers who now had to consider new alignments "between the needs of the unit and the characteristics and needs of the people in it." The academic manager's task was made more challenging by the fact that a threatened reduction in funding caused several accounts to be frozen, which meant that they could not be drawn upon immediately and some of the programs planned for early in the academic year had to be cancelled or postponed. A great deal of time and energy were therefore spent in replanning and finding ways to cope with new fiscal realities. The funding problems also had impacts on individual members' expectations regarding satisfaction of tangible and psychological needs for participation. For one thing, lack of funding momentarily eliminated team members' opportunities to attend seminars and workshops for professional self-development (tangible needs), while on another level the lack of funding raised questions about the institution's commitment to the project and its status (psychological needs for esteem and status).

Fully conscious of this, the academic manager worked closely with the team as a unit and as individuals, seeking ways to retain the unit's program and status while stressing the importance of each individual's needs. Eventually, the funding was unfrozen, and the program that had been planned for the second semester of the year was conducted without major constraints. However, the team did not remain unscarred. One of the new members resigned at the end of the first semester, stating in effect that he did not believe he was serving the team, nor that the team was serving him—a clear statement of the importance of alignment between unit and individual needs. The individual stated this as a fact, not as an accusation. Thus, while the conscious effort to use the Linking Elements Concept may not have worked in so far as retaining this individual's participation was concerned, it did work to the extent that the individual could verbalize accurately and without rancor why he was choosing to cease participation.

Without going through the point-by-point analysis from the organizational and individual perspective of the Linking Elements Concept, as provided for year one of this project, it still should be obvious that the concept was being employed during year two. However, structural changes in the unit, new individual perspectives, and external factors outside the unit's control added new dimensions that had to be considered in the employment of the concept. This is to be expected. It is noted here to alert the academic manager to the fact that the Linking Elements Concept can and does provide for changes in the situation and to further alert him or her to the proposition that unit and individual needs and goals change and therefore that constant attention to needs and goals is extremely important, as was noted in the prior discussion on the use of the Linking Elements Concept for systematic analysis.

This was very much on the academic manager's mind when the team convened in late spring to develop goals and action plans for its third year. The fiscal and other constraints placed on the team during year two were to continue during year three, the difference being that funds would not be frozen, they simply would not be available (except in limited amounts). Therefore, the extent and quality of unit goals for the third year (the EQ of EQIFAPPO) were extremely important considerations for the team. In line with the anticipated constraints, the extent of the program was reduced and some activities that had been conducted in the past were curtailed. The guiding question became "Which of the program goals are most important, and what is absolutely necessary (not just desirable) in order to address those goals?" Working in this fashion, the team developed a program for the third year that took into account severe new limitations, but did not lose sight of the broad philosophical reason for being—quality of instruction.

At the same time, concern was being expressed for year-three goals. Concern was also surfacing regarding the team structure for year three. The mechanism in place called for replacing four senior members with new members. Further, the team had already lost one of the new members, who had not been replaced. There were concerns regarding loss of the resources of the senior members, concerns regarding continued fiscal support for an eight-person team, and concerns about the provisions that needed to be made for new team members (that is, other EQIFAPPO concerns: *I*nvolvement, *F*requency of goals review, *A*ccountability, *P*articipation, *O*perational/developmental goals concerns).

Deliberating over these concerns, the team and the academic manager agreed that the resources of the retiring team members should not be lost. These team members were to continue as alumni to be called on when their particular skills were needed to assist the team in areas of particular interest or concern. They would no longer receive released time to be participating, planning members of the team, but identity with the team was to be retained by keeping them informed and involved.

Regarding concerns for continued fiscal support of an eight-person team, it was agreed that this could no longer be afforded. One new member had already resigned, and a second new member was accepting another post that would extensively curtail the time she could devote to the team. As a consequence, only two new members were left. However, the revolving, evolving team concept was still judged to be a good one, so the two remaining members (now the senior team members), in view of the limited fiscal support and the new goals, selected two new members to join the team for its third year. Thus the team had come full circle, returning to a four-person team, but the strategic goal of an evaluative/operative team had been achieved. It simply underwent structural modifications in response to contextual changes.

With respect to the concerns about the provisions that needed to be made for new team members (that is, the other EQIFAPPO concerns), these became concerns of and for all team members (new or old), and attention was paid to them through periodic team and individual meetings. One of the greatest concerns evidenced during the third year was with operational/developmental goals considerations. To address this, the team spent some of its limited resources to bring in an outside consultant to work with them on determining how they could meet their own individual developmental goals while working toward the goals of the unit. This analysis permitted each team member an opportunity to make some determination regarding whether his or her tangible and psychological needs were being sufficiently met to warrant continuation on the team and continuation of the team concept and activity. All agreed that it was worth continuing the team, and each agreed it was worth continuing as a team member. This was done despite external forces that suggested that a fourth year might bring even further fiscal constraints and reduction in fiscal support.

Again, a point-by-point analysis from the organizational and individual perspectives of the Linking Elements Concept could be done, but the repetition seems unnecessary as long as the reader realizes that all these points must remain in consideration at all times if linking elements is to work. They are never ignored; the dimensions merely are altered with the circumstances. Therefore, one must constantly be aware of the meaning of his or her organizational and individual perspectives and remain alert to external forces that can impact on them.

Assumptions and Assertions

Not only must the academic manager be constantly aware of organizational and individual perspectives, but he or she must also not lose sight of the assumptions underlying the Linking Elements Concept. Viewing the case history just described along with these assumptions, the following assertions would not seem out of order:

Assumption	*Assertion*
1. A manager's actions are shaped by three primary influences: the environment, the people who report to him or her, and the manager's personal characteristics.	1. Throughout the life of the project, all influences changed. First, the environment became less supportive (at least fiscally); secondly, the people reporting to the manager changed each year by design (that is, *new* people were assigned each year and added to an existing group of people); and third, the manager's personal characteristics altered at least somewhat: he grew older, his interest in the project fluctuated, other activities commanded his interest, and so forth. All these changes influenced actions the manager could and did take relative to the project.
2. A person cannot motivate other people, but only create an environment in which the others can find motivation.	2. A key concept of this project was that each team member would stake out what was important to him or her of the project's program goals.

Assumption

Assertion

Others could share in that stake, but it belonged to the person who claimed it. This concept has not changed throughout the life of the project. This concept was an environmental factor that permitted individuals to find motivation, especially once they were aware that it was an operational concept.

3. Decision-making and communication skills are required for all management activities; as these skills are improved, it is likely that other skills will improve as well.

3. Given the changes that occurred over 3 years and the role of the manager as an administrative liaison as well as manager, communication skills became increasingly important. The team was given the opportunity to make several decisions of a programmatic nature, but could not do so without accurate and up-to-date information and an understanding of the implications of that information. Much work was done, therefore, on communicating, and outside consultants were used to assist the manager and team members in improving communication skills.

The work with outside consultants on improving communication skills also increased team members' skills in goal setting, task assignments, and dealing with organizational detail. Each year's team, however, needed this work on communication

Assumption

Assertion

skills because the team
changed each year and new
communication mixes
developed.

4. A major determinant of success of an organizational unit
is the extent to which unit
needs are aligned with employee needs and characteristics.

4. Perhaps more than any other
assumption, this one remained
constant throughout, in terms
of the attention received. It
was an important consideration in unit goal setting, in
team-member selection, and
in providing opportunity to
address individual needs and
characteristics.

With the impact of external
forces, changes in unit goals,
and changes in the team
structure annually, alignment
was a constant concern of the
manager and the team
members. The team even conducted its own training and
employed outside consultants
to help with alignment—
especially when forces outside
the team's direct control impacted on that alignment.
Such developmental activity
should be an ongoing part of
any professional development
program.

5. There is some measure of
validity to the findings of all
serious, prominent researchers
and theorists, and a com-
prehensive concept must take
these findings into con-
sideration.

5. The nature of the project
described particularly lent
itself to examining and acting
out ideas of prominent researchers and theorists in
management. Instruction can
and does involve management
concepts. This project, which
addressed instructional quality

Assumption   *Assertion*

provided team members an
opportunity to be project
managers as well as instructional developers, and in doing so, many (including the
overall academic manager)
began to develop more comprehensive approaches for
dealing with ongoing con-
cerns.

Summary and Conclusions

In this chapter an effort has been made to identify the roles and responsibilities of academic managers and to address concerns they are likely to
have as they attempt to achieve the goal of "enhancing the intellectual
climate" through the management of available resources. Because of the
long history of participation, democracy, and direct faculty involvement
that exists in many institutions of higher education, academic managers
must especially have skills and acumen in working with committees, interest
groups, and individuals whose collective or individual needs and goals may
be in conflict with the needs and goals of the organization.

It has been suggested that academic managers, at whatever level, who
understand goals-management programs and can systematically examine
practices using EQIFAPPO have a tool that will assist them in functioning.
It has been further suggested that academic managers need an opportunity
to participate in development programs. People who have management
responsibilities must receive management-development assistance.

Finally, it also has been noted, particularly through the case study cited,
that the Linking Elements Concept applies. Opportunity for its use to
upgrade management competence exists for the academic manager as well
as for managers in other fields. An academic manager, therefore, does not
necessarily have to follow linking elements guidelines at all times, but
failure to note an existing opportunity to apply the thorough diagnostic or
remedial process, it is suggested here, can be a gross oversight. Academic
managers, leaders if you will, must understand the complexities of their
function in relating their organizations and the people who staff them.
Leaders of the eighties, if they are to make progress toward the larger goals
of their institutions, must, in the words of Maccoby, "contend not only
with individuals or groups that do not want to give up power and control,

but also with a heavy, depressed collective spirit, a deadly mixture of anxiety, competitiveness, hopelessness, and secret guilt about self-betrayal for career and comfort."[9] Understanding linking elements may help such leaders to contend.

Notes

1. Unpublished conference materials, Resource Center for Planned Change, American Association of State Colleges and Universities (AASCU), Washington, 1978.

2. Ibid.

3. Charles Perrow, unpublished draft of address presented at Rutgers Graduate School of Education Conference, New Brunswick, N.J., March 1978, p. 2.

4. Ibid., p. 12.

5. A typical example can be seen in the New Jersey system, whereby a single contract is negotiated for all nine state colleges. This is negotiated at the state level, with local institutions (both management and labor) having only limited opportunity to influence the negotiations.

6. Overall responsibility for grants and development may often be assigned to the chief fiscal affairs officer or the chief developmental affairs officer, but the chief academic affairs officer may have such overall responsibility in some situations and certainly has responsibility for academic resource grants.

7. In one 3-year period the writer was personally involved in evaluations or preparation for evaluations for a required accrediting association (MSA), a major national accrediting agency (NCATE), a major state/national accreditation (NASDTEC), a state evaluation (Department of Higher Education), and in establishing a local evaluation procedure.

8. See Ed Kiersh, "Presidential Searches: Divided We Stand," *Change Magazine*, vol. 11, September 1979, pp. 29-35, for a discussion of the uses made of search committees by interest groups.

9. Michael Maccoby, "Leadership Needs of the 1980s," in *Current Issues in Higher Education, 1979, No. 1, Perspectives on Leadership*, Washington, AAHE, 1979, p. 22.

Student Affairs

Robert A. Laudicina

There are many different perceptions of student affairs held by professionals in the field. They differ primarily in emphasis. Without question, everyone will agree that recruitment and retention of students is the core of the job. However, there are those who feel that activities, student organizations, and group processes should be the primary areas in which student affairs works to achieve best performance. Others, however, would consider individual growth of students as far more important. A third group might consider campus physical appearances and service levels to students as the most important. Depending on the philosophies held by student affairs directors or the chief student personnel officer (CSPO), the emphasis would then reflect itself in the way service areas receive more or less attention and, of course, differential funding within the student affairs group.

Thus student affairs professionals who hold the first view could be called *integrators*; they would place emphasis on group interaction to build a sense of community through shared interests. They would see programming and orientation as a means to social integration. Student organizations and programming receive considerable attention as a means for developing shared interests among students. Integrators believe that initiating as many face-to-face relationships as possible is likely to encourage students to remain as students and thereby develop their capacities through student governance, clubs, and cultural activities. Integrators utilize orientation and various group activities to encourage student, faculty, and staff interaction.

Those with the second view could be considered *bilateralists*. Their emphasis would be on individual development in one-to-one focus—counseling, testing, assessing, and developing. Helping students assess themselves and develop their abilities is an important concern. Rather than watching students blindly tumble into academic or career paths, bilateralists believe careful testing of all students should be required at the earliest possible time in a student's college career. Bilateralists typically seek an articulated program of testing, student assessment, and career planning. Bilateralists are also likely to believe that strong development programs in reading and math are a *sine qua non* for maximizing student retention.

Finally, the third group, which could be called *environmentalists*, would place emphasis on student rights, due process, and legal concerns, as well as on housing, student financing, student employment, building maintenance, and amenities. Their interests rest primarily with providing better service levels in admissions, registration, and financial aid and better facilities in housing and student union buildings. They believe that prospective and registered students are likely to respect and appreciate an institution whose services are efficiently run and responsive to student needs. Environmentalists also are likely to be concerned about complying with relevant government regulations regarding financial aid, consumer interests, and equal educational access for all applicants.

The differences between these three views are not as clean-cut as presented here, of course. There is disagreement on emphasis, but basically all see the need for competence in all activities as essential to superior performance. The following diagram depicts the comprehensive view that recruitment and retention are interlocked and that success in one makes it easier to achieve goals in the other.

Recruitment of student is achieved through:

— Promoting equal access for all prospective students.

— Providing reliable and meaningful information about policies and procedures.

Retention of student is achieved through:

— Social integration

— Community building

— Individual development of students

— Physical amenities

It is not the function of this book to evaluate the relative merits of these philosophical approaches to student affairs. Rather, its purpose is to provide a management framework that could allow all three philosophies to attain the maximum advantage from the human and financial resources at the disposal of student affairs personnel. If the managers in the student affairs department are competent as managers as well as in their respective disciplines, then they will achieve most with their resources, however limited they might be.

Student affairs personnel have been called many things: surrogate parents, benevolent dictators, consensus seekers, professional articulators of student rights and responsibilities, teachers, coordinators, cultivators of student resources, and more. They have been asked to assume many functions: student discipline, recreation, housing, health, counseling, placement, orientation, athletics, admission, financial aid and more. Student affairs professionals make available the means necessary for students to develop personally and intellectually. They help students coordinate talents and interests with the requirements of life outside the classroom and campus. They also have become the contacts to ensure that the institution provides fair value to students for goods and services received.

The student affairs function in the college community has been dramatically transformed during the last several decades as a result of changing relationships between students and the institutions they attend. There has been a shift from autocratic direction and discipline, often through a benevolent counselor relationship, to what now is often referred to as a "contract"—where students expect, as rights, what once were considered to be privileges.

The changes to legal adult status of students, moreover, has strengthened the hand of students who demand that goals and service levels as stated in brochures and catalogs be actually provided. Students now insist on a significant voice in the formulation of rules, regulations, and policies that may affect them.

Student affairs staffs typically are organized with the following departments reporting to the chief student personnel officer:

1. Admissions
2. Financial aid
3. Counseling
4. Residence
5. Student activities
6. Placement
7. Health services
8. Minority programs
9. Athletic programs (occasionally)

A typical organizational structure for the Student Affairs Department is depicted in figure 8-1.

Goals for the Student Affairs Function

In addition to its primary mission, a student affairs group may be charged by the institution to attract higher-quality students. The assignment can demonstrate how the function could apply a goals program and the EQIFAPPO concept. The strategic goal could be "to increase, by the end of the recruiting season, to 30 percent the proportion of student acceptances who rank in the top 15 percent of their high school classes."

Supporting this strategic goal could be operational goals like

1. To obtain funds for an additional 15 merit scholarships to newly admitted students based on academic performance and extracurricular activities, these scholarships to start with the fall term, 1981

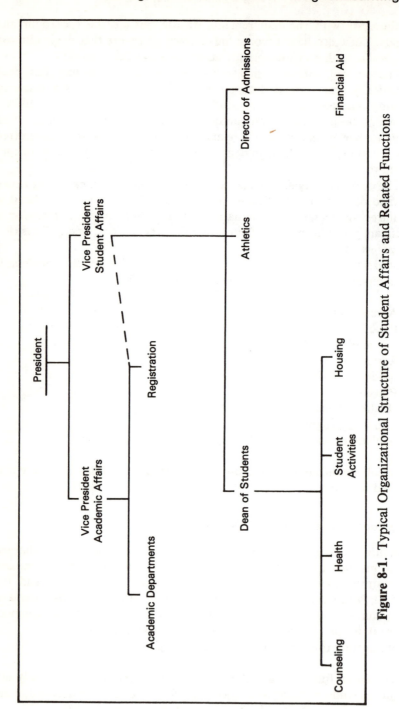

Figure 8-1. Typical Organizational Structure of Student Affairs and Related Functions

2. To intensify recruiting operations in private and quality public high schools within a 100-mile perimeter to achieve 1,000 applications from the top 15 percent of their respective graduating classes
3. To establish a special program of more intensive cultural and intellectual activities that will be available to all students meeting certain scholastic requirements or admission standards, specifications for the program and attendance goals to be completed by July 1
4. To develop a publicity program that would spread information about this program beyond the 100-mile perimeter to attract an additional 500 applications from qualifying students

Some of the action steps for the goal of obtaining funds for the merit scholarships would be performed by the financial aid director and could involve

1. To determine by December of 1980 how much money could be made available from existing financial aid funds for this program
2. To meet with the department of athletics to obtain views on funds that could be made available from athletic aid budgets
3. Preparing and mailing an appeal to corporations and foundations who might wish to sponsor some of the scholarships and following up with telephone calls

Some of the operational goals involve effort by people in other departments over whom the managers in the student services function have no organizational authority. As was discussed in chapter 4, the responsibility of these managers would be limited, of course, to appropriate steps, such as meeting with relevant people in the other departments, making suggestions, exploring in detail what could be done, obtaining agreement to the extent possible, following up so that agreements are not forgotten, and notifying the chief student personnel officer of any obstacles that arise.

Despite even the most competent action steps, it is still possible that the strategic goal of increasing the percentage of students in the top 15 percent of their class may not be achieved; however, if all these steps are indeed taken, the likelihood of achieving them is much greater than if the process had not been arranged in this semiformal way or had not been thought through as carefully. Furthermore, the goal-setting process, by clarifying that primary responsibility for goal achievement at the next higher level, ensures that people at those levels are available to intercede when obstacles develop. Such support is often crucial, and observance of EQIFAPPO principles provides guidance so that support is placed at those goals which deserve highest priority. For instance, the vice president of development and the vice president of student affairs may jointly seek grants from outside, if competent, serious effort by the people in charge of financial aid, recruiting, and admissions does not bring the planned results.

While, at first, this process appears to place extra burden on people at higher levels, the opposite is closer to the likely effect. When higher-level managers can effectively delegate, through goal setting, they become involved only with the achievement of those goals where competent effort, with resources available at lower levels, is inadequate. This much involvement is rarely more extensive than the workload under other systems.

Developing Competence

Student affairs personnel are varied in background and typically bring a wide range of skills to the goal of student development. Health service officers, financial aid counselors, reading specialists, physical activities directors, marketing personnel, and even business managers may all be on the same student affairs team, each with varied technical backgrounds, personal attitudes, and psychological and tangible needs. Given the probable diversity of any student affairs staff, it is clearly essential that the competence of individual staff members for their respective responsibilities be factually evaluated and that programs be made available for improving any weaknesses.

Some learning experiences that are often needed include knowledge of procedures and budgeting, as well as workshops assessing the changing trends in associate professional areas of the institution. Specialists and experts in various fields can be invited to speak at such seminars, and some students can be invited to add a point of view essential to this function. There is considerable beneficial fallout from a training and development program of this type, since both staff and students can more clearly identify respective roles and therefore work more effectively with each other.

Psychological Rewards

Helping young people grow and develop is often its own reward. People in student services, managers, professionals, and nonprofessional employees all have substantial contact with young people, their successes, and their failures. Within the limits of their abilities, they can address student needs and concerns and thereby satisfy their own personal and professional needs. Although there are frustrations and many disappointments, work in student services can be richly rewarding for those whose interests steer them toward human service careers. Obviously these psychological rewards from the work itself can come in rich measure only if management of the function can develop the climate that helps people reach for and enjoy success.

Admissions

Admissions can be considered as the marketing arm of the college or university with regard to student recruitment. Its function is to identify what types of students might be most appropriate for admission and where such students can best be found, communicate the benefits of attendance at the institution to those students, perform the procedural functions necessary to evaluate capabilities and to make specific selections, and ensure that information to prospective students is accurate and that admission procedures comply with federal guidelines and other authorities that regulate college admissions, especially those which prohibit discrimination against women, minorities, and handicapped persons.

A typical admissions department therefore performs many, if not all, of the following functions:

Assessment of academic and student life strengths within the institution

Preparation of catalogs and publicity releases that will bring these strengths to the attention of prospective students

Preparation of student recruitment plans and school visitation schedules

Application review and selection of students by admissions committee

Preparation of acceptance notices to students and coordination of follow-up by financial aid, counseling, and other student services

Preparation of new student orientation programs

Analysis of characteristics of students who accept and students who reject admission to the institution

Preparation of reports concerning student interests and needs for relevant offices such as student activities, housing, health services, or counseling

The admissions process has experienced extensive changes over the past decade primarily because a seller's market existed prior to the seventies. In those years, admissions officers simply reviewed applications to select candidates who best met institutional criteria. The great stringency of financial resources and the larger number of options open to students have since made admissions much more of a selling function with primary emphasis on attracting the kind of students the institution desires. At the same time, in view of the increasing interdependence of the departments of the college or university, admissions has to rely heavily on the development of joint strategies that will create the environment or atmosphere that helps attract and retain students. This means that active cooperation is required with academic departments as well as with those in administration to achieve an environment that encourages a high percentage of retention.

Such coordination may involve:

1. Creation of a student-faculty admissions committee to help identify market areas, assess academic standards for prospective students, augment the admissions staff during campus visitation days, and serve as liaison to faculty departments and student governance boards
2. Achievement of common views on the numbers and profiles of students to be admitted in a given year with university financial personnel, various academic departments, and housing personnel
3. Cooperation with university development and/or public relations departments on publications and media copy
4. Provision of university counsel with all application and publications material as well as admissions policies to ensure compliance with regulations
5. Analysis of acceptances by students for review by deans, faculty, financial aid, counseling, housing, and student activities personnel for preparation of appropriate orientation programs.

In order to ensure that admissions personnel, students, and faculty who participate in recruitment activities clearly understand their roles and are capable of performing their responsibilities requires an understanding of institutional mission, campus history, and organizational and governance structures. For the institution to project a professional image to the outside world, all these people have to be very knowledgeable in the facilities and programs that the college offers. Indeed, federal regulations require that statements, not only promotional materials, to prospective students be accurate and that they fairly represent facilities, programs, and resources that a college and its students might enjoy. To achieve the level of technical competence required of those who initially meet and talk with prospective students, appropriate learning experiences have to be made available. The American Association of Collegiate Registrars and Admissions Officers (AACRAO) generally maintains and offers such programs for admissions personnel, but inhouse programs are more practical for faculty, students, and other staff members involved in the admissions effort.

Topics that could be considered if a knowledge/skill list is to be prepared for an admissions official could include knowledge of the following concerns and, of course, the skill in communicating them to prospective students, families, and other interested persons:

Federal regulations, particularly those involving equal access, consumer information, and foreign student admissions

The institution's enrollment histories and projections based on population trends

Marketing and recruiting techniques

New academic programs

Auxiliary services, particularly housing, food, bookstore, student employment, and so forth

Financial aid programs

Campus visitation and tours procedures

Guidance counselor procedures

Working in admissions can be very rewarding. Admissions jobs are generally highly enriched because they provide direct contact with prospective students, often with opportunities to help them start on their college careers. It can be especially gratifying to those who enjoy being on the front line and meeting and talking with young students about their career choices and the ways in which they wish to plan their lives. Competent management can use the many positive aspects of the positions in admissions to create a highly positive work climate, despite some negative aspects such as extensive travel required by some positions, which keeps the incumbents away from home for considerable periods of time; difficulty for individuals over 30 years of age to remain in the admissions field; and the need for immediate feedback of the extent to which programs have met with success; that is, how many students, and with what class rank, have decided to attend. While this knowledge of results can be motivational to some people, it often has a depressing effect, especially in the highly competitive environment where challenging goals are difficult to achieve.

A Case

Florhans Fells College, a private women's college with approximately 600 students, enjoys a quality faculty and a fine program and facilities, which, though aging, are still attractive and well maintained. Nevertheless, enrollments are declining, primarily because of competition from low-cost state colleges, but also because of a static liberal arts program. A series of meetings has been held between faculty and administration to agree on a course of action that might be best suited to encourage more students to attend. It was recognized that the educational offerings needed some revamping and that the quality of faculty members and the attractiveness of the institution's facilities as well as its basic program should be made more visible to prospective students. The obvious need for detailed planning brought a decision to hold a retreat at which the senior administration officials as well as all academic department heads, deans, and even some student representatives would be provided with an opportunity to present views and discuss the possible courses of action. It was hoped that the retreat also would bring greater commitment on the part of the various groups to effectively assume their respective responsibilities in helping the college achieve whatever plans would ultimately be decided on.

The retreat was held, and while it brought a fairly distinct plan and goals for administration personnel, it failed to bring a really meaningful consensus among faculty members concerning the type of programs to be offered and the staffing policies to be used. Still, the admissions department received reasonably clear direction to update the available literature, to step up the recruitment program, and to widen the role of faculty and students in the admissions effort. Specifically, Admissions Director Donaldson was asked to investigate the relative costs and benefits of direct mailings to prospective students, newspaper advertisements, and student-faculty visitation teams to targeted private and public schools and to make decisions on the basis of this assessment.

On the question of resources for the expanded activities, the conference was less clear. It was recommended, however, that the president review the budgets and see what could be done to provide the necessary monies for new admissions programming. An analysis of the budget in light of inflationary demands on projected limited resources indicated that very little, if any, additional money would be available for admissions to achieve its more ambitious goals. As a result, Donaldson was asked by the president to accomplish most, if not all, of them without increases in budget beyond unavoidable cost increases such as mandated salary increments. The admissions department and its organizational ties are depicted in figure 8-2.

Admissions Director Donaldson is a task-oriented individual who enjoys the respect of the staff, although he is not exceptionally well liked because he appears to always place job performance ahead of legitimate needs of people. The difficult assignment that faces him in this situation presents some interesting opportunities. Success would not only bring benefits to the college, but also would undoubtedly create a uniquely rewarding climate for the admissions staff. There are formidable obstacles, of course, but the rewards to Donaldson and to those staff members who contribute could be significant. One strategy, based on the Linking Elements Concept, that contains considerable potential is outlined in the case analysis that follows.

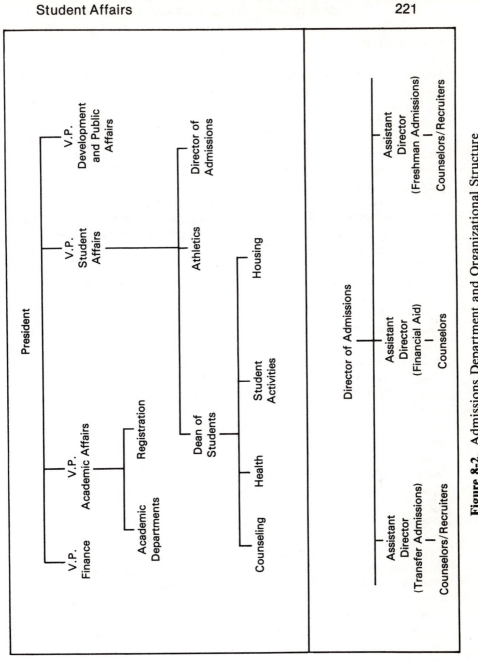

Figure 8-2. Admissions Department and Organizational Structure

Case Analysis

The problem facing Admissions Director Donaldson, of course, is not unique. Obviously, the steps toward a solution require coordination with and the cooperation of other departments. Still, most of his efforts have to be directed toward helping his team reach much higher levels of achievement.

If he is willing to accept the discipline that the Linking Elements Concept requires, until it becomes an established procedure, Donaldson could plan a broad approach that would include a gradual shift to a more participative management style.

1. In an initial planning session with the three assistant directors, Donaldson could clarify his conviction that greater commitment on the part of staff members will be needed to achieve a significant change. At this point he would have to carefully explain why he believes that the admissions department has to take the lead in helping the college reverse the deteriorating trends. He would have to provide some evidence that he is prepared to adapt a more participative style, that he himself is more than willing to accept his share of the workload and is ready to support others where needed. This team could review what goals should be considered and tentatively decide priorities.

2. The assistant directors could then meet with their staffs to explain the need for commitment by the admissions department. They could then review the department goals that apply to their respective functions, jointly with their staff members, and decide on accepting them or on any modifications they would consider desirable. They also could discuss respective operational goals and even major action steps. These action steps could concern creating a student/faculty admissions committee to review applications, augment the admissions staff, and serve as representatives from respective academic departments; updating of the campus handbook for new students with student activities personnel; inviting junior college counselors to the campus for a review of academic programs and facilities available; developing, with placement services, a student job corporation so that more new students might find employment; establishing, through the counseling center, a skill-development program (reading and math) that would be available at no cost to entering students; investigating the use of direct mail and newspaper advertising to attract new students; identifying those alumni who would be willing to visit prospective students and discuss the advantages of attending Florhan Fells; and placing a series of articles on important faculty members and their contributions to the community and region with relevant newspapers, magazines, and radio.

This might not be the time, in light of the heavy demands, to consider any specific development goals of staff members except that managers, as much as possible, should support activities of staff members with on-the-job coaching with respect to any new duties.

3. After these staff meetings, the goals could be formalized in brief write-ups, regular goals-review sessions could be scheduled, and accountability could be clarified in line with EQIFAPPO principles.

At the same time, it would be of significant help if the admissions director disciplined himself to spend more time with individuals in the group, offering personal help whenever difficult tasks have to be performed, running interference for staff members wherever they face difficulties with people outside the department, and providing extensive evidence that he is fully prepared to do whatever the team considers necessary. The entire approach, consisting of goal setting, supportive activities by the admissions director, and somewhat more emphasis on coaching where desired, could quickly create significant psychological rewards for the other members of the staff. It would lead to the identification of procedural obstacles that have previously reduced the effectiveness of the group and would thereby eliminate unnecessary or wasteful efforts that have taken time in the past. It also would point to areas where students, volunteers, or more effective methods could be used so that, in a relatively short time, the staff could in fact achieve considerably more without much additional effort.

Success and the awareness that the team is accomplishing more than before could lead to higher levels of motivation. It is well within the realm of possibility that within a short period of time, staff personnel might actually not work harder than before, but considerably more would be accomplished. In addition, the director of admissions could add to the satisfaction staff members obtain from their work. This would require consistency in the change of style he initiated at the meeting with the assistant directors. Moreover, this would provide more positive impulses for the members of his staff and for those from whom he must seek support.

Having taken the lead through increased effort and attention by his staff, Admissions Director Donaldson is in an excellent position to request that similar programs be initiated in other departments, if they have not already started there. Supportive activities by other student service departments that would especially aid the admissions program by bringing greater student retention could include

1. In Registration:
   a. Establishment of procedures for students considering separation from the college that require a meeting with the student's academic adviser or counselor
   b. Analysis and dissemination, with recommendations, of data regarding student requests for transfers, leaves, and withdrawals
2. Counseling:
   a. Establishment of a skills-development program (reading and math) for all students

   b. Providing outreach programs in residence and commuter centers that enhance personal development.

3. Financial aid:

Establishing contacts with community banks, businesses, and government agencies for the purpose of expanding employment and other financial aid opportunities to students

4. Student activities:

   a. Cultivating those resources which promote personal growth among students—leadership training, media, and club activities

   b. Establishing management workshops for students interested in planning and implementing organizational activities

5. Residence:

Providing opportunities for students, staff, and faculty members to meet and discuss various topical issues and concerns within a residence setting

Registration

The registration office serves as a data bank for student course schedules, course availability, course costs, and curriculum and catalog requirements. It coordinates scheduling of courses with space or room availability. The registration office also maintains records of student withdrawals from individual classes.

A registration office is usually called on to prepare and distribute class-schedule information for purposes of academic advising and student counseling. Registration personnel also usually are the very first people whom students approach when they have questions about their schedule or about catalog requirements, or when they need to talk with someone about withdrawing from school.

At one time considered to be merely record keepers, registration personnel are now recognized as the primary information agents within a college's organization, and they are expected to properly distribute valuable information and analysis on course availability, space availability, student withdrawals, and catalog requirements to students, staff, and faculty.

The need to manage growing data bases in support of institutional activities and the need for registration personnel to regularly interface with all academic and student affairs departments prescribe the goals for the function. For instance, a strategic goal and related operational goals could be

Strategic: To provide the information and develop procedures which would reduce, by 25 percent, the number of students who withdraw or transfer from the institution each semester

Operational: To establish procedures within 30 days that would ensure that students considering withdrawal from the college would meet with an academic advisor or counselor

Operational: To prepare a registration information flowchart by (*date*) that identifies agreed upon administrative responsibility for various retention activities.

Operational: To prepare for every Tuesday morning staff meeting, reports and analysis/comparisons of student withdrawals and requests for transcripts or transfer information, complete as of the preceding Friday close.

Registration is, without question, one department in which coordination with other departments is of great importance. Without timely input on course offerings from the academic departments, and without adequate information from admissions about new student requirements, the registration department cannot provide the smooth support that a quality relationship with students demands.

More so than in other departments, managers in registration have to pay attention to the coordination needs of the institution with their respective functions. In this regard, flowcharts, preferably in network-diagram format can be of great help.[1] Such a chart informs all those involved in the information-collecting process and in the use of data output from registrations when, where, and how they can expect the information they need. A sample chart is shown in figure 8-3.

If such a chart is drawn up by a committee with appropriate representation from every department, then every department can set appropriate goals to ensure that its share of the task is completed on time. Coordination with academic departments and student affairs offices also may be aided by a schedule of meetings with admissions and faculty chairpersons to confirm courses scheduled for particular semesters, curriculum requirements which those courses satisfy, and college policy relative to closed and cancelled courses.

Proper direction to students can be given only if registration personnel are fully aware of course availability, curriculum requirements, and policy changes. Joint working relationships with allied departments are even more critical for an institution's retention program. Indeed, registration personnel have to be a formal part of any retention program that might be developed and should act as referral agents to the counseling department for personal problems students might have. Many students who decide to leave school often request a transcript from the registration office. A student, unhappy with his or her academic program or unable to immediately pay semester bills, also may discuss with registrar personnel his or her

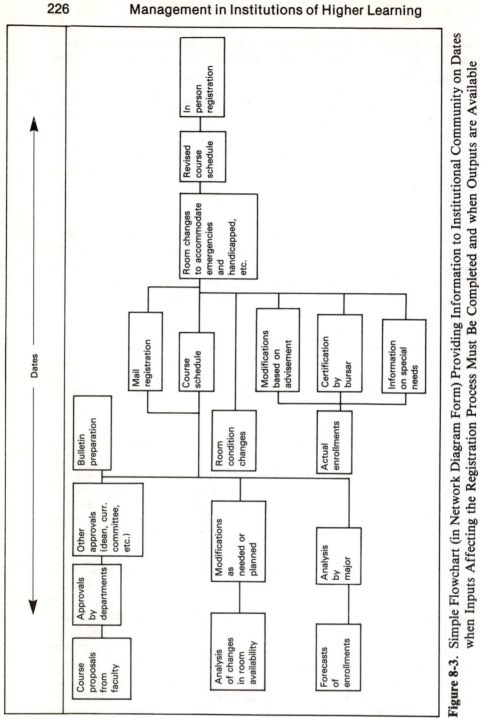

Figure 8-3. Simple Flowchart (in Network Diagram Form) Providing Information to Institutional Community on Dates when Inputs Affecting the Registration Process Must Be Completed and when Outputs are Available

thoughts about leaving school. It is important, therefore, for the student affairs office to have a direct linkage with the registrar's office so that strategies can be developed to help students who are not progressing toward their degrees and/or who are not satisfying major or degree requirements.

The daily responsibilities of registration personnel in direct contact with students require thorough knowledge of catalog requirements and campus procedures. Knowledge/skill demands and training to eliminate gaps therefore should cover federal regulations concerning tuition refunds, educational loans, course representations, confidentiality of student records, and necessary arrangements for handicapped persons, as well as the interpersonal skills that can help bring good relations with students and other departments. In-service training also should include a review of classroom, auditoria, and space resources, admissions programming, and the ways in which publications and course schedules are provided to student clientele. Training in the use of computers and statistical analysis of output data can substantially upgrade the quality of service the registrar delivers to students and staff.

Working in a registrar's office can be as rewarding as working in other student-contact areas of an institution. Sometimes registration personnel represent the only administrative people with whom a student will meet and talk about college work and career interests. As a result, members of the registrar's staff can have access to the satisfactions, as well as the frustrations, that stem from improving complex information management systems from working with students and providing guidance to them.

Despite the problems that such work can bring, there can be many joys, especially if managers are competent in helping their staff members achieve successful completion of challenging tasks, in supporting them when difficulties arise, and, of course, in maintaining an open communications climate in which they can feel that they are valuable parts of an effective team.

Counseling

Counseling services at most colleges and universities range from limited diagnosis and short-term problem assistance to sophisticated psychological and learning services aimed at self-improvement and career planning/assessment. A counseling center can help students gain wider opportunities for educating themselves and thereby increase chances for achievement of personal and career goals.

Until recently, few counseling professionals considered themselves managers of a service department within the student affairs division. Some staff psychiatrists or clinical psychologists may have believed, and indeed still believe, that their work, to be effective, must be accomplished outside of the regular flow of student personnel services. With more and more emphasis on retention of students, however, counseling center personnel are likely to appreciate the need for managing their activities in cooperation with other service departments.

Few counseling centers, for example, would simply wait today for a student in trouble to show up at their door. They are more likely to engage in outreach activities, orientation programming, and other assertive counseling activities, including

1. Testing of all freshman for interests, study habits, and reading deficiencies
2. Reading, math, and study skills development programs
3. Special counseling for students placed on academic probation
4. Assessment workshops for students interested in changing their academic or career interests
5. In-service training for residence assistants and peer counselors
6. Human sexuality seminars
7. Encounter groups
8. Research activities on drug and alcohol abuse

Each of the preceding activities, of course, requires appropriate goal setting and management. A strategic goal and an operational goal follow as examples:

Strategic: To achieve, by the end of the second year, elimination of reading deficiencies of all entering students whose aptitude scores were below college minimum levels

Operational: To design, by April 1, 1981, a reading-development program that would utilize reading specialists, pretests and posttests, and counseling of students on appropriate study habits

Because of their extensive education, it may seem that counselors should require little if any continuing training. Changing student lifestyles, from liberal to conservative, new campus needs for retention of students, and student deficiencies in verbal and quantitative skills, however, demand that counseling personnel do participate in sustained and systematic training activities. For example, student anxieties may surface in the form of increased alcohol abuse, and counselors more familiar with student drug cultures will need to redirect their reading and research activities. Counselors, moreover, must remain sufficiently flexible to operate both within and outside the campus community. This is especially so because women's centers, volunteer and social service agencies, libraries, and even coffee houses may become appropriate locations for counseling service activities. Divisional efforts to promote student retention, furthermore, can be most effective when counseling personnel interact with student club and governance activities. The visibility of an adult member of the campus community who is responsive to student problems can be of particular advantage to student morale.

Developmental activities for counseling personnel often can be most effective in research and in functions where they serve as group facilitators. However, counselors may direct their study and research to those immediate and long-term student needs most in evidence on a particular campus. They also may engage in training activities for student groups who are involved in first-line counseling work, such as residence counselors. Special workshops for leadership and personal development also are likely forms of training activities with which counselors may become involved. Such workshops, particularly when conducted jointly with a residence or student activities staff group, can be especially helpful to students and counselors alike.

Counseling might seem initially to be a strongly satisfying and rewarding activity. Counselors, however, often do not know to what extent their efforts have helped an individual. Furthermore, a substantial percentage of the students they see are unhappy about some aspect of college or personal life and do not, or cannot, respond favorably. Nevertheless, when counselors set realistic goals and support each other in professional projects, their work can be very rewarding. This is especially true if the director or department head is a skilled manager, capable of encouraging the counselors in their search for more effective, innovative approaches to the solution of campus problems.

Financial Aid

Perhaps more than any other student affairs work, financial aid has grown in prestige over the last decade. A student's opportunity to attend an institution of his or her choice is often tied directly to financial support, and financial aid has therefore taken on an increasingly important role in the retention process. The various functions of financial aid officers include

1. Assessment of students' financial aid needs
2. Awarding grants and loans to eligible students to help them maintain registration
3. Providing financial counseling
4. Educating students about their consumer rights and responsibilities
5. Providing on-campus or off-campus employment

As might be expected, financial difficulties are a prime source of student discontent and are often listed as a reason for leaving college. In this regard, then, the help of a financial aid officer often can make a difference in whether or not a student maintains his or her registration. Retention of students, while obviously important to all student service departments, remains an instant and highly visible departmental objective for any financial aid office. With substantially increased workloads, owing in large part to new government regulations permitting all registered students to apply for interest-free loans, financial aid functions obviously have increasing need for competent management.

The financial aid process, to be most useful in serving institutional objectives, requires careful coordination with the admissions effort. Requests for federal funds, on the one hand, must be matched with actual student recruitment efforts, on the other. Federal payment for some staff services also must be matched with new government requirements for student consumer information, internal controls, validating systems for student registration, and even administrative review of a student's academic progress. As students are admitted to an institution, financial aid personnel must be ready and competent to inform, discuss, and counsel students on available jobs, loans, and grants as well as the source and amount of each type of aid that might be available. They also must provide reports containing data and analysis on the number of applications evaluated, the number of students aided, the numbers and type of programs, and the funds involved. Systematic goal setting can ensure that these functions are performed and improved on a continuing basis. Sample strategic goals and examples of operational goals follow.

Strategic: To increase by 50 percent the number of job opportunities made available to registered students for the academic year 1981-1982

Operational: To establish, by June 1, a student job services corporation that will place 100 students by October 1, by (1) systematically identifying qualified students for on-campus and off-campus employment opportunities; (2) training students for specific jobs that may be required in the community; and (3) interfacing with community businesses and government agencies to identify and obtain commitments on available opportunities

Operational: To establish with relevant academic departments, credit opportunities for students whose jobs relate directly to course studies

Operational: To establish, by August 1, with relevant student affairs departments, 20 specific job opportunities that can be accomplished by students, for students (that is, peer counseling, tutoring, food services, housing maintenance), in which course credits can be given.

Given the need to retain students once they are admitted and the obvious need to find sources of income for students who need part-time jobs, particularly in times of high inflation, a chief student personnel officer (CSPO) is very likely to encourage a financial aid director who wishes to establish a systematic pool of job opportunities for students. As noted in the case study, effective coordinating activities are critical in order to achieve goals, and a financial aid director would probably lobby extensively with fellow student service departments so that the sample goals noted earlier could be achieved.

Operational goals to establish a student job services corporation, for example, might require coordinating activities with the career placement office, food service, housing, and student activities. Since a student job corporation could include sales of various goods, that is, food, candy, gifts, clothing, laundry services, and even travel plans to students, it is immediately clear that cooperation with the groups just mentioned and substantial planning with student groups would be essential. Without proper communication and coordination, the sale of food, for example, is likely to infringe on the duties of individuals operating the campus food service. Nevertheless, if carefully explained to existing food service personnel, a dormitory or after-hours snack service operated by students might be appropriate and could handsomely support several student jobs.

Meetings with off-campus employers could be initiated through the CSPO and the placement director. Community businesses are likely to provide employment for students, because this may lead to increased business. Some alumni might be able to provide jobs or even serve as supervisors for the purpose of certifying work that may be appropriate for academic credit. Establishing a work-for-credit program (cooperative education) may not be an easy task, but it is of sufficient advantage to both students and the institution that the CSPO should be willing to support such an effort by initiating contact with academic deans and department chairpersons. Government funds are available to support cooperative education programs, and there is much to say in favor of work experience as a basis for extending academic credit.

Demands made on financial aid officers are frequent and varied. Government, students, parents, and even the institution itself generally see financial aid in self-serving ways. Government demands accountability for the expenditure of funds, of course, but also wants its dollars returned through higher skill and performance levels in the citizenry—not to mention more tax dollars obtained from fully employed individuals. Students and parents see financial aid as a way to secure education that would otherwise be beyond their fiscal reach. Scholarship aid, which was at one time a symbol of status and prestige, has become much less so today because of massive federal financial aid monies available. Institutions see financial aid as a means to achieve institutional objectives, that is, attracting more students, holding down tuition increases, and enhancing the institution's image before the community and general public. Training for financial aid officers, therefore, is critical given the diverse demands and conflicts inherent in such work.

Training topics for financial aid officers obviously include substantial exposure to federal regulations dealing with institutional requirements with respect to loan and grant eligibility, as well as consumer information, and the guidelines for work-study and cooperative education. Such training should increase the amount of funds that reach an institution as well as promote more effective and equitable distribution. Financial aid officers must be sensitive, of course, to the financial needs of students, but also to the possibility of personal problems that require a different kind of professional review. Appropriate counseling and communication techniques might be acquired through an inhouse training program. Additional areas in which a financial aid professional might develop his or her competencies include information processing, statistical analysis, publications, and grant development.

In summary, financial aid officers are subject to competing demands and the typically harsh realities of student needs, family problems, and seemingly insufficient resources with which to cover the ever-increasing costs of a college education. It is, of course, immediately gratifying to develop a financial aid package that will permit a student to attend college and at the same time satisfy institutional enrollment requirements. Competent managers in financial aid who develop a climate in which their staff members work toward the realization of department goals help their people achieve these higher satisfactions.

Student Activities

Student activities functions include many social and recreational activities and some extracurricular educational experiences. The student activities department typically manages not only these social and recreational functions, but also the food services, the book store, and the campus gift shop, if one exists. This department also is involved with the student news media and student governance matters. In light of these various functions, student activities provides significant employment opportunities for students and can add measurably to their development as mature members of the society's economic community while still in school.

Social, recreational, and extracurricular activities can have a very great impact on the institution's ability to recruit and retain students. A well-managed student activities function, including meaningful club activities, cultural activities, art shows, theater and music events, and vibrant media programs, can provide the kind of stimulating experiences that make an institution desirable for students.

Student activities personnel, perhaps more than any other student affairs unit, are in the unique position of working directly with students, providing support for their organizations, and coming to grips with their problems. As such, activities directors face demanding tasks, but these tasks offer great potential for creative, exciting, and challenging solutions.

Teaching, informing, and consulting with students on how to set goals, establish priorities, set performance standards, and evaluate properly is certainly a critical responsibility for activities directors. This work helps students gain leadership skills and higher competency in organizing student functions. If student activities professionals are accustomed to working with goals and plan carefully, they will impart the same discipline and competencies to students with whom they work in these diverse activities.

Activities directors, then, are involved with students in a group process that should set goals, establish performance criteria, and provide diverse organizational and educational opportunities for students. Appropriate goals for a student activities office might include the following:

Strategic: To increase by 20 percent for the 1981 fall term the number of students directly involved in planning, budgeting, and programming processes for all student organizations

Operational: To develop, by August 1, 1980, a leadership training program for all freshman students that would emphasize planning and budgeting in programming activities

Operational: To identify, by September 1, 1981, 50 students in the freshman class who would be given special training in personnel management, that is, preparing job descriptions for student organizations, interviewing techniques, and supervision

Operational: To identify, by September 1, 1981, 50 freshmen students who would be given special training in budget management, that is, forecasting income and expenses, allocating resources, and financial controls

Although it might seem that an activities office could program music and theater events or other activities without being concerned about extensive coordination, this is hardly the case. Any serious attempt to teach students proper planning techniques, for example, would certainly require collaboration with relevant academic and administrative departments. Indeed, no successful music or drama event could likely be held without the support and aid of the department of buildings and grounds. Further, a drama or music department, for example, also would prove to be a useful resource to draw on while planning cultural activities. Committees that include students and staff are usually excellent vehicles for promoting cooperation between student activities and other departments that may be involved directly or indirectly in activities programs.

In light of these many broad activities, student activities personnel should be rather knowledgeable not only in working with students and their problems, but also as managers of activities. Therefore, each professional in this field needs to have the competencies of supervisors in other administrative areas.

Housing

The mission of residence management is to provide a quality environment for personal growth and academic study. Creating and maintaining educational programs that improve the quality of residence life for students is certainly a compelling objective for student affairs personnel who specialize in housing.

Previously, housing directors were little more than building superintendents; that is, they arranged for the purchase of furnishings, worked with admissions on the numbers of students who might have requested housing, provided head counts for food services, and coordinated safety efforts with campus security. Such housing activities still exist and require good management techniques, but other functions have become more critical to the educational function of residence personnel.

Resident advisers (RA's) working under the direction of the housing director provide first-line academic advising and personal counseling to students. RA's also are responsible with others for initiating social programs and orienting new students to the campus. Developing the skills of these untrained resident advisers is an important educational responsibility for housing personnel. RA's need to understand the objectives of residence management and the ways in which residence management believes it can achieve those objectives.

Residence life provides a unique opportunity for individuals and groups to create an environment for learning. Given the cooperation of relevant staff and faculty, residence forums, small group discussions, and miniseminars can all be held within a residence setting. Student needs such as career planning and health education can be studied, while topics such as student vandalism, abuse of drugs or alcohol, and new sexual lifestyles also can be examined by RA's, housing personnel, and students themselves.

With such varied educational responsibilities, residence directors will want to carefully define strategic and operational goals, of which the following are examples:

Strategic: To initiate a peer counseling program, by September 1, 1981, to include 25 RA's trained in programming, reading development, financial aid counseling, and career planning

Operational: To obtain sufficient funding, by March 1, 1981, from relevant student affairs budgets (student activities, counseling, financial aid, and placement) to support training activities

Operational: To enlist, by April 15, 1981, training personnel from relevant student affairs departments who would work directly with RA's to develop effective peer counseling techniques

Operational: To secure approval for summer training workshops by March 1 (2 weeks each) in each of the preceding areas so that RA's can be properly trained for September orientation week

Coordinating the various functions and services of a housing office is obviously no easy task. Interdepartmental communications must be precise and may need to be repeated several times. The distribution of keys and food service cards are typically handled through a residence office and may require active interface with other administrative offices, including the admissions office and the finance office.

In the strategic objective just noted, the promise and potential for active collaboration of RA's, housing staff members, and faculty is obvious. A small group framework directed toward specific training activities can be a highly effective means of ensuring grassroots support for student affairs programs so often needed among student leaders and faculty members.

In order to achieve a viable peer counseling program, the director of housing would need to secure from fellow student affairs directors both dollars and training personnel. The CSPO will likely be highly supportive of the director of housing's goals for such a program and probably would facilitate any necessary contacts with other departments. By emphasizing interdepartmental cooperation and the real promise of achieving several kinds of benefits from peer counseling activities, the director of housing is likely to make real progress in achieving program objectives.

Training for housing personnel is likely to be varied, especially because of the diverse management and student-development tasks inherent in the position of residence director. Residence directors and RA's face many serious questions daily concerning student needs, interests, and problems. Training for housing personel, and particularly student advisers, is therefore a requirement for effective operation. Without training and assessment of work activities, job objectives are likely to remain unfulfilled. Managers will find that the following checklist identifies the more important areas in which training may be needed:

1. Interpersonal relationships
2. Behavior modification
3. Programming
4. Management and budget skills
5. Living/learning activities
6. Student rights and responsibilities
7. Community development

The hours of a housing director are typically long and not easily spent. Given the potential for noise, drug abuse, and vandalism, the morale within the housing office can fluctuate daily. Indeed, the delayed delivery of bedframes or the failure of a residence adviser to properly inform the counseling center of a student in personal trouble can influence the climate. A housing director, however, who sets appropriate goals and ensures that the department is moving, through appropriate coordination procedures, toward the achievement of those goals can have a significant effect on the climate. An effective director can help his or her people achieve the rewards of a close residence community, good fellowship, and substantially pleasant group activities by applying the techniques identified in the Linking Elements Concept.

Health Services

Campus health services may range from small, one-nurse dispensaries to hospital-sized facilities complete with specialized practitioners in psychiatry and gynecology. Whatever their size, health services can play an important educative role in student development. The functions of a Health Services Office include treatment of students, maintenance of medical histories, study of diseases and illnesses that may be likely to affect students, training of residence advisors in first aid, and programming to include health education for all students.

Ideally, a health services director will emphasize preventive medical care, so that students may learn a lifelong orientation to good health. For instance, a sample strategic goal and related operational goals could be

Strategic: To prepare the materials and develop procedures, by September 1, 1981, that would instruct all freshmen students in basic techniques of preventive medicine

Operational: To obtain and code medical histories for all incoming students from the admissions department by August 1, 1981

Operational: To write and have printed, by August 1, 1981, educational units on various topics, for example, drug abuse, human sexuality, hypertension, diet, cancer, and so forth, that will be distributed to students.

The health services director may feel that an articulated program of health education should be available to all students on a regularly scheduled basis. Programs can be presented at coffee hours held once a week. This is often a helpful way for health and counseling centers to coordinate activities and minimize the fears that students may have. At the same time, ongoing programming maximizes the possibility for helping to solve a student's problem. Health services on a college campus should exist to support the educational objectives of the campus community by fostering awareness of ways to maintain mental and physical health.

College-age students are probably among the healthiest subgroups in the general population. Because of this fact and the fact that current budgetary concerns of most colleges limit the extent of medical services available, health service delivery now generally includes fewer doctor hours and more nurse and college health aide hours. Budget restrictions have precipitated the need for increased training, especially since students are more involved in the actual delivery of services and in medical-record maintenance. The following is a checklist of the areas in which training might be provided to students and staff members in health services:

1. Federal regulations relative to privacy and other legal considerations, including privileged communications and malpractice
2. Contemporary sexual lifestyles
3. Alcohol and drug abuse
4. Preventive medicine
5. Mental health
6. Information processing
7. Crisis intervention
8. Cooperative education
9. Behavior modification

Of course, technical competence is a major requirement for effective members of the health services team. The director who helps his or her people obtain the skills needed for high-level performance provides services to the institution, to the students who require treatment, and to the employee who is moving along a chosen career path.

Placement

Perhaps no other student service today is as important to a student's future as the placement office, often called the office of career planning. Helping students plan rather than blindly tumble into careers represents a primary responsibility for college placement officers. Simply posting available part-time jobs and inviting companies and government agencies to visit a college campus is far less than what is minimally required for an effective office of career planning. Placement officers today must be able to provide those educational programs which help students to maximize their career growth opportunities. Such programs must provide the means for both personal and intellectual growth and help students understand the need for preparing career strategies. The functions of a placement office include career counseling and planning activities, recruitment of students for available jobs, resume preparation assistance, interviewing analysis, and cooperative education. Helping students develop identifiable career roles is a primary function for placement officers. Indeed, placement personnel should emphasize career development, rather than job placement, and students should be encouraged to think about career planning and the need to set personal and academic objectives relative to their interests and abilities.

The following is a sample strategic goal that a placement staff might wish to pursue. Operational goals that might support such a goal also are noted.

Strategic: To establish, by September 1, 1982, a cooperative education program with at least 100 participating students in accounting, marketing, and management areas

Operational: To identify and obtain written confirmation, by September 1, 1981, of at least 200 local and regional corporations that would be willing to participate in a cooperative education program where academic credit would be assigned for work experience

Operational: To prepare the materials and schedule, by October 15, 1981, interviewing and resumé development workshops for those students interested in cooperative education

Operational: To obtain written confirmation, by January 1, 1982, from faculty representatives in accounting, marketing, and management areas who would be willing to serve for the 1982-1983 fall term as cooperative education supervisors

Coordination with the college of business, the counseling center, and, of course, local companies would be necessary before these objectives could be achieved. The placement director might initially prepare a letter to local and regional corporations inviting their participation in a cooperative education program and then meet jointly with the counseling center and college of business to define the precise program desired. Additional coordination steps obviously would include scheduling meetings with representatives of corporations wishing to participate in cooperative education programming. Follow-up workshops with faculty would, of course, be appropriate as well. Proper communication with faculty members concerning courses and curricula required for changing occupations also would have to be initiated by the placement director.

In the face of increased student anxiety concerning job opportunities and heightened consumer awareness about the value and worth of a college education, placement directors cannot easily avoid the need to do more—job solicitation, resumé development, career counseling, indeed anything that will help students feel more comfortable about finding a career. Placement personnel also might maintain contact with community business people and alumni; these people can provide a wide-ranging network for student use.

A checklist follows that offers a guide to the areas in which placement counselors need to develop competencies:

1. Federal regulations, particularly those concerning student privacy and equal employment opportunity
2. Cooperative education
3. Resumé development workshops
4. Interview training
5. Information processing
6. Student retention
7. Community development

Rewards for placement directors are often immediate—learning from a student that he or she has received a job. Success in this area can readily be measured, much more so than in many other student personnel functions. A department that consists of highly competent people who have clear and meaningful direction is likely to achieve a high measure of success and the resultant satisfactions.

Conclusion: Comprehensive Planning and Student Affairs

Comprehensive planning, as described previously, involves the definition of organizational missions; the analysis of relevant data, events, and resources; the establishment of goals; the articulation of operational means for securing those goals; the actual implementation of action steps; and the evaluation of progress toward organizational goals. Making a goals program operationally sound, however, requires that managers provide an environment in which people find the incentive and desire to achieve. Establishing goals and developing the operational means to achieve those goals will not alone spell success. Adherence to EQIFAPPO concepts represents for managers a means for promoting positive motivational impact of goals.

At the beginning of the chapter it was pointed out that the primary functions of student affairs activities revolve around recruitment and retention. Community building and social integration are central strategies for helping to achieve high-level performance. In all activities, compliance with government regulations must be maintained. A student affairs department that can achieve high levels of competence in these areas is likely to be outstandingly successful.

To help with a review of the function, a sample departmental audit questionnaire is provided that can serve as a model for the development of a more comprehensive one suited to the special needs of an individual institution.

Sample Audit for the Student Affairs Function

1. Recruitment and retention
    a. Is there clear articulation by the (CSPO) of the student affairs mission at the institution? (with staff and with students?)
    b. Are staff and students involved in setting strategies (operational goals and action steps) for recruiting and retaining students best suited to the programs and facilities of the institution?
    c. Is there active involvement by student affairs managers and students in recruitment and retention committees, particularly with regard to providing institutional research data and government statutory requirements?
    d. Are regular reviews held to consider the progress of recruitment and retention committees and to identify the special work or needs of team members?
    e. Do managers and staff members receive recognition for contributions and achievements, and are they held accountable when achievement or performance are inadequate?
    f. Do employees in student affairs feel that they have influence over their work and can identify areas of success and failure?
    g. Are personnel and student assistants evaluated on the basis of criteria that are known, understood, and accepted?
    h. Are training programs provided for personnel and students involved in recruitment and retention efforts at your institution?

2. Community building and social integration

    a. Are strategies (operational goals and action steps) for enhancing the personal and intellectual growth of students discussed regularly with staff and students?

    b. Are strategies (operational goals and action steps) for increasing student participation in and the institution's contribution to cultural life on campus and in the community regularly discussed with staff and students?

    c. Are priorities for the improvement of student life facilities (student center, residence halls, and media) set jointly with personnel and students, and are they clearly communicated?

    d. Is there active involvement in cultural life and social activities programming by student affairs management, particularly with regard to providing community and institutional support?

    e. Are the progress of cultural and social programming toward institutional goals and the individual contributions of personnel and students evaluated regularly?

    f. Are appropriate means for evaluating social life, drug use, alcohol use, sexual lifestyles in existence?

    g. Are those staff members and students who contribute to community building/social integration goals adequately recognized, and are those who fail to carry their fair share appropriately held accountable?

    h. Do employees and involved students believe that they can influence community building/social integration efforts and identify areas of success and failure?

    i. Are achievement criteria for evaluation of personnel and student contributions known, understood, and accepted?

    j. Do training programs exist for residence and student activities programming?

3. Government regulation and student affairs

    a. Are institutional and divisional legal responsibilities to staff personnel and students clearly communicated and understood?

    b. Are strategies (operational goals and action steps) for informing student consumers of institutional statutory obligations relative to financial aid, privacy, sex discrimination, and discrimination in employment discussed with staff members and students?

    c. Are strategies (operational goals and action steps) for helping students learn more about their legal rights and responsibilities set jointly with appropriate management and staff involvement?

d. Is there an active relationship between staff and student leaders interested in providing legal, financial, and insurance information to students?

e. Is progress of staff personnel responsible for informing and consulting with students about their legal, financial, and insurance needs evaluated regularly, and is recognition provided where appropriate and accountability for lack of achievement placed appropriately?

f. Do employees and student assistants feel that they have influence over their work and can identify areas of success and failure?

g. Are personnel and student assistants evaluated on the basis of criteria that are known, understood, and accepted?

h. Do training programs exist for personnel and students involved in informing and consulting with students about their legal, financial, and insurance needs?

Note

1. Popular network diagrams for this purpose are CPM (Critical Path Method) and PERT (Program Evaluation and Review Technique). Such a technique need not be used vigorously, but can provide a uniform picture to all those in the faculty, in student affairs, and in administration who are involved in various phases of the registration/space allocation/course assignment functions. At the same time, it can communicate the dates when inputs are needed for decisions. For instances, it would show when faculty departments have to submit course recommendations, when they have to be approved, and so forth. For further information see Gary E. Whitehouse, *Systems Analysis and Design Using Network Techniques* (Englewood Cliffs, N.J.: Prentice-Hall, 1973), and Jerome D. Wiest, *A Management Guide to PERT/CPM (Englewood Cliffs, N.J.: Prentice-Hall, 1969).*

Administration and Finance in Higher Education

Elliot I. Mininberg

The truism that the major resource of an organization is its people is one that is often expressed, but probably accepted only philosophically by most managers in industry, government, or public institutions. People have a tendency to see an organization through its external elements: the buildings, the facilities, the products. Even the success or failure of an intercollegiate athletic program is viewed as a major element of an institution's vibrance and vitality. Just as carpeting and attractive glass-enclosed offices give the impression of permanence and success for a business organization, an attractive campus with clear, ivy-covered walls and lots of recreational opportunities makes a favorable impression on new students.

It is true, of course, that for the short term, the financial resources, external image, adequacy of the equipment and machinery—all the physical resources of an organization—have a great deal to do with its current performance. However, buildings deteriorate, machines become obsolete, offices decay, and therefore, over the longer term, the real forces that make for success or failure are not the current strengths. In business terms, the balance sheet is only a reflection of the competence of the past, while the indicators of the strength for the future lie in the competence and motivation of the people who use these resources.

It is in this conflict between what will make short-term success and what will build a foundation for permanent future success that the real work of the administrative officers rests. In higher education, there is pressure from faculty for the requirements that will make their environments immediately more pleasant, more effective, and more efficient. There is also pressure from students who request and often demand facilities that enhance their current feeling of well-being so that life in college is more interesting, exciting, and pleasant. From these conflicting demands, and many others, the chief administrative officer must choose an appropriate balance that will provide guidance for the setting of priorities with respect to specific decisions.

The chief administrative officer must maintain integrity in the custodial role while constantly keeping in mind that over the long run it is the quality of the instruction that will achieve success and provide the wherewithal that will allow satisfaction of the other needs. Complicating these decisions is the difficult task of evaluating output in the academic areas. While it is easy to evaluate the appearance of the grass on the basis of the bare spots or the external maintenance of the building by its appearance, it is much more difficult to determine the quality of instruction by the faculty.

Unfortunately, the resources available to the chief administrative officer in supporting the mission of the college are greatly limited by the fact that a very large proportion of the resources available to the institution are used for salaries. Another large chunk is mandated as fixed expenses, such as debt service and physical maintenance, utilities, insurance, and other irreducible requirements. Other fiscal constraints come from the board or other regulatory agencies that have authority over the activities of the institution. When all these requirements are subtracted from the resources available in any one year, the importance of the human resources becomes that much more apparent. It is only through stimulating prudent management on the part of every member of the institutional community, including those who do not often perceive themselves as managers, that the administrative function can hope to achieve outstanding performance.

It is because flexible resources are so limited that the administrative officer more often finds himself or herself in a position of having to deny to others that which they feel is due to them. It is not surprising, therefore, that frequently the financial officers are perceived by those who seek what they consider to be satisfaction of reasonable needs as gate keepers concerned with the physical trappings of the institution rather than with the need to establish a climate in which people can find maximum motivation to attain higher levels of achievement in their work.

How a new administrator is perceived, however, also is largely determined by the way that individual sees himself or herself and by the way the administrator is able to articulate to the community awareness of and a commitment to the basic instructional mission. This awareness and commitment must exist not only at the highest level of the administrative staff, but also must be reflected throughout the organization. Herein lies the challenge in the administrative function. The commitment to accept this challenge and to achieve expresses itself in the way the chief administrative officer develops or fails to develop appropriate goals with the respective heads of the administrative departments and managerial subunits. The chief administrative officer's ability to create a climate of cooperation and mutual respect with these people as well as with other people in the academic departments is crucially important. From an appropriate climate comes recognition of the administrative department's professionalism, which, with common acceptance by the academic departments that the administrative personnel are indeed performing their function in a competent way, provides the foundation for the mutual cooperation that is so essential.

In order to achieve this primary guiding mission for the administrative function, the chief administrative officer typically works through eight major functional units: personnel, business services, computer services, safety and security, facilities maintenance, intercollegiate athletics, institutional planning, and auxiliary services.

Personnel

There are two primary functions that a personnel department performs:

1. The mechanical/technical functions of administration
2. A less clearly defined function of the management and development of human resources

The Administrative Function

Personnel is a highly regulated area in which the administrators are greatly dependent on prescribed regulations set down by national and local authorities, as well as by the board of trustees. The personnel department must maintain a thorough and well-organized mechanism for ensuring that all compensation decisions, whether they concern wage and salary or fringe benefits, are promptly implemented and maintained. The major goal of compensation administration is to achieve awareness on the part of every employee, in academic as well as nonacademic departments, that the institution is indeed doing its very best to ensure that every individual within the institutional community receives fair treatment relative to the outside world and other members of the community.

Wage and Salary Administration: Administratively, the personnel department must see to it that there are appropriate procedures for wage and salary administration and for the attainment of these compensations. This means that the personnel department must be aware of wage and salary practices in colleges and universities throughout the country, as well as in similar functions within the geographic area.

Personnel's responsibilities in compensation administration include the following:

1. Time keeping, including time records on employees and students who perform compensable work.
2. Payroll deductions, including savings bonds, fund drives, and encumberances
3. Authorizations for payments such as those pertaining to overtime, docking actions, bonuses, uniform-maintenance allowances, housing-

maintenance allowances, pay advances, retroactive pay adjustments, and, of course, termination pay.

These functions are primarily of a repetitive nature. Most of the work is fairly routine, and as a result, strategic and operational goals concern primarily accuracy quantity of work performed, ensuring privacy of information, and timeliness of services rendered. Equally important is the maintenance of the files necessary for application of these functions to employees who are unique in various ways, such as temporary employees. There are also other miscellaneous duties, such as appropriation of error reports and log sheets and the search for causes of errors when they occur and their reconciliation.

Fringe-Benefits Administration: Closely related to the activities of salary and wage administration is personnel's responsibility for fringe-benefits administration. In this area there are a very large number of functions that have to be peformed, including administration of

1. Health and medical benefits, such as basic health coverage and major medical; special coverages, such as for diagnostic procedures; sick-leave payments; any health-maintenance plans that exist, such as prescription drug plans, vision care plans, and dental plans; and medical care (or Medicare) for retired employees, for those who are indigent, and for those on disability status
2. Pension benefits, which include the basic enrollment, application of prior service, withdrawals, loan applications, retirement applications, certifications, actual payment of benefits, selection of benefits options, Social Security benefits, and life insurance payment administration
3. Mandated benefits, which include Workmen's Compensation and disability benefits, all of which involve the completion of reports and maintenance of files

In addition to ensuring accuracy and speed when providing these functions, personnel's goals with respect to fringe-benefits administration include (1) obtaining the best possible package for available funds or buying the prescribed package for the least cost, and (2) ensuring that employees are informed of benefits available to them and are aware of appropriate applications. For example, employee options relating to fixed and variable annuities are constantly changing. The personnel office has an obligation not only to offer the best packages, but also to ensure that employees are properly aware of their options so that choices are based on full understanding.

The personnel department also serves in an advisory function to supervisors who work with unionized employees. In addition, one of the important things that the personnel department has to do is to ensure that the supervisors are aware of the importance of appropriate documentation and deliberate care in the handling of grievances and disciplinary actions. Disciplinary actions very often are challenged by the union and then go through grievance steps to arbitration, where the arbitrator will rule against the institution because of inadequate documentation on the part of the supervisor. The personnel department, therefore, has the responsbility to provide whatever information is necessary to ensure that all the steps are taken in proper sequence, that all rules are followed, that the individual is not subject to discrimination, and that there is adequate documentation in all disciplinary actions.

Recruitment, Employment, and Separation: This function of the personnel department concerns all the activities related to the search for employees in nonacademic functions. This is distinct from the personnel department's responsibility with respect to academic personnel, where it performs only administrative functions, but where decision making with respect to recruitment, employment, and employment status is made by the particular department or academic unit.

The recruitment, employment, and separation functions are somewhat less routine, but still highly subject to procedures. They include

1. Recruitment functions such as handling requests to initiate hiring action, monitoring positions in relation to allocation of resources, making recommendations pertaining to minimum position qualifications, posting vacancy notices and placing ads, and performing other recruiting activities.
2. Employment functions such as conducting employment interviews, providing physical examinations and other testing, scheduling interviews, and referring applicants.
3. Position classification functions such as preparation of job descriptions, conducting job evaluations, preparing ogranizational charts, evaluating requests for changes, and undertaking any necessary audits or reviews to ensure appropriate balance and consistency.
4. Separation functions such as processing of status changes, including promotion, lateral transfers, and reassignments, as well as separations. This also would include conducting exit interviews and notifying separating employees of their remaining rights and the steps they have to take to protect their rights.

These functions also carry the burden of social equity. The activities just described can be used by a personnel unit to either select highly competent people who fit into the social climate of the organization or to screen out those who the personnel people believe will not be readily accepted however competent they may be. It is not difficult to see the implications here for violation of both the spirit and the law of Affirmative Action for classes of people who have historically been deprived of access to more desirable positions.

Union Relations: With respect to union relations, the personnel department is involved in a number of activities, including the following:

1. The personnel department must anticipate the demands of any unions who represent employees of the institution so that an appropriate data base can be formed for the college to consolidate its position prior to negotiations.

2. It must obtain information about contract clauses that are detrimental to the effective performance of the mission of the college and integrate appropriate requests for changes into the college's position at negotiations. For example, if the personnel unit has received a significant number of grievances and expressions of work discontent, all of which focus on a particular implementation practice of the existing contract, this fact can be brought into play at the negotiating table so that a rewording of that particular paragraph or section of the agreement can be reached to eliminate either the discontent or the ability to continually grieve it.

3. It must ensure that the contract clauses are administered equitably and fairly. This implies reasonable, fair, but also businesslike interpretation of various clauses of the contract when other questions about their meaning arise. One of the difficulties associated with doing this, of course, lies in the interpretation of whatever management intent may exist. Under increasingly strong union awareness of the meaning of the minor subtleties of each clause, supervisors are very often led to believe that the union position is a stronger one and that, in the case of confrontations, management is more likely to concede.

4. It must create an awareness on the part of supervisors that management indeed has full rights under the contract and that the gradual erosion of management rights that often occurs is primarily due to supervisory acquiescence, which is not always necessary. The other side of this coin, of course, is excessive intransigence or militancy on the part of supervisors who feel that management rights are being unfairly encroached upon and the lack of awareness on their part of how to counter such pressures.

The personnel department has a very important role in helping supervisors become aware, through counseling and other appropriate steps, that management positions can be upheld provided that the steps taken to uphold them are reasonable, appropriate, and thoroughly executed.

5. The personnel department must represent and appropriately consider the needs and rights of "silence" constituencies at contract time. Inevitably, with every contract, two parties are highly visible, namely, management and union. In reality, in every contract, additional constituencies are involved. Sometimes, there are employees who are not unionized; sometimes there are employees who belong to the union, but do not subscribe to union philosophies or viewpoints. Then—and here is where an educational institution really differs—there are, of course, the students, who are neither union nor management, but who are greatly affected by the terms of the agreement. Of course, when there is more than one union, the members of other unions are affected by the terms and conditions that are agreed upon in the contract being negotiated.

The ultimate impact of this sort of thing is visible in the negotiations of the New York City Police and Fire Departments contract, in which there is a demand for equity even though the contracts are negotiated at different times of the year. If the personnel department does not know this demand going into negotiations, the department may not be able to accomodate the secondary demand after agreement is reached on the first. In higher education, the importance of this may be seen in a contract that permits a reduction in the number of different preparations each faculty member is required to teach each semester, which in turn might result in a student demand for alteration in the hours of instruction and/or number of sections of a specific course to be offered.

Management and Development of Human Resources

In addition to the routine administrative functions the personnel department has to perform, it also serves as the adviser to all other departments of the institution with respect to the management and development of human resources. The functions are necessary to achieve an appropriate climate in which people can find maximum motivation to achieve and grow.

With respect to all of its functions, the human resource management/development group, in effect, becomes the conscience of good, competent management, in terms of either the Linking Elements Concept or any other equivalent philosophical framework. The human resource management/development function, therefore, has responsibilities of a consultative nature and, in some areas, of providing support with respect to (1) compensation programs; (2) benefits programs; (3) recruiting, employment, and separation; (4) supervisory practices; and (5) training and development.

As discussed in chapter 5, the tangible benefits must meet the basic requirements of equity in relation to the higher education community throughout the country, as well as more specifically, those positions in higher education which exist within the same geographical area. However, since the personnel department's function is primarily one of a consultant recommending actions to be taken by either the board of trustees or the top management of a college with respect to compensation and fringes, it also must keep in mind the fundamental thought that compensation and fringes are primarily of a hygienic nature. Granting benefits and compensation that are clearly substandard with respect to equitable principles will lead to considerable dissatisfactions. However, granting compensation and benefits in excess of those enjoyed by others will bring very little in the way of addition to the motivational climate of the institution. On the contrary, it may very well be a detracting force.

With respect to recruitment, employment, and separation, of course, the manner in which these functions are performed reflects the concern for individual rights and the need of individuals to be respected and accepted. In addition to engendering respect for the individual and a positive attitude toward the institution at the start, the functions of recruiting, selection, and employment (and separation, of course) have considerable impact on the general technical competence level of administrative and other staff employees and therefore deserve high priority in ensuring that they are discharged competently.

Supervisory Practices: In a way, the personnel department has the responsibility to monitor supervisory practices to ensure that employees are indeed treated fairly, so that the institution is seen as a responsible employer that offers its people a high quality of work life. Many supervisors are selected for their positions on the basis of considerable competence in their respective functional areas. A good technician in data processing is likely to become a supervisor in data processing. A competent counselor is likely to wind up as the head of the counseling function. The same, of course, also happens in academic departments, where very often the most distinguished faculty member will be asked to assume the position of department chairperson. Competent people in their functional areas do not necessarily make good supervisors until they have received the training and development necessary to help them achieve a greater level of administrative competency. As this book points out, there is more, much more, to supervision and management than pure common sense or competence in a specific discipline.

One need not look any further than the incidence of vacancies for college presidencies throughout the country to get confirmation of this important point. The reason why so many college presidents do not achieve lasting tenure is because many of them are not competent as administrators. They may be outstanding scholars in their respective fields, but that does not necessarily provide them with the ability to cope with the covenants and managerial problems of their presidency. In a much simpler vein, the skills required in playing a violin are very different from those required to lead an orchestra. The point is the one made earier: there is such a thing as the art and science of management that must be mastered for competence in positions that have managerial requirements.

It does take time, however, for training and developmental experiences to help an individual become a competent supervisor capable of developing a climate that will lead to motivation and employee satisfaction, as described in the Linking Elements Concept. In the meantime, while individuals in supervisory positions are developing the competence to establish that climate, the personnel department has a monitoring, advising, and possibly counseling function as well as a support function when supervisors face difficulties. As a parallel, the personnel department can be viewed as a broker of services that are necessary to achieve the higher-level competence that must exist in every functional department. This applies to supervisory practices as well as it does to training and development, which will be discussed later.

In this function as broker/monitor/supporter, the personnel department is the appropriate unit to maintain the corrective ear to the ground for the institution, listening for dissatisfactions that are occurring and determining where there is evidence of inadequate attention to human relations. The personnel department can then provide the services necessary to that department, whether they be counseling, training and development, direct intervention through team building, or direct assistance in dealing with the problem.

Training and Development: There are, as in the other functions, several philosophies that may be present in different personnel units. Many personnel departments have separate training and development sections who offer staff-development programs and who see their function as developing staff members toward greater competence. Others view their role as support to the line managers and will help line managers understand more clearly what their role is with respect to the development of subordinates and then provide whatever support programs may be required and requested by these departments. The difference is most clearly defined in those personnel organizations which attempt to offer courses that are mandatory to all staff members and those which offer discretionary courses. This means that the various department heads or subdepartment heads can either nominate some of their people for these courses or the individuals can go voluntarily.

Just as in industry, where the training and development function will usually offer tuition refund programs, in an educational institution, tuition payments might not be required. However, distinct from noneducational institutions, the personnel department may arrange for flexible hours of employment to accommodate attendance at appropriate courses within the institution itself.

At one institution that offered courses for employees to upgrade skills without employee cost not only did the program improve the competence of those who participated in it, but it also raised morale and caused employees to think differently of their work environment. It also brought people from different parts of the institution into contact with one another, a feat that previously could not have been orchestrated in a more complex way.

Role of the Personnel Department in the Institution

With respect to the Linking Elements Concept, the personnel department's role is a primary one that is generally referred to as a staff role. A staff role can be a rather forceful one at times if it is discharged in a competent and effective way, with a full understanding of inherent strengths and weaknesses. A manager who clearly understands the Linking Elements Concept will acknowledge clearly that it is the responsibility of the individual organizational unit supervisor, regardless of where that unit may be, to ensure that the unit will achieve the highest performance through establishment of the best possible control and the highest possible level of quality of work life or morale that the environment and situation permit. If the individual supervisor in the student affairs department, or in an academic area, is to perform this comprehensive function of achieving the most appropriate climate and achievement orientation within that unit, then he or she must make all the necessary decisions with respect to each of the linking elements. This automatically precludes the personnel department from direct intervention and limits personnel's role to one of support.

The completely administered personnel function will recognize and support the need for the individual manager or supervisor to fully assume the role the Linking Elements Concept describes. This does not lessen the personnel department's role in ensuring that supervisors perform their functions appropriately. On the contrary, this role is one of great importance in various areas: in monitoring and finding the weaknesses that exist within the organization and in identifying the support the personnel department should provide. It must determine to what extent the authority of the institution should be used to achieve greater compliance or greater understanding of the department supervisor and, finally, actually provide auxiliary and supportive services on which the individual supervisor can draw.

What does this mean in practical terms? If, for instance, the vice president of student affairs has difficulty with supervisory competence in a specific area within that function, it should be possible for him or her to call on the personnel department to review the situation, identify the supervisory practices that may be causing the difficulty, identify the problems as perceived from the employee's point of view, and then recommend appropriate steps that can be taken, including offering the services such as counseling and training. In so doing, the personnel department ensures that it helps the vice president of student affairs to develop competence in the respective functional unit rather than assuming a transference of responsibility to itself.

Often there is a tendency on the part of competent personnel administrators faced with what they perceive as lack of competence in many areas to consider themselves to be in charge of a particular personnel function and to insist on adherence with the way they perceive the needs of the respective functional units. This view is understandable in light of the fact that most supervisors assume their supervisory responsibilities without adequate preparation for them.

There are, of course, two ways to deal with the problem from the point of view of the personnel officer. One is to assume a more and more direct advisory role in the decision-making process. The other is to see it primarily as a function of developing the respective manager to assume the responsibilities more competently. It is obvious that the first approach is fully self-defeating The personnel department neither has adequate staff to provide this kind of detailed decision-making support to every functional department, nor would such involvement lead to confidence and development of self-reliance on the part of the respective supervisors.

In many ways, this pressure to take charge is quite similar to the pressure on the individual supervisor in any function to maintain control through direct involvement in all important decisions. This was already discussed extensively in chapter 4 during participation in decision making. As a result of their positions, personnel administrators must be even more aware that they are undermining their real function when they become too deeply involved in the direct management of individual units.

There is, of course, the problem of balance here. For instance, one of the major universities on the East Coast was operating for years under a highly capable president who was able to generate a positive, achievement-oriented climate within the organization, particularly with respect to academic achievement. Unfortunately, that particular president was not equally effective in the management of the business affairs of the university. The result was a deterioration of the financial position of the university, which originally started with an adequate endowment and ultimately found itself going deeper and deeper into deficit budgeting. When this highly respected administrator was replaced by a more business-oriented president, the entire atmosphere throughout the university changed toward greater control. People lost the feeling of belonging and the feeling of achieving self-realization through their work. Morale decreased, but the financial problem was gradually brought under control, at some cost in the quality and diversity of instruction and the quality of work life for the members of the community.

Neither of these two presidents necessarily had to sacrifice too much in order to come closer to achieving his objective. In each case, the personnel department could have stepped in and provided assistance. It could have identified problems in the institution and provided advice on ways those problems could be handled. These might include suggested approaches, for instance, on how the initial president could achieve financial soundness by paying more attention to the goals related to that function without sacrificing any significant degree of quality of work life. Or, personnel might have recommended strategies to the second president for maintaining an appropriate achievement-oriented climate within necessary budget structures.

How a high-level administrator, whether he or she is the president or a personnel director, can achieve this appropriate balance is, of course, to some extent a matter of that particular individual's strength. In most cases, however, it is most likely achieved through appropriate selection of the functional department heads, and through the development of these people in terms of what has been defined earlier as a high level of maturity as members of the management team.

Setting Goals in the Personnel Department

There are, of course, an infinite number of goals that can be set on the very many functions in the personnel department. A few examples can help to illustrate the point. In wage and salary, the strategic goals could concern achieving measurably higher satisfaction on the part of employees toward the compensation system by a certain date. Specific operational goals could be to reduce the incidences of errors in checks, to increase the rapidity with which special payments are made, and to achieve cost reduction in processing of salary checks. Similarly, with respect to fringes, a strategic goal could concern the improvement in benefits without increase in cost through negotiations with insurance carriers or more effective management of the funds.

Strategic goals in recruitment, employment, and separation concern primarily the quality of new employees and the effectiveness with which transfers and promotions enhance the technical competence of the organization. However, operational goals can be seen in reducing the number of open positions and the time required to fill positions, increasing the speed with which classifications are completed or classification questions are resolved, and improving the effectiveness with which any controversial decisions are explained and questions about them are clarified.

In union relations, the strategic goals concern the levels of cooperation with the unions and the relative cost of contracts when compared with similar institutions or comparable contracts in the area. Operational goals would concern specific goals relating to numbers of grievances, favorable clarification of vague clauses, and negotiations on new contracts.

Strategic personnel goals related to supervisory practices concern the climate that supervisors create. This climate is, of course, very difficult to measure, since the only practical devices are attitudinal surveys and not many institutions use these on any regular basis. Less effective measures include records of the numbers of complaints and informal discussions with staff members in various functional areas. These are not as precise and, therefore, are less likely to provide valid data for specific goals. However, whenever a problem does arise, whether it is brought to the attention of the personnel department by a dean, a department head in student affairs, or a member of the top management, goals can, be set of course, on correction of the problem. Whenever possible these goals should relate to supervisory or managerial development rather than to replacement.

Business Services

The major functions the business office performs concern the receiving and dispersement of the financial resources available to the institution, whether it is a publicly owned institution where the processes are heavily regulated or a private one with considerably more leeway. In either case, however, business services operates under guidelines set down by either the regulatory agencies or the board of trustees. Obviously, there is greater opportunity for the professionals in business services to present the department's view to the board of trustees than to a regulatory agency in a far away location. As a result, there are some distinct differences in the way the business functions are performed in a publicly owned institution as opposed to a private one. In general, however, the similarities are far greater than these differences, and what is even more important, the management function and the activities of managers that lead to excellence in the field are very similar indeed.

Business Services are provided to the institution through a series of subordinate offices that include in most institutions (1) a budgeting office, (2) a revenue and dispersement office frequently called the bursar's office, (3) a purchasing office, (4) an accounting office, (5) an internal auditing office (in some institutions), and (6) an administrative services office.

Budgeting

There are primarily two major types of budgets: an *operating budget* and a *capital budget*. Both budgets are planning documents that spell out how anticipated revenues will be spent by the various departments of the institution. Generally, the operating budget is for a 1-year period, while the capital budget is for a longer period of time, sometimes projecting far into the future the major changes that are contemplated for the institution. The capital budget concerns primarily buildings and major pieces of equipment. The operating budget includes all the ongoing expenditures of the institution, including salaries, supplies, materials, minor equipment items, and insurance.

For budgeting purposes, the institution is broken down into separate cost centers. During the budgeting process, each cost center is provided with specific budgets for various activities and functions, such as salaries, materials, and supplies, postage, duplicating costs, possibly even telephone costs, or any others that are measurable and direct, so that the costs can be traced specifically to the cost center incurring them.

The budget reflects the resolution of the conflicting demands that have been reconciled through the governance process and ultimately reveal themselves as priorities through allocations within the budget. For example, an academic department might request considerable increases for the coming year in its respective departmental budgets for faculty salary increments, for additions to faculty/staff in those areas where student demand is growing, and for additional graduate assistants for research purposes. At the same time, the student affairs department may ask for additional personnel for counseling and placement services, as well as residence staff to cope with the increasing stress on young people in college and the threat this places on retention of students. At the same time, the security department might need additional staff to increase its foot patrol during evening hours and reverse a trend toward petty thefts. These conflicting demands may be resolved through the budget-setting process, and the final figures on budget lines reflect the amounts available to the respective areas for internal decisions on how to meet their needs in the most effective ways. When the budget process operates properly, the priorities in the budget reflect the mission of the institution and the strategic goals that have been set.

One pitfall that often obstructs the development of an intelligent, most useful budget is the tendency, when there are three such competing demands and limited resources, to split those limited resources in some reasonably equitable way among these three demands. Very often this can be a highly detrimental policy. It may be more advantageous for the institution to totally eliminate one of the three and allocate the monies appropriately among the other two. There is, of course, the other dimension of time, and it is an important managerial discipline to set the priorities in such a way that the matters deserving highest priorities are appropriately funded during the current period, while the lesser priority matters are postponed for later periods. This is preferable to the situation in which several activities are being funded inadequately so that none can operate effectively.

An institution whose governance process is able to provide effective guidance will achieve a budget without the many pitfalls that can exist. The budget can be a positive instrument that helps an institution make the most effective use of all its resources. When the budgeting process is not operating effectively, as often occurs, then some areas that are central to the mission of the institution and have high priority can be in great need of funds, while other areas of far less importance can have budget resources available to them.

The concepts discussed under EQIFAPPO (see chapter 4), but especially under the accountability and performance-evaluation sections, are where the key lies to development of appropriate budgets. If people are clearly aware that accepting a lower budget during a period when for some reason there is a lull in needs does not automatically preclude higher budgets in future years when the needs are greater, then there is less necessity to demand "protective budgets." An example can be seen in the department that ends a fiscal year with excess funds available and elects to spend these dollars for matters of low importance or urgency just to avoid returning money to the budget office out of concern that failure to do so would reflect negatively on future budget requests.

Well-organized budgets provide regular reports to the managers in charge of the cost centers and serve as tools for managers to use the discretionary resources to the greatest benefit of their particular function. In the budget, more so than anywhere else, it is obvious that a department chairperson is indeed a manager. It is the department chairperson who must guide the department to the decisions on how the discretionary monies are to be spent, and any department chairperson who attempts to avoid this responsibility will see monies spent less effectively than one who accepts the responsibility and effectively guides the department toward appropriate decisions. Very often in these instances, the monies not spent are lost to the department, and if the budget was a competent one in the first place, then the mission of the particular department and the institution suffers because of this loss.

The discussion so far has concentrated on the importance of seeing a budget as a planning document. For the period of time for which a budget is set (which is usually a year), an institution will experience changes in conditions and environment that cannot be accurately predicted at the beginning of the budget period. For this reason, those budgets which best serve the institution's needs have flexible elements built into them. Their flexibility can be achieved through facilitating transfers of money within each cost center and through the transfer of money from one activity to another, but also between cost centers, again through effective decision making within the governance process.

The budgeting office itself has a monitoring function to see that funds allocated in the budget are indeed spent appropriately. However, the budgeting office generally has both limited authority and access to information. For this reason, an auditing office (where one exists internally) or the external auditor has responsibilities in supporting this effort. For instance, a department may have $3,000 in travel money, and while this money could, under the budget, be spent on one single $3,000 trip for one staff member, this would undoubtedly be inconsistent with the intent of the allocation. Therefore, budgetary safeguards are necessary, even though many exist within the governance process itself. Managers who set goals in the manner suggested in this book are not likely to experience this problem.

The budget is important as a planning tool that can help a goal-setting process work appropriately. Many of the goals are, in effect, the achievement of a specific activity within the budgetary limitations, so the budget infringes in one way or another on almost all institutional and departmental goals. If one wishes to see how well a goals program is working, therefore, looking at the budgeting process and the satisfaction that people express with its effectiveness is an excellent place to get reliable indication.

Revenue and Dispersements

The people in this functional area accept the revenues for the institution from many sources, such as, tuition, fees, scholarships, some financial aid monies, rental income, special functions, and fund raising. All these funds are contributed to what is considered the general fund of the college, from which the normal budgeting expenses of the institution are met. In addition to these general fund revenues, most institutions have other income, which is dedicated to specific purposes and comes from endowment funds and particular projects designated in gift form. These funds are usually not processed by the fiscal and accounting office, and they are not in the regular budget. These monies are received and dispersed by either an institutional treasurer who reports independently to the president or vice president for administration and finance or an auxiliary office established specifically for this purpose.

The revenue and dispersements office, which often is headed up by a person called the bursar, is often the largest unit within administration and finance. Even though most of the work performed here is highly routine, such as entries into records either on a computer or maintained on paper by hand, the major contribution of the bursar's office is in the opportunity it provides the institution to make the most effective use of the monies currently available. Particularly in times of high interest rates and rapid inflation, the speed with which information is available on how much cash is at the institution's disposal, how much cash will be needed in the immediate future, and where these monies are can help the financial officers make the most effective use of these funds and gain the greatest income from them while they are uncommitted.

Most of the work in these functions is highly routine, and despite all the changes in techniques and available data-processing equipment, there remains some of the aura of the old bookkeeping office with people sitting on high chairs with green shades over their eyes. The reason for this lies in the meticulous manner in which the work must be performed. Enormous masses of data are processed, and the opportunities for cumulative errors (that is, transposed numbers or misplaced decimal points) are significant. The need for managerial competence in this environment is very high if the institution is to offer a reasonable level of quality of work life to the people working in this area.

Purchasing

Purchasing is closely related to revenue dispersement. Generally the people working in purchasing offices are in close proximity for improved interaction. In fact, all the dispersement activities are triggered by the actions of the people who buy the supplies and other materials used by the institution. Even services are purchased through the purchasing office, and the only significant expenditure of funds that does not affect the purchasing officer is salaries. Purchasing work, although also rather tedious, is much more enriched in many ways than much of the work in the revenue and dispersement office. The purchasing buyers have the opportunity to meet vendors, and the more varied environment that these experiences provide makes for considerably higher quality of work life by itself.

There is a negative aspect to the often heard generalization that the purchasing department does not operate at the highest level of competence. Frequently, since the function of the purchasing office is to buy at the best possible price, purchasing people are perceived as sacrificing quality and special requirements for the sake of economic expediency. A competently managed purchasing department that approapriately communicates its goals and adequately explains its activities can silence negative generalizations by establishing open lines of communications with the departments making requisitions. Open communications can promote more effective working relationships so that the best interests of the institution can be served within the budgetary limitations.

Within the institution, the purchasing department is, without doubt, the one most susceptible to potential corruption because of relationships with competing vendors and the conflicts of interest that can occur. As in government, the question as to when a gift is a token of appreciation and when it goes beyond that and impacts on the decision-making processes, of course, is a very difficult line to establish. Managers in the purchasing department therefore need to apply judiciously the strategies discussed under the linking element that concerns adherence to rules, as discussed in chapter 5.

Accounting

There is an absolute need for control devices to ensure that the fiscal integrity is maintained and that the records of receipts and dispersements somehow "add up" and no funds "disappear." This function is the accounting function. It culminates in regular monthly, quarterly, and annual reports to the heads of the institution as well as to external agencies or boards concerned with the activities of the institution. Obviously, even alumni and those interested in the future of the institution need summary reports to tell them how the financial resources of the institution are used to further the mission. All systems require checks and balances, and the appropriate functioning of these checks and balances is monitored through the creation of these reports and auditing by internal and external audit personnel.

As in a business, an institution must prepare the two reports that reflect its financial condition and provide some information about its potential and viability for the future. These two reports are (1) an income and expense system, which is called by a different name by various institutions (see table 9-1), and (2) a balance sheet (see table 9-2). The income and expense statement summarizes in general format all fiscal activities for the period it covers. It, therefore, is a report of activities that have occurred. The balance sheet provides a glimpse of the status of the assets and liabilities of the institution as of the moment for which it is prepared.

In addition to the balance sheet and income statement, formal financial statements very often also provide a statement of changes in financial position that shows where financial resources were obtained and what they were used for. Sometimes the statement includes an analysis of working capital. An example of this is shown in table 9-3. This table shows how the budget for selected functions has been allocated, including further breakdowns for the various cost centers in business services. The budgetory program ledger (see figure 9-1) is a computerized expenditure-control report issued monthly by the college financial system. It is used for purposes of monitoring, controlling, and modification as necessary.

Auditing

The purpose of the auditing function is threefold: (1) to determine whether the records accurately reflect the way money has been spent, (2) to determine

Table 9-1
Dormitory Operating Account: Statement of Income and Accumulated Equity for 6 Months Ended December 31, 1979, Unaudited

Revenues:	
Room rentals	$ 443,670
Room and board summer session	143,122
Meal ticket income	307,210
HUD debt subsidy grants	71,740
Interest income	39,238
Excess receipts	191,390
Work study grants	26,940
Miscellaneous income	15,101
Total revenues	$1,238,411
Costs and expenses:	
Food service concession	$ 270,359
Bond interest	253,288
Depreciation	137,378
Salaries and wages	171,030
Fuel and utilities	69,724
Repairs and maintenance	36,085
Employee benefits	21,290
Other	53,896
Total costs and expenses	$1,013,050
Net income	225,361
Accumulated equity at beginning of year	529,224
Accumulated equity as of December 31, 1979	$ 754,585

whether the money has been spent in accordance with the intentions of the allocations, and (3) to provide recommendations for changes in accounting procedures and record-keeping procedures that will eliminate any problems that have been uncovered.

As a rule, the second of these functions is performed by staff members, while the first and third functions usually are performed by an external accounting firm specifically designated for this purpose by the board of trustees. In publicly owned institutions, this external auditor frequently is a government agency or an arm of a government agency that performs audits for all institutions and agencies within that governmental unit. Frequently, even publicly owned institutions will use a private accounting firm to audit the special auxiliary funds or segregated funds that are not controlled by the public owner of the institution.

Administrative Services

The last major segment of the business services office is concerned with all those functions not specifically covered by the others. These include risk man-

Table 9-2
Dormitory Operating Account: Balance Sheet, December 31, 1979, Unaudited

Assets	
Current assets:	
Cash and cash equivalents	$ 49,143
Investments at cost	260,000
Accounts receivable	470,807
Excess rental payments	28,444
Accrued interest and other receivables	20,689
Prepaid expenses	4,672
Total current assets	$ 833,755
Buildings and equipment—net	8,499,848
Construction in progress	257,434
Other assets:	
Debt service reserve funds	703,781
Project renewal and replacement funds	147,763
Construction fund	495
Deferred charges	31,361
Total assets	$10,474,437
Liabilities and Equity	
Current liabilities:	
Current portion of capitalized lease obligation	$ 123,500
Accounts payable	84,047
Due to/from Montclair State College	
and related organizations	221,305
Total current liabilities	$ 428,852
Long-term portion of capitalized lease obligation	8,516,000
Donated surplus	775,000
Accumulated equity	754,585
Total liabilities and equity	$10,474,437

agement (insurance and related activities that protect against disastrous events or large losses of property), inventory management, central storage and supply, mail and duplicating services, telephone and other internal communications, and other less common administrative services, including such diverse activities as student identification cards, bulletin board maintenance, and shuttle bus services.

While each of these may seem to be an insignificant aspect of an institution's activities, each has to be managed by a highly competent individual able to organize many diverse activities and operate them without waste to the greatest benefit of those involved. Inventory, mail services, and duplicating can be potentially significant sources of annoyance to the other members of the institutional community because these services are so essential to the

Table 9-3
Fiscal Year 1980 Allotments: Vice President for Administration and Finance

Object Code	Account	Reserves	Allotment	Adjusted Allocations	VPA&F Office 721	Inst. Planning 722	Office 724	Mngrs. Office 725	Pur-chasing 725	Accounts Payable 727	Revenues 728	Budgets 729	Total	Computer Center 741
										Business Services				
	Salaries													
120	Officer and employees													
120	New positions													
120	Special projects (Blankets)													
120	Debits/(credits)													
120	Overtime													
	Total	(28,660)	108,930	79,270										42,000
	Materials and Supplies													
210	Printing and office				650	630	600	6,170	2,100	1,700	2,890	1,520	14,980	
240	Education	700	700		65	260	1,600	220	50			70	1,940	760
	Services													
301	Travel	3,220	7,150	3,930										
302	Telephone	—	235,000	235,000										630
307	Advertising													
308	Subscriptions and memberships	380	4,100	3,720	250	330	110						110	
321	Postage	—	135,000	135,000										
324	Official reception	1,425	3,590	2,165	33	65	1,770						1,770	
326	Data processing	38,000	253,000	215,000										215,000
344	Rent: data processing equipment	9,897	109,400	99,503										99,503
345	Rent: other	(275)	3,340	3,615	34		570	780			315		1,665	
365	Staff training	—	11,680	11,680										
390	Other	(2,020)	3,300	5,320	1,168	110		1,640			770		2,410	2,140
	Maintenance Property-Recurring													
410	Office equipment	11,600	27,700	16,100										
	Maintenance of Property-Nonrecurring													
460	Office equipment		5,000	5,000			5,000						5,000	
	Extraordinary													
513	Compensation awards		40,000	40,000										
	Additions and improvements													
710	Office equipment	28,000	60,000	32,000			32,000						32,000	
740	Education equipment	5,400	5,400											
	Total	68,327	955,630	887,303	2,200	1,395	41,650	8,810	2,150	1,700	3,975	1,590	59,875	359,033

PROGRAM FA210000
REPORT NO FA2100R1
DEPT 110156 PHILOSOPHY/RELIGION PROJ 000 FUND 10000 GENERAL STATE FUND FISCAL YR 80

BUDGETARY PROGRAM LEDGER

DATE 02/13/80
PAGE 853

OBJ	RPT DATE	REFERENCE	DESCRIPTION	ORIG BUDGET	CURRENT BUDGET	ENCUMBRANCES	PAYMENTS	BALANCE
12000	12/05/79	BAL FWRD	SALARIES OFFICERS & EMPLOYEES	.00	248,336.00	.00	29,452.40	218,883.60
12000	12/13/79	52J 8003531	P/R T			.00	90.36	
12000	12/13/79	52J 8003583	P/R 21			.00	11,746.76	
12000	01/07/80	52J 8003791	P/R 22			.00	11,746.76	
12000	01/07/80	52J 8003792	P/R 24			.00	11,746.76	
12000	01/16/80	52J 8003891	P/R 25			.00	11,746.76	
12000	01/16/80	52J 8003892	P/R 26			.00	11,746.76	
12000	02/01/80	52J 8004229	P/R 01			.00	11,714.94	
12000	02/01/80	20J 8004482	ALLOT 934		750.00	.00	.00	
12000	02/01/80	52J 8004525	P/R 2			.00	11,714.94	
12000	02/13/80	END BAL	SALARIES OFFICERS & EMPLOYEES		249,086.00	.00	111,706.44	137,379.56
12200	12/05/79	BAL FWRD	SALARIES SPECIAL SERVICES	.00	.00	.00	150.00	150.00
12200	12/13/79	52J 8003463	P/R V			.00	855.00	
12200	12/13/79	52J 8003497	P/R U			.00	2,250.00	
12200	12/13/79	52J 8003531	P/R T			.00	161.95	
12200	01/16/80	52J 8003890	P/R Y			.00	2,250.00	
12200	02/08/80	52J 8004512	P/R A			.00	3,135.00	
12200	02/13/80	END BAL	SALARIES SPECIAL SERVICES			.00	8,801.95	8,301.95
19100	02/08/80	52J 8003890	P/R Y			.00	50.00	50.00
19100	02/13/80	END BAL	SALARIES BONUS			.00	50.00	50.00
21000	12/05/79	BAL FWRD	PRINTING AND OFFICE SUPPLIES	.00	1,100.00	.00	232.65	867.35
21000	01/16/80	30J 8003981	DEBIT 678			.00	434.79	
21000	01/25/80	30J 8004088	DEBIT 777			.00	100.00	
21000	02/08/80	30J 8004723	DEBIT 1021			.00	87.84	
21000	02/13/80	END BAL	PRINTING AND OFFICE SUPPLIES		1,100.00	.00	855.28	244.72
24000	12/05/79	BAL FWRD	EDUCATION SUPPLIES	.00	440.00	.00	20.70	419.30
24000	01/07/80	99P 0004399	0A40884 NON IDENTIFIED VENDOR		.00	24.77	.00	
24000	02/13/80	END BAL	EDUCATION SUPPLIES		440.00	24.77	20.70	394.53
30100	12/05/79	BAL FWRD	TRAVEL	.00	975.00	.00	.00	975.00
30100	02/13/80	END BAL	TRAVEL		975.00	.00	.00	975.00
71000	12/13/79	20J 8003471	ALLOT 686		206.70	.00	.00	
71000	01/07/80	30J 8003476	DEBIT 564		.00	.00	206.70	
71000	02/13/80	END BAL	OFFICE EQUIPMENT		206.70	.00	206.70	.00
		****PROJECT 000 TOTALS		.00	251,807.70	24.77	121,641.07	130,141.86
		****COST CNTR 156 TOTALS		.00	251,807.70	24.77	121,641.07	130,141.86

Figure 9-1. Computerized Expenditure-Control Report

completion of daily tasks. For example, when something that a department urgently needs cannot be obtained from central stores, or when mail services are delayed or mail is misrouted, or when duplicating services cannot provide clean copies effectively, or when telephone calls cannot get through, each can have a significant impact on the effectiveness with which the entire institution operates.

It would not be hard to picture the frustration of a faculty member who has spent several years on a research project and is finally putting the finishing touches on the last report, which is due, in several days, to the federal government, who cannot get several pages of the manuscript typed, duplicated, bound, or prepared for mailing. It is all too easy for administrative people to shove these problems aside, indicating that they are commonplace in all large and complex bureaucratic entities. However, it really does point up the need for effective management of this area by a competent person. The cliché that we are only as strong as our weakest link is particularly true in this instance.

Computer Services

There are many facets to the management of computer services within an institution. Among the many concerns are (1) the effective use of the equipment, (2) the time allocations for equipment usage, (3) management of the various staff people (operators and keypunchers, programmers, systems analysts), and (4) the type of hardware to be used.

There are many areas where alternatives must be selected. For example, an appropriate-sized computer can be installed on campus or the institution can become a member of a time-sharing network employing large computers. Another consideration concerns the way the equipment is to be used; the convenience of on-line, live interaction must be compared with the usually more effective and efficient method of batch processing.

A manager in computer services has to cope with staffing at fairly broad extremes. The people who input information work in a highly repetitive environment, often under considerable pressure. At the other extreme are the systems analysts who translate the needs of the various departments into a conceptual framework. Programmers then put these concepts into the correct format, which is also rather conceptual work. The creative people in systems and programming may need to work flexible hours when they feel most creative, and the manager may have to coordinate these needs. Likewise, since computer people speak a language uniquely their own, the manager may have work to do in establishing clear lines of communications with interfacing departments.

Institutional functions in the academic, business, and student affairs are becoming increasingly dependent on computers for processing, storage, and retrieval of data. As a result, the staff at computer services is frequently involved in usage conflicts. The enormous capability of computers often serves as a line for unnecessary data gathering, storage, and processing. Unnecessary computer usage can present a significant drain on the institution's resources.

The director of computer services, therefore, should serve as a conscience for use of the data base and provide rational guidance to the institution on the use of the computer and the value of its services. In an academic environment, where knowledge is so central to all activities, the need to accumulate and analyze data may exert strong pressure to expand computer services beyond optimum size. Because of the computer's importance, many institutions have formed committees to monitor the activities of the computer function, to recommend policy and set standards, to influence budgets, and to ensure the privacy and security of the data bank.

Still other institutions have instituted a position entitled data base administrator, and the basic responsibility of this person is to fashion the priorities of work to be undertaken by the computer center. This individual ordinarily reports to a committee including the director of institutional research and other senior officers of the college or university. The administrator is further responsible for the maintenance of an integrated data base for decision making and formulation of policy. He or she is the primary management information systems officer and is responsible for this critical area.

Safety and Security

The safety and security function in an institution serves to satisfy four primary needs of the community: fire protection, protection of life and property, emergency medical services, and traffic control and parking. The first contact the public has with the institution is often through the safety and security department, usually at the information booth staffed by a security officer. Furthermore, no matter where an institution is located, it inevitably has close ties with the larger community or municipality within which it functions. Liaison with the protective agencies in those communities is of utmost importance for the protection of health, life, and property.

Just as there is a relationship between this function and the community, so there are often close relations between segments of this function and individual units within the institution. If there is a medical school, or a school of fire science, or a school of police science, then obviously there are close relationships between these schools and the respective segments of the safety and security department.

Besides the major functions just described, a host of miscellaneous ones also are performed by the safety and security department, including special services for the handicapped; logistic coordination of special events, such as graduation exercises, cultural affairs on campus, and athletic contests; conduct of fire drills; response to emergencies, such as bomb scares, threats, and other pranks or problems raised by hazing activities of fraternities and sororities; and escort services for prestigious guests.

With the possible exception of the emergency medical services, the functions are generally organized in a paramilitary fashion. People in police and security services, as well as in fire services, are trained to see their primary function as meeting emergencies, even when, as is true of the security staff, most of the work is relatively routine. It is interesting that this attitude toward the work in safety and security exists in rural and suburban communities as strongly as it does in inner-city areas. This is despite the fact that in rural and suburban communities, the overwhelming proportion of time is spent on completely routine activities such as traffic control, fire prevention, maintenance of equipment, aiding the handicapped, and escort services, while only a minute fraction of the time is actually spent in the battling of emergencies.

Since the most important moments of service, however, come during emergencies, the organization, as well as managerial attitudes, is geared primarily toward these relatively rare moments. People serving in emergency units often feel as strongly as those in academic functions that general managerial principles do not apply the same way in these functions. Nevertheless, studies and analysis of the work of competent individuals in all these functions have shown that superior performance is achieved by those who understand their responsibilities as managers and supervisors and who discharge them appropriately, paying attention to the identical principles that managers do in other functions, whether they be business or nonbusiness affairs.

There are many issues that managers in safety and security have to resolve, and most of these have significant impact on the general climate of the institution. As a result, there is often strong interest on the part of other members of the institutional community in how these issues are resolved, and managers in safety and security have to be skilled in dealing with the external forces as well as the internal ones. An example of one of these issues is the way the safety and security staff achieves compliance with rules and regulations pertaining to drug and alcohol abuse. Here, with other rules and regulations, enforcement must recognize the unique character of institutions of higher learning and the different levels of tolerance needed to be displayed toward the different constituencies that exist on the college campus. Treatment must be accorded to students and staff members in such a way that neither feels discriminated against nor perceives special treatment for one of the other groups.

How these issues are resolved has great impact on the image safety and security staffs enjoy from outsiders and from students. For instance, whether the security people are seen as "cops" or as protectors is even more important here than it is for a police force in the community at large. Directly related to this image is the question of firearms for the officers. Should all officers be provided with guns or only the supervisory staff? Should they have mace or billy clubs? What communications equipment should they have access to? What should be their authority with respect to issuing of tickets and warnings in relation to local police and so on?

Competent management with an unusual awareness of how things impact on public relations is needed to resolve these issues in such a way that they satisfy the college community and the community at large and, at the same time, provide the highest possible level of quality of work life for the members of the department. These questions have heavy impact on training and development as well, because the higher the level of unpreparedness on the part of officers, the greater the need for careful, consistent, and continuous training in the use of force.

Facilities Management

The activities involved in facilities management concern not only the construction of new facilities and major repairs, but also the three normal maintenance functions of prevention, routine maintenance, and repair. The new construction and major repair function is generally performed by a small planning office, often called the office of institutional planning.

Maintenance functions are performed primarily by three types of employees: (1) trades people such as painters, electricians, plumbers, masons, carpenters, and vehicle mechanics; (2) custodial staffs who perform the housekeeping duties; and (3) groundspeople who maintain the campus and the external surfaces of the buildings. Projects frequently require teams or task forces composed of several groups. For instance, a heating, ventilating, and air-conditioning project concerning the installation of a new heating system might require the services of an electrician, a plumber, a carpenter, a painter, and possibly an engineer. Housekeeping personnel also might work in teams to help move materials and clean up debris from this project, while groundspeople may be needed to restore any damage done to the landscaping.

These team efforts or small group projects are particularly important to the institutional climate and require skilled supervisory and managerial talents, particularly in terms of necessary coordination procedures. Productivity within trades is difficult to maintain at high levels, and it is important that promotion of skilled people takes place through the ranks and that leadership carry with it a responsibility for performance on these special projects.

There are many difficult aspects to management in these functions. Usually the work crew is widely dispersed, which makes it difficult for a supervisor to retain control. Besides, many functions have to be performed on a 24-hour basis, which creates some difficult scheduling problems. Many of the people in these functions find it difficult to think in terms of goals and results. Many, particularly in the housekeeping and groundskeeping functions, live permanently on the right side of the life-cycle curve.

The Equal Employment Opportunity and upward mobility issues are frequently most serious in these functional areas. An institution, which by its very mission is designed to provide educational services, is expected to aid the potential for upward mobility of all groups, and yet, because of the nature and background of many of the people who serve in these functions, it is difficult to provide meaningful counseling and educational services to them. Usually, institutions discharge, or attempt to discharge, the obligation by offering and providing tuition-free access to courses. Some institutions even provide these tuition-free privileges to the offspring of employees who meet minimum longevity requirements.

While these efforts are intended to provide educational opportunities for people in the maintenance functions, this is not necessarily the most appropriate way to assist them. From a practical point of view, people in the lower socioeconomic strata (from which most of the people in this function are drawn) do not have the background to take advantage of these opportunities. An institution that considers its obligation to end when it offers the tuition refund opportunity is really discharging only a portion of its obligation for career assistance. A variety of efforts in the form of planning, guidance, and individualized attention should be provided to people in this function, and at a level that meets their needs in an appropriate manner.

Good institutions, of course, provide appropriate physical facilities such as locker rooms, clean and attractive uniforms, and reasonably up-to-date equipment to help maintenance staff members gain the maximum satisfaction from their work, to instill a sense of pride, and to help further the public image of the institution. For the director of facilities and the vice president of administrative services, there are some very difficult tradeoffs involved here. On one side, to lift the competence of the staff and to gradually develop motivation for career advancement requires a highly competent manager with considerable education and broad awareness of the social and managerial implications of an appropriate career development program. On the other, imposing management from outside of the work force sharply closes career opportunities for the current members.

In most institutions, this issue is not faced as clearly as it could be. The decisions involved here are of great difficulty and require long-term, consistent implementation. For instance, it appears to be fairly obvious that optimum approaches would involve using career-ladder appointments and supporting encumbents adequately, with external talent drawn either from outside consultants or the management staff within the department. An alternative approach might be to help managers develop appropriate internal competence, to shift those individuals to other functions within the institution, and to encourage that people from the work force be hired for the open positions. Neither of these approaches is short-term. Each, obviously, may face immediate opposition, since each can easily be interpreted as a face-saving rather than a sincere attempt to help develop adequate people internally. In light of the enormous effort, a competent approach to the problem requires full awareness that long-run benefits will possibly far outweigh the very high current costs if effective action is taken on the problem.

Another difficult situation with which management in this function has to cope is the long-established union allegiance of trades people and the income-level problems that are unique to trades people. Because of the uncertainty of employment in most trades, the hourly wage earned by trades people in private industry is generally very high relative to positions requiring similar skills and effort in more permanent positions. Therefore, whenever trades people are engaged on a permanent basis by an organization, whether in an institution of higher learning or elsewhere, there is a very unfavorable comparison between the salaries offered by these organizations and the wages paid to trades people, particularly in the building trades.

Unions, although recognizing the difficulty, do seek to maintain membership. As a result, some colleges have to deal with many different trade unions and have to establish contracts with them. Invariably, these contracts are unique for the union because of the nature of the institution and the type of employment; and therefore, they present a problem for the union. At the same time, maintaining parity between contracts with a group of unions poses difficult negotiating and quality of work life obstacles.

Institutional Planning

As mentioned briefly in the section on the facilities maintenance function, the planning office works closely with architects, general contractors, and engineers on new construction and major repairs. The planning office prepares proposals for consideration by the board of trustees, enters into contracts with the professional firms providing architectural and engineering construction services, and then monitors the actual construction activities.

This office is also responsible for working with a variety of campus constituents in setting priorities and determining the order and sequence within which work will be done. Of course, goal-setting and coordination procedures must be applied by planning office managers. Space allocations and the use of facilities are other typical topics for reconciliation by the planning office.

The planning office is also charged with developing plans for achieving savings, either through the recommendations that establish capital expenditures or through maintenance projects. Planning also may provide additional important input into the budgeting process, because it provides the estimates that serve for the establishment of expenditure budgets for all facilities-related costs, including energy, which in the modern world are so difficult to predict.

Intercollegiate Athletics

Few activities involve as many emotions as the area of intercollegiate athletics. Not only is the institutional community deeply involved, but so are enormous pressures from alumni and from the world at large. Since there are national and divisional classifications, the complexity and resources required for the administration of intercollegiate activities will differ according to that classification. The different levels of activity of Division 1, Division 2, and Division 3 schools have significant impact on budget allocations, recruitment activities, scholarships, and a host of other related alternatives.

Intercollegiate athletic activities constitute one area of an institution that holds the potential for large amounts of income if the institution is able to field teams that are successful. Indeed, many large institutions have underwritten many of their academic costs through income produced from intercollegiate athletic enterprises. It is not only admissions to competitive events, but a host of ancillary income activities such as food services and the selling of programs, benchwarmers, and any number of other things that add to the physical viability of the total institution through the efforts of its intercollegiate athletic program. Caution must be exercised to ensure that academic values do not take a back seat to athletic income and reputation.

The status of the intercollegiate athletic teams can have, in addition, great impact on the image of the institution in the nation, on the attractiveness of the school to applicants, and on the ease with which the institution can raise funds both for endowment and operational expenses. The functional activities within this are fairly self-evident, and they stretch from the routine activities of management of gym and facilities, to the provision of supplies and sports information, to the development of talent where it exists.

There are two major types of college athletics. One concerns the intercollegiate activities, and the other concerns the intramural ones. Both can be important to the ability of an institution to recruit and retain students. Staffing for this department constitutes several rather diverse groups. There are the people who manage the routine activities just described, including facilities, supplies, and information, and there are those who perform the professional activities, such as full-time coaches and team managers. In addition, there are the large numbers of part-time student aides who perform routine operations such as ticket booth staffing, program distribution, and seating and ushering; sometimes these people also perform the functions of part-time coaches. In addition, there are support functions, such as cheerleaders, rally coordinators, booster clubs, and alumni groups. Managing this large part-time force, which sometimes shows intense devotion, can present some unique challenges to managers.

Although the history of collegiate sports is dominated by activities of male teams, society increasingly demands greater equality between male and female teams. Title IX of the Education Amendments of 1972 and interpretations by the courts of the various sections of the Civil Rights Act of 1964 mandate equalization not only in funding, but also in the quality of attention and the number of opportunities provided for each sex. In light of the rather heavy expenditures required for football programs, they have been exempted from equalization with respect to women's sports. However, the institutional thrust for equalization does require some balance with respect to full-time coaches and the amount of money allocated to support the various activities. At the time of this writing, a major series of questions has been raised by the NCAA with respect to the clarity of the Title IX requirements. For example, it is currently not clear as to whether the federal government is talking about compliance based on head count or based on some other benchmark as yet unidentified. The important feature here is that institutions of higher learning carry a moral obligation that goes beyond the legal requirements that may be imposed, and the satisfaction of these moral obligations is the fulfillment of the spirit behind the Title IX requirements. Hopefully, a by-product of the move to equalize the balance between men's and women's sports will be the deemphasis of the importance of sports in relation to one's academic preparation for life.

All these considerations place heavy demands on competence in management of the function. Here too, appropriate goal setting, appropriate attention to technical competence, and appropriate policies to establish high quality of work life for all constituencies are not easy for a manager to achieve. However, application of the concepts presented in this book can help managers in this area to ensure that their units achieve high levels of performance.

Auxiliary Services

Auxiliary services encompass many different functions, including management of the campus gas station, the institution's candy store, and student pub; management of the campus book store; administrative functions that support the residence program; and management of funds for student scholarships and research. Unique to this unit is the fact that ordinarily it is an income-producing unit that, in a way, operates independently, almost the way any other private business would operate. The academic environment, of course, places unique stresses on that type of operation and a need to satisfy both the institution and the student body. Students often expect these functions to operate at cost, or very close to it, and this places additional strains on the technical business management competence and communications competence of the managers.

Auxiliary services often have business responsibilities that reach outside the institution. This would include the use of or sale or rental of services and facilities to the community. Since the halls and food service facilities frequently lie dormant, they represent valuable resources which, if properly marketed and managed, can bring income to the institution.

Auxiliary services, although they are not essential to the core mission of the college or university, can greatly enhance the reputation of the institution and significantly contribute to the quality of life within the campus community. As an example, one large northeastern university maintains a butcher shop, a vegetable store, and a retail dairy outlet, all of which bring benefits to the institutional community as well as to the larger community of which it is a part. At the same time, these help to bring income to the institution.

The institution needs to be particularly sensitive to the possibility that local businesses such as motels, hotels, and catering services will perceive the institution as competitive with local enterprise. A manager of auxiliary services must be particularly sensitive to the institution's needs in relation to the broad public relations position the institution establishes with respect to the community within which it functions.

Appendix A:
Decision Making

New managers usually need to practice the skills of decision making. Most managers who have taken a course or attended a seminar in decision making have come to appreciate the importance of thorough analysis in decision making. Today, the decision-making process is no longer the way it was when managers made most decisions unilaterally. Many people often have to be involved, and the skills needed to help a group arrive at a good decision are sometimes more important than thorough knowledge of the decision-making process.

Few people realize how significantly their lives can be affected by the application of good decision-making skills. Careful planning and well-thought-out decisions can lead to better use of limited resources. The general application of management principles to one's personal life also can help to bring about more meaningful relationships with others.

Inexperienced decision makers often err by regarding decisions as a choice between two alternatives. Some decisions, of course, are that simple. For example, one either stays in bed or gets up. In most situations, however, there are a fairly large number of alternatives from which to select. Granting a privilege, for instance, may seem at first to be a simple yes or no matter, but there are many ways to say yes or no. An employee requesting a new uniform or a change in vacation may be told yes, but in such a way that future requests are discouraged. Or no may be said in such a manner that the person making the request thoroughly understands the reasons behind the decision and feels no bitterness. Unskilled managers often say no in such a way that difficulties and hard feelings result.

Recognizing the possibilities that do exist is much easier when one follows a formal decision-making process. Therefore, it is appropriate to discuss decision making in the abstract, that is, as a process that helps one select those courses of action likely to be most successful.

Types of Decisions

There are many different kinds of decisions. At one extreme, there are those which are so simplistic that most people probably do not even think of them as decisions, such as, which pencil to pick up when writing or whether or not to blink one's eyes at a particular time. On the other hand, there are those decisions which are extremely complex, such as those involving career choices where little information is available at the time that critical decisions have to be made. Other complex decisions might involve whether to purchase a new photocopier or how to resolve a conflict between groups in a department. Between the extremes just presented, there are many other decisions; some can be solved intuitively, while others require more rational approaches.

Basically there are three types of decisions:

Problem-solving decisions: These deal with specific deviations from expected results or defined standards. They frequently emerge when a difference between "what is" and "what should be" is observed. A problem exists, and it must be addressed fairly quickly.

Opportunity decisions: These decisions are not the same as problem-solving decisions. They are frequently less urgent. They are often generated by observing a difference between "what is" and "what could be." In most organization units, numerous opportunities for improvement exist. The managerial role, therefore, becomes one of selecting which opportunities are most desirable based on the overall objectives and mission of the unit.

Project-management decisions: These are decisions concerning the day-to-day operation of the unit, and they are made neither as a result of problems nor in connection with specific opportunities. They are routine decisions, such as what should be included on this month's budget report or which high schools the recruitment team should visit next week.

Overview of Decision Making

While the decision making chart depicted in figure A-1 appears rather overwhelming, it is quite simple to apply once understood. The chart provides a thorough explanation of the technical aspects of decision making (the traditional step-by-step process to decision making) with which many managers are probably already somewhat familiar; it also shows how the human element of the decision-making process—the important considerations for involving others in decisions—fits in with the technical process.

Following are some of the general features of the decision model:

Although it conveys a formal step-by-step process for analysis, this process is not a rigid one that should be applied formally to all decisions. While the model shows a series of logical decision steps, many can be shortened as a manager becomes more expert in using the process.

The model is intended to be used only with complex decisions. It would be foolish to use this intricate process for decisions that can be made easily through experience and intuitive judgment.

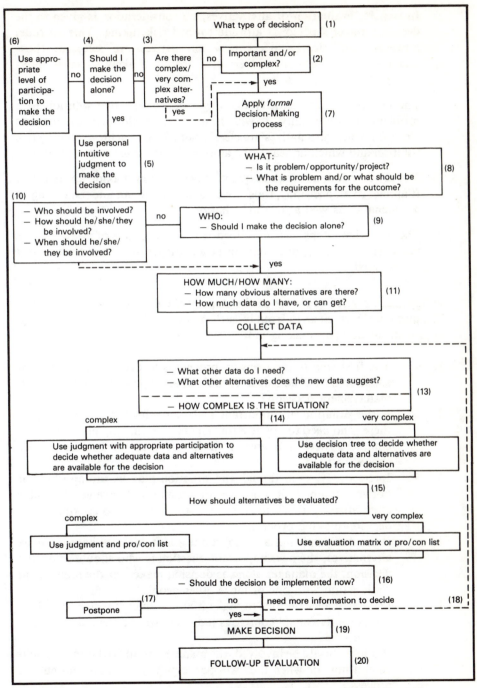

Figure A-1. A Practical Guide to Decision Making

In step 15, evaluation of alternatives, no consideration is given to the decision maker's personal attitude toward risk taking. This attitude, however, will clearly affect how alternatives are selected; those managers who are more conservative are more likely to select alternatives that have less risk.

The model will not identify the single best alternative solution to a problem or opportunity. It will, however, help sharpen a manager's views on which alternatives are clearly not likely to achieve an effective solution and which appear to be among the best alternatives available.

The process does not require quantitative decision-making approaches. It applies to all decisions, those that do not require an understanding of mathematics as well as to those that do.

The overview steps are described from the point of view of the manager. Of course, one need not be a manager to use the process as it is described.

Following is a brief overview of the steps in the decision-making process. The numerical references in front of each step are coded to the numbers that appear in the decision making model (figure A-1):

1.   The first step in the decision process is to determine the type of situation or decision. Is it a problem, an opportunity, or a project-management decision?

2.   Is the situation an important and/or complex one? If it is not, there is no need to utilize a formal decision-making process; if it is complex, there is a greater likelihood that the formal process should be used.

3.   Interestingly, even though the situation may be unimportant or not very complex, it is possible that it may still have very complex alternatives; if this is the case, it is still advisable to use the formal decision-making process.

4.   If the decision is not a complex one and it does not have complex alternatives, the next important question is who should make the decision, the manager alone as decision maker, or the manager in conjunction with one or more other people?

5.   If the manager decides to make it alone, since it is a simple decision, intuitive or subconscious judgment will be adequate to make the decision.

6.   If others should be involved, the manager decides who they should be and how or when they will participate in the decision-making process.

7. As mentioned earlier, in cases where the situation is important and/or complex or has very complex alternatives, the formal-analysis process should be applied.

8. The manager identifies the nature of the decision: Is it a problem, opportunity, or project decision? This step appears to be a simple one and is often taken for granted. Frequently, though, if a problem or opportunity is not defined precisely or is defined incorrectly, an excellent solution may be achieved but for the wrong reason. More important, even, specific requirements or conditions that the outcome should satisfy are developed at this stage.

9. & 10. The manager now decides whether to make the decision alone or with others; if others are to be involved, who should they be, how extensively should they be involved, and at which point(s) should they be involved in the decision process.

11. Preliminary alternatives are now developed on the basis of the limited evidence available.

12. Additional data are collected to refine existing alternatives.

13. Additional data will generally lead to other alternatives and possibly to the need to obtain still more data.

14. At this stage, the manager determines the complexity of the situation and decides whether adequate data have been obtained and whether the number of alternatives is adequate.

15. Based on the complexity of the decision, the manager determines what type of evaluation would be appropriate to isolate those alternatives which appear to be most desirable.

16. He or she then determines whether or not the decision should be made at that moment.

17. If not, it should be postponed.

18. If it should be made, but cannot because inadequate data are available, steps 13, 14, 15, and 16 are repeated.

19. Finally, a decision is made by selecting an alternative from those which are most desirable.

20. After the decision is implemented, the manager evaluates it closely to determine whether future adjustments have to be made to ensure that the alternative selected comes as close as possible to meeting the requirements specified earlier.

Decision Trees

Decision trees help to define and evaluate alternatives. A decision tree *depicts* the question that should be asked at every step in a decision: What alternatives are available at this point, and what consequences should be expected from each?

A decision tree starts by asking what alternatives exist at the moment. For example, a very simple tree could be built for a short trip from one's home to the school. Assuming that three routes are available, that the trip must be made during rush hour, and that it is important to get to the school by a specific time, the possible alternatives might be (1) a limited-access highway or (2) two major truck routes, each of which has some stretches containing traffic lights. These alternatives are depicted in figure A-2.

Once the first branches of the tree have been drawn, the consequences for the end point of each branch need to be considered. The consequences, as depicted in figure A-3, are

1. For the limited access highway: (a) the possibility of heavy, slow-moving traffic, about 40 minutes; (b) the possibility of complete blockage due to an accident, maximum probable time 2 hours; and (c) no obstruction, free traffic flow, 15 minutes.
2. For truck route 1: (a) heavy traffic, slow moving, about 60 minutes; (b) total obstruction, good connection to limited-access highway at four points, 1¼ to 1½ hours; and (c) normal traffic, 35 minutes.
3. For truck route 2: (a) heavy traffic, slow moving, about 65 minutes; (b) total obstruction, good access to side streets, 95 minutes; and (c) normal traffic, 30 minutes.

Some experts say that probabilities should be estimated for each branch of the tree. Others say that probabilities are not that practical and that decisions should be based on the decision maker's judgment about the value of the various alternatives without mathematical analysis. The important point about decision trees is that they help to identify alternatives that are not immediately apparent.

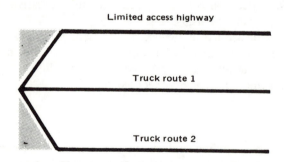

Figure A-2. A Diagram of the Simple Decision Tree

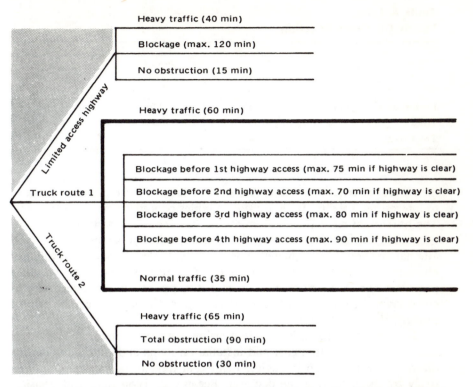

Heavy traffic (40 min)

Blockage (max. 120 min)

No obstruction (15 min)

Heavy traffic (60 min)

Blockage before 1st highway access (max. 75 min if highway is clear)

Blockage before 2nd highway access (max. 70 min if highway is clear)

Blockage before 3rd highway access (max. 80 min if highway is clear)

Blockage before 4th highway access (max. 90 min if highway is clear)

Normal traffic (35 min)

Heavy traffic (65 min)

Total obstruction (90 min)

No obstruction (30 min)

Figure A-3. A Diagram Illustrating the Consequences for Each End Point of the First Set of Branches for the Simple Decision Tree Shown in Figure A-2

Decision trees need not be drawn for most situations, because in most cases, alternatives are quite obvious. Anyone who makes use of the decision-tree technique for complex decisions, however, finds that it can bring a certain discipline to analysis that is absent without it. One other advantage of the technique lies in its ability to clearly communicate alternatives when several people are involved in seeking out the best approach. However, the technique has one major disadvantage—it is cumbersome. Therefore, it should be used with discretion, and only for those decisions for which it can provide enough of an advantage to justify the effort.

Decision Matrices

Any decision that has at least two dimensions can be organized as a matrix that gives some insights into the relative advantages and disadvantages of

Table A-1
Matrix for Route Selection

	Shortest Possible Time (Minutes)	Longest Probable Time (Minutes)	Reliability (Assurance that Estimate is Accurate)
Limited-access highway	15	120	Low
Truck route 1	35	90	Medium
Truck route 2	30	95	High

the various alternatives. Tables A-1 and A-2 illustrate two matrices that lead to interesting insights. Both are simple tables containing only a few boxes. The horizontal rows list all alternatives that are worth serious consideration; each vertical column then designates a criterion against which each alternative should be evaluated. For example, table A-1 partially evaluates alternatives identified in the decision tree (figure A-3), and table A-2 compares the desirability of several pieces of equipment. (It is not necessary to construct a decision tree for each matrix, but a decision tree can be helpful to identify alternatives.)

It is important to notice that in decision matrices there are always tangible items such as initial cost and installation items and continuing expenditures. There are also intangible items that have to be evaluated subjectively by those making the decision. Because decision trees and decision matrices ultimately require judgment about intangibles, they do not give a precise result, and no single answer emerges. For this reason, involving several knowledgeable people in decisions brings greater objectivity. Similarly, when considering the impact of a decision on people, a group is usually more accurate than an individual.

The value of matrices lies in the thorough analysis they require. Detailed analysis helps to ensure that better decisions will be made more often. Strict adherence to the decision-making process and use of decision trees and decision matrices do not guarantee good decisions, but they do tie together to provide considerable support when a manager faces a difficult decision. Moreover, they ensure that poor decisions will be made less frequently.

To summarize, therefore, the *steps in the decision-making process* ensure an orderly and organized approach to the decision sequence. The *decision tree* provides a framework for reviewing possible courses of action and helps stimulate creative thinking. And finally, *decision matrices* are useful in evaluating which alternative represents the best choice.

The following items might be listed among the purposes of such decision aids:

1. They provide a path and tools to help arrive at the best possible course of action when difficult decisions need be made.
2. They aid in forming a thought process that can guide decisions, thereby helping to bring about what is commonly called "good judgment."
3. They provide a shorthand record of the thinking that led to the decision.

Table A-2
Matrix for Evaluation of a Machine Being Considered for Purchase

	Cost	Maximum Capacity	Operating Costs per Hour	Special Advantages	Special Disadvantages	Operator Preferences
Manufacturer A	X dollars	R units	O dollars	Simplest to operate	Highest expected maintenance	High
Manufacturer B	Y dollars	S units	P dollars	Best controls and access for maintenance	Difficult to convert to other products	Medium
Manufacturer C	Z dollars	T units	Q dollars	Easiest to convert to other products	Uses most space	Medium

Appendix B:
Conflict Resolution

In an institution of higher education, as in any complex organization composed of various self-interest groups, conflict will exist and might originate from many sources. Not all such conflict is damaging. Some, such as constructive competition can even be beneficial. This appendix addresses the manager's or leader's role in managing undesirable conflict.

In perhaps its most basic form, conflict is the result of differences in ideological or philosophical outlook between people or between groups, or in the benefits which different courses of action bring to each of them. For example, it would not be uncommon for the editorial staff of the student newspaper to be in conflict with the administration on a policy issue or on one concerning budget.

Interpersonal conflict also can result from personality differences between individuals or from clashing of emotional needs. Still other instances of conflict stem from differences in perception. People see problems in different lights, and their responses are conditioned by their viewpoints. For instance, a student government officer, the director of buildings and grounds, and the faculty union leader may have widely differing opinions with respect to the allotment of parking spaces for faculty and students. More serious problems of this nature occur when the goals of an organization and the characteristics and needs of the individuals working in that organization are in conflict.

Then, too, there are status differences. A math professor may resent a student who corrects computational errors made on the chalkboard during an explanation of a difficult concept. When this happens, problems may well develop between the individuals that might lead to serious conflict.

For any conflict to be reduced and resolved, someone has to assume responsibility and leadership in moving away from the problem toward a more constructive relationship. In higher education, this responsibility often falls on the shoulders of managers and leaders. The two types of conflict that primarily concern managers and leaders are (1) conflict between the manager or leader and another person, and (2) conflict between other people with whom the manager is concerned.

Most behavioral scientists believe that conflict situations are best reconciled when a climate of open communications is established. The following step-by-step procedure is useful to open communications and brings a satisfactory outcome to a conflict situation:

1. Reduce the emotional level. The skills discussed in Transactional Analysis and in counseling and the Johari window can be very useful here.

If the conflict involves other groups, the skills of mediators or intermediaries can often bring a reduction in emotional tensions. Rarely, at this point, should high-level officials of the institution be involved, and certainly not those who ultimately must make the final decisions to determine the institution's position. For instance, in a confrontation between minorities and the newspaper, or in a confrontation pertaining to faculty retention, it would rarely be advisable for the president of the institution to be involved in the early stages when emotions are high and before the issues have been clarified and resolution has been attempted.

2. In the second step, the person attempting to resolve the conflict will seek to clarify where the real conflicts of interest lie. In many instances, this identifies misunderstandings or misconceptions that can be removed in discussion. Conflict is often resolved at this stage entirely.

3. The third step concerns the identification of alternatives that can be considered for resolution of the conflict. These range from severe win-lose situations, in which one party wins significantly while the other takes extensive losses, to the far more desirable win-win situation, in which both parties gain something from the resolution of the conflict. The possibilities include

a. Postponement of the conflict. This may be excellent strategy when the possibility exists that unfolding events will either remove the source of the conflict or change conditions so that the conflict will be in a different environment where it may be easier to resolve. Postponement, therefore, sometimes can lead to a win-win situation.

b. Use of authority by the person with such authority. This generally is a win-lose situation, except in the rare instances when all parties involved desire such a resolution as preferable to the continuation of the conflict or when exceptionally enlightened decisions are made by the authority figure. Use of authority is also desirable in rare instances such as severe violation of rules by one party or behavior detrimental to health and safety.

c. At the other extreme from use of authority is full concession to the other party, which also is a win-lose situation. There are useful applications, however, when the conflict involves relatively less important matters, where concessions to the other side may have long-run benefits that outweigh the disadvantages of the concession. In this case, what is a win-lose situation for the short run turns into an ultimate win-win situation.

d. In addition to these alternatives, which always are possible, there is a series of compromises that generally produces a lose-lose situation. Each party, however, loses less than it would if it conceded or if authority were used. In compromises, the parties to a conflict accept less than what they are seeking, but do attain something that improves their positions when compared to what they might lose in the conflict.

e. There are also alternatives which careful discussion can sometimes uncover. These are what are frequently referred to as "creative solutions," in which each party gains over the preconflict situation and therefore can consider itself to have won something from the conflict. Solutions of this type are the most desirable ones, and individuals skilled in conflict resolution, such as mediators, competent managers and administrators, will always attempt to continue discussions until either such a solution has been found or it becomes clear that none exists.

Selected Bibliography

Argyris, Chris. *Intergrating the Individual and the Organization*. New York: Wiley, 1966.

Baldridge, J. Victor, David V. Curtis, George Ecker, and Gary L. Riley. *Policy Making and Effective Leadership*. San Francisco: Jossey-Bass, 1978.

Beckhard, Richard. *Organization Development: Strategies and Models*. Reading, Mass.: Addison-Wesley, 1969.

Bennis, Warren G. *Organization Development: Its Nature, Origins, and Prospects*. Reading, Mass.: Addison-Wesley, 1969.

Blake, Robert R., and Jane Srygley Mouton. *Corporate Excellence through Grid Organization Development*. Houston: Gulf Publishing Co., 1968.

Drucker, Peter F. *The Effective Executive*. New York: Harper and Row, 1966.

Gellerman, Saul W. *Motivation and Productivity*. New York: American Management Association, 1963.

Graves, Clare W. "Deterioration of Work Standards." *Harvard Business Review* (September-October 1966):117-126.

Hersey, Paul, and Kenneth H. Blanchard. "Life Cycle Theory of Leadership." *Training and Development Journal* (May 1969).

Hersey, Paul, and Kenneth H. Blanchard. "So You Want to Know Your Leadership Style?" *Training and Development Journal* (February 1974):22-37.

Hersey, Paul, and Kenneth H. Blanchard. *Management of Organizational Behavior*, 2d ed. Englewood Cliffs, N.J.: Prentice-Hall, 1972.

Herzberg, Frederick. "One More Time: How Do You Motivate Employees?" *Harvard Business Review* (January-February 1968):53-62.

Jellema, William W., ed. *Efficient College Management*. San Francisco: Jossey-Bass, 1972.

Lahti, Robert E. *Innovative College Management*. San Francisco: Jossey-Bass, 1973.

McGregor, Douglas. *The Human Side of Enterprise*. New York: McGraw-Hill, 1960.

Miles, Raymond E. "Human Relations or Human Resources?" *Harvard Business Review* (July-August 1965).

Myers, M. Scott. "Who are Your Motivated Workers?" *Harvard Business Review* (January-February 1964):73-88.

Myers, M. Scott, and Susan S. "Adapting to the New Work Ethic." *The Business Quarterly* (Winter 1973):48-58.

Rausch, Erwin. *Balancing Needs of People and Organizations.* Washington: Bureau of National Affairs, 1978.

Richman, Barry M., and Richard N. Farmer. *Leadership, Goals, and Power in Higher Education.* San Francisco: Jossey-Bass, 1974.

Index

Index

About the Contributors

Robert A. Laudicina is vice president and general manager of Automatique, Inc., a food-service and restaurant consulting group. Previously, he was dean of students at Fairleigh Dickinson University, Madison, New Jersey. He is a past president of the Eastern Association of College Deans and Advisors to Students.

Dr. Laudicina has published and lectured widely in the areas of administration, personnel, and law, including a presentation to a NASPA conference entitled "Law and Management in Higher Education." He received the B.A. and M.A. from Rutgers University and the Ph.D. from Columbia University.

Elliot I. Mininberg is vice president of administration and finance at Montclair State College. Previously, he was assistant deputy chancellor of New York University.

Dr. Mininberg has made numerous presentations to professional groups, including "Administrative Effectiveness in State Colleges and State Universities," delivered to the American Association of University Administrators. He received the B.A. from the University of Bridgeport and both the masters and doctoral degrees from New York University.

Richard J. Nichols presently serves as acting dean for advanced studies, research, and development at Kean College of New Jersey. He has more than twenty years of experience in education, ranging from teaching in New Zealand on a Fulbright Grant to college administration.

Concerned with organizations and the human relations within them, Dr. Nichols has served as a consultant to institutions and agencies on professional development, goal setting, long-range planning, decision making, and problem solving. Dr. Nichols received the Ed.D. from Ball State University.

Bernhard W. Scholz is currently acting dean of the College of Arts and Sciences at Seton Hall University, where he is also a professor in the Department of History. He is the author of *Carolingian Chronicles* and of several articles on the Middle Ages. Dr. Scholz received the Ph.D. in medieval history from the University of Würzburg.

Nathan Weiss has served as president of Kean College of New Jersey since 1969. He joined the Kean faculty in 1961 and taught for eight years in the department of history and social science. He became chairman of the department in 1967.

In 1971 Dr. Weiss was named to the National Committee on Policies and Purposes of the American Association of State Colleges and Universities. In 1977 he was elected president of the New Jersey Chapter of the American Society of Public Administrators. He has published articles on political science and teaching of political science in numerous magazines and professional journals. He received the B.A. in history from Montclair State College, the M.A. in political science from Rutgers University, and the Ph.D. in government from New York University.

About the Editor

Erwin Rausch is president of Didactic Systems, Inc., Cranford, New Jersey, a management training and development firm that distributes the widely used *Catalog of Ideas for Results Oriented Managers/ Trainers/Communicators*. Before starting his own firm, he served for almost 20 years as vice president of the Wing Company, a division of Aero-Flow Dynamics, Inc., and as director of manufacturing for the Bogen-Presto Division of Lear Siegler Corporation.

Mr. Rausch is originator of the didactic simulation/game technique and author of *Balancing Needs of People and Organizations—The Linking Elements Concept*, which provides the basis for the discussions in this book. He is editor of the text *Management in the Fire Service*, which applies the same concept to fire departments, and author or coauthor of numerous training materials, including the series *Handling Conflict in Management*. For fifteen years, he has taught evening courses at Rutgers University, Kean College of New Jersey, and Fairleigh Dickinson University.

Mr. Rausch is a panel member of the American Arbitration Association and has been a member of the American Management Association's Manufacturing Planning Council and its Advisory Committee for Education and Training Conferences. He received the B.M.E. from Cooper Union, the M.S.I.E. from Columbia University, and the M.A. from New York University.